T0320727

Critical Concepts, Standards, and Techniques in Cyber Forensics

Mohammad Shahid Husain
Ministry of Higher Education, Oman

Mohammad Zunnun Khan
Integral University, India

A volume in the Advances in
Digital Crime, Forensics, and Cyber
Terrorism (ADCFCT) Book Series

Published in the United States of America by
   IGI Global
   Information Science Reference (an imprint of IGI Global)
   701 E. Chocolate Avenue
   Hershey PA, USA 17033
   Tel: 717-533-8845
   Fax: 717-533-8661
   E-mail: cust@igi-global.com
   Web site: http://www.igi-global.com

Library of Congress Cataloging-in-Publication Data

Names: Husain, Mohammad Shahid, 1981- editor. | Khan, Mohammad Zunnun,
   1988- editor.
Title: Critical concepts, standards, and techniques in cyber forensics /
   Mohammad Shahid Husain and Mohammad Zunnun Khan, editors.
Description: Hershey, PA : Information Science Reference, 2020. | Includes
   bibliographical references and index. | Summary: ""This book explores
   critical concepts, standards, and techniques in cyber forensics. It also
   examines the software used in cyber forensics"--Provided by publisher"--
   Provided by publisher.
Identifiers: LCCN 2019031653 (print) | LCCN 2019031654 (ebook) | ISBN
   9781799815587 (hardcover) | ISBN 9781799815594 (paperback) | ISBN
   9781799815600 (ebook)
Subjects: LCSH: Computer crimes--Investigation.
Classification: LCC HV8079.C65 C75 2020 (print) | LCC HV8079.C65 (ebook)
   | DDC 363.25/968--dc23
LC record available at https://lccn.loc.gov/2019031653
LC ebook record available at https://lccn.loc.gov/2019031654

This book is published in the IGI Global book series Advances in Digital Crime, Forensics, and
Cyber Terrorism (ADCFCT) (ISSN: 2327-0381; eISSN: 2327-0373)

British Cataloguing in Publication Data
A Cataloguing in Publication record for this book is available from the British Library.

For electronic access to this publication, please contact: eresources@igi-global.com.

Advances in Digital Crime, Forensics, and Cyber Terrorism (ADCFCT) Book Series

ISSN:2327-0381
EISSN:2327-0373

Editor-in-Chief: Bryan Christiansen, Global Research Society, LLC, USA
Agnieszka Piekarz, Independent Researcher, Poland

MISSION

The digital revolution has allowed for greater global connectivity and has improved the way we share and present information. With this new ease of communication and access also come many new challenges and threats as cyber crime and digital perpetrators are constantly developing new ways to attack systems and gain access to private information.

The **Advances in Digital Crime, Forensics, and Cyber Terrorism (ADCFCT) Book Series** seeks to publish the latest research in diverse fields pertaining to crime, warfare, terrorism and forensics in the digital sphere. By advancing research available in these fields, the **ADCFCT** aims to present researchers, academicians, and students with the most current available knowledge and assist security and law enforcement professionals with a better understanding of the current tools, applications, and methodologies being implemented and discussed in the field.

COVERAGE

- Telecommunications Fraud
- Digital Crime
- Digital surveillance
- Encryption
- Malware
- Malicious Codes
- Cyber Terrorism
- Data Protection
- Identity Theft
- Database Forensics

IGI Global is currently accepting manuscripts for publication within this series. To submit a proposal for a volume in this series, please contact our Acquisition Editors at Acquisitions@igi-global.com or visit: http://www.igi-global.com/publish/.

Titles in this Series

For a list of additional titles in this series, please visit:
http://www.igi-global.com/book-series/advances-digital-crime-forensics-cyber/73676

Utilization of New Technologies in Global Terror Emerging Research and Oportunities
Emily B. Stacey (Swansea University, UK)
Information Science Reference • ©2019 • 141pp • H/C (ISBN: 9781522588764) • US $135.00

Applying Methods of Scientific Inquiry Into Intelligence, Security, and Counterterrorism
Arif Sari (Girne American University Canterbury, UK)
Information Science Reference • ©2019 • 396pp • H/C (ISBN: 9781522589761) • US $195.00

Countering Cyber Attacks and Preserving the Integrity and Availability of Critical Systems
S. Geetha (VIT Chennai, India) and Asnath Victy Phamila (VIT Chennai, India)
Information Science Reference • ©2019 • 334pp • H/C (ISBN: 9781522582410) • US $225.00

Mobile Network Forensics Emerging Research and Opportunities
Filipo Sharevski (DePaul University, USA)
Information Science Reference • ©2019 • 337pp • H/C (ISBN: 9781522558552) • US $185.00

Psychological and Behavioral Examinations in Cyber Security
John McAlaney (Bournemouth University, UK) Lara A. Frumkin (Open University, UK)
and Vladlena Benson (University of West London, UK)
Information Science Reference • ©2018 • 334pp • H/C (ISBN: 9781522540533) • US $225.00

Combating Internet-Enabled Terrorism Emerging Research and Opportunities
Emily Stacey (Swansea University, UK)
Information Science Reference • ©2017 • 133pp • H/C (ISBN: 9781522521907) • US $115.00

Combating Security Breaches and Criminal Activity in the Digital Sphere
S. Geetha (VIT University, Chennai, India) and Asnath Victy Phamila (VIT University,
Chennai, India)
Information Science Reference • ©2016 • 309pp • H/C (ISBN: 9781522501930) • US $205.00

National Security and Counterintelligence in the Era of Cyber Espionage

For an entire list of titles in this series, please visit:
http://www.igi-global.com/book-series/advances-digital-crime-forensics-cyber/73676

701 East Chocolate Avenue, Hershey, PA 17033, USA
Tel: 717-533-8845 x100 • Fax: 717-533-8661
E-Mail: cust@igi-global.com • www.igi-global.com

Editorial Advisory Board

Table of Contents

Detailed Table of Contents

Today one of the major difficulties facing all organizations is cybercrime. Cybercrime is any crime related to computers or the internet. Cybercrimes cover a vast range, from sending fake emails to downloading and distributing copyrighted material. Cyber forensics is among one of the important branches of computer science. It deals with cybercrime investigation. In this chapter, the author provides an overview of cyber forensics. The chapter focuses on its importance and some of the techniques and tools used by cyber forensic investigators.

Chapter 2

This chapter includes the evolution of cyber forensics from the 1980s to the current era. It was the era when computer forensics came into existence after a personal computer became a viable option for consumers. The formation of digital forensics is also discussed here. This chapter also includes the formation of cyber forensic investigation agencies. Cyber forensic life cycle and related phases are discussed in detail. Role of international organizations on computer evidence is discussed with the emphasize on Digital Forensic Research Workshop (DFRWS), Scientific

Working Group on Digital Evidence (SWDGE), chief police officers' involvement. Authenticity-, accuracy-, and completeness-related pieces of evidence are also discussed. The most important thing that is discussed here is the cyber forensics data.

Abhishek Kumar Pandey, Babasaheb Bhimrao Ambedkar University,
India
Ashutosh Kumar Tripathi, Babasaheb Bhimrao Ambedkar University,
India
Gayatri Kapil, Babasaheb Bhimrao Ambedkar University, India
Virendra Singh, Babasaheb Bhimrao Ambedkar University, India
Mohd. Waris Khan, Babasaheb Bhimrao Ambedkar University, India
Alka Agrawal, Babasaheb Bhimrao Ambedkar University, India
Rajeev Kumar, Babasaheb Bhimrao Ambedkar University, India
Raees Ahmad Khan, Babasaheb Bhimrao Ambedkar University, India

The digital age has undoubtedly revolutionized the life and work of people. However, this sheen of digital technology remains challenged by the spate of cybercrimes that imperil the privacy and data of the end-users. The alarming rise in cybercrimes has become a major concern for cyber specialists. In this grim context, digital forensics has emerged as a boon for cyber specialists because it has proven to be an effective means for investigating cyber-attacks. This chapter reviews the existing tools and approaches in the field of digital forensics in cybersecurity. This chapter also discusses the current challenges and problems that are faced by a forensic investigator. In addition, it enlists the different categories of digital forensics. The study concludes by underlining the importance and the need for extensive research in digital forensic tools.

Abhishek Kumar Pandey, Babasaheb Bhimrao Ambedkar University,
India
Ashutosh Kumar Tripathi, Babasaheb Bhimrao Ambedkar University,
India
Gayatri Kapil, Babasaheb Bhimrao Ambedkar University, India
Virendra Singh, Babasaheb Bhimrao Ambedkar University, India
Mohd. Waris Khan, Babasaheb Bhimrao Ambedkar University, India
Alka Agrawal, Babasaheb Bhimrao Ambedkar University, India
Rajeev Kumar, Babasaheb Bhimrao Ambedkar University, India
Raees Ahmad Khan, Babasaheb Bhimrao Ambedkar University, India

Security issues are ever-evolving in today's scenario due to the heterogeneous nature of software applications, multimedia features, multilingual interactive and responsible features, and rapid rise in third-party software products. The main objective of this chapter is to focus on the difficulties and components that the users have to contend with on the internet. This chapter investigates and manages ongoing malware attacks. It also explains the significance of the research, malware investigation, social engineering, and user awareness in the field of malware attacks. Cyber-attacks are the most common problem in recent years, and the increasing number of malware is becoming a challenging task for security experts. This chapter underlines key issues along with various aspects for experts to discuss and focus on reducing the threats posed by malware and planning the strategy for prevention in the future. The chapter provides an effective future direction for researchers to produce impactful outcomes.

Chapter 5

Parkavi R., Thiagarajar College of Engineering, India
Nithya R., Thiagarajar College of Engineering, India
Priyadharshini G., Thiagarajar College of Engineering, India

In this rapidly growing era of technology, terrorist organizations do not ultimately depend on weapons, army, bombs, and lethal weapons to inflict terror. As the entire earth is developing at a rapid pace, so do the terrorists. The strategies adopted by them have become cannier and more sinister. In addition to that, they no longer involve in training, making tedious plans, undergoing physical training, and subjecting their allies to physical attacks. Rather, they impose serious threats by attacking their victims by vandalizing the online infrastructure. This can be done conveniently from any part of the globe, thus enabling them to use the dark side of the internet. This chapter focuses on digital terrorism attacks, its impact, and it furnishes certain methods for prevention.

Chapter 6

Abhineet Anand, Chitkara University Institute of Engineering and
Technology, Punjab, India
M. Arvindhan, Galgotias University, India

Digital forensics is the science of preserving and analyzing digital data; this data can then be used in court cases as well as for crime detection and prevention. Digital forensics began in the 1970s and was initially used as a tool for fighting financial crime. Today, with computers and digital devices being an integral part of our professional and private lives, digital forensics are used/needed in a wide variety of disputes. Data Acquisitions is described and discuss different techniques or methodology obtain the data, facts, and figures from different resource and at a different level of the system.

The year 1978 was the year when the first computer-related crime took place; it was alteration or deletion of data. The day-by-day level and intensity of cybercrime has strengthened and is getting stronger in nature in the current era. So, to achieve accuracy during the investigation, an intensive investigation environment or lab is needed. This will help the investigation team in various ways. More advanced techniques and tools are used in a current age lab setup, and solutions to forensically examine a variety of digital devices apart from computers are made.

With the advent of computers, there came computer-related crimes; hence, there comes the need for cybercrime judicial proceedings. And for any trial, evidence plays an instrumental role in bringing the victim to justice. So, there is a need for digital evidence. Digital crime evidence forms a core for the field of computer forensics. Breaking down the term digital crime evidence to be understood in simple words, it is the collection of data and information that plays a crucial role in digital crime investigation and that is usually stored and transmitted in electronic formats. Digital evidence is defined as any data stored or transmitted using a computer that supports or refute a theory of how an offense occurred or that address critical elements of the offense such as intent or alibi. This data is commonly a combination of text, audio, images, and videos. This evidence is generally invisible, fragile, time-sensitive, and integrity will be lost if they are mishandled.

Steganography has been considered as a major instrument used for an unauthorized and destructive purpose such as crime and warfare, and forensics has been used for a constructive purpose such as crime detection and fraud detection. Hence, the combination of both steganography and forensics plays a major role in the present internet era for information exchange between two parties. It has been propelled to the forefront of the current security techniques. The main objective of the technique is to provide an imperceptible way of transferring secret messages to the recipient. Another issue to be noted is that the term steganography completely differs from cryptography. The above-stated analysis is used in digital forensics. There are many steganography software tools available for ordinary computer users.

Chapter 10

    Mohammad Zunnun Khan, Integral University, India
    Mohd. Shahid Husain, Ibri College of Applied Sciences, Oman
    Mohd. Shoaib, Aligarh Muslim University, India

With the advent of information and communication technologies, e-mail is one of the prime tools for communication. Almost everyone uses emails for business communications as well as for sharing personal information. E-mail is vulnerable against cybercrimes. This chapter focuses on the basic concepts of web forensics and then provides an insight about the e-mailing policies, email architecture, and existing investigation techniques used by forensic investigators. Most of the organizations implement some standard e-mailing policies; however, it is not sufficient to handle and prevent the digital crimes. We need to monitor and investigate emails for proper check. This chapter discusses some prominent tools and techniques through which forensic experts can gather and analyze data about suspected email accounts for investigation and produce evidence in the court of law.

Chapter 11

    Radiah Othman, Massey University, New Zealand

This chapter discusses some of the stages involved in detecting and investigating financial statement fraud in the digital environment. It emphasizes the human element aspects – the fraudster and the forensic investigator, their skills and capability. The explanation focuses specifically on the context of financial statement fraud detection and investigation which requires the accounting knowledge of the investigator. It also highlights the importance of the investigator to be a skeptic and have an inquiring mind of who had the opportunity to perpetuate the fraud, how the fraud could have been perpetrated, and the motive(s) to do so.

   Mohd. Akbar, Integral University, India
   Mohammad Suaib, Integral University, India
   Mohd. Shahid Husain, Ministry of Higher Education, Oman
   Saurabh Shukla, University Teknologi of Petronas, Malaysia

The cloud computing environment is one of the most promising technologies in the development of computing resources. The cloud service providers provide almost every resource for computing to their users through the internet. With all its advantages, cloud computing has major security issues. Especially in the case of public clouds, anyone can misuse the services for performing unlawful activities. The traditional approaches used for cyber forensics and network forensics are not adequate for the cloud environment because of many technical constraints. There is a need for setting up effective countermeasures that can help an investigator to identify and track unlawful activities happened in a cloud environment. Cloud forensics is an emerging area of research where the researchers aim to provide effective digital forensic techniques that help in the investigation of digital crimes in a cloud environment. The cloud environment helps to extract data even from devices that are not physically accessible. However, cloud forensics is not as easy as it seems; a lot of the success depends on the cloud service model implemented in the context. Getting the support of cloud service providers in accessing the potential sources of evidence necessary for investigation is also a major concern. Another critical aspect of cloud forensics is dealing with legal issues. This chapter discusses the basic concepts of cloud forensics, its challenges, and future directions.

   Mohammad Haroon, Integral University, India
   Manish Madhava Tripathi, Integral University, India
   Faiyaz Ahmad, Integral University, India

In this chapter, the authors explore the use of machine learning methodology for cyber forensics as machine learning has proven its importance and efficiency. For classification and identification purposes in forensic science, pattern recognition algorithms can be very helpful.

   Mohammad Suaib, Integral University, India
   Mohd. Akbar, Integral University, India
   Mohd. Shahid Husain, Ministry of Higher Education, Oman

Digital forensic experts need to identify and collect the data stored in electronic devices. Further, this acquired data has to be analyzed to produce digital evidence. Data mining techniques have been successfully implemented in various applications across the domains. Data mining techniques help us to gain insight from a large volume of data. It helps us to predict the pattern, classify the data, and other various aspects of the data based on the users' perspective. Digital forensics is a sophisticated area of research. As the information age is revolutionizing at an inconceivable speed and the information stored in digital form is growing at a rapid rate, law enforcement agencies have a heavy reliance on digital forensic techniques that can provide timely acquisition of data, zero fault data processing, and accurate interpretation of data. This chapter gives an overview of the tasks involved in cyber forensics. It also discusses the traditional approach for digital forensics and how the integration of data mining techniques can enhance the efficiency and reliability of the existing systems used for cyber forensics.

In this chapter, the authors collected and defined different types of case studies based on cyber forensics. They tried to gather the latest as well as the oldest case studies. This chapter will help those who want to study different categories of cyber care and their forensics studies. The following scenarios are specific examples of the problems that have been faced by various organizations in the past. For reasons of client confidentiality and legal sensitivity, actual names have been changed.

Foreword

This book introduces the readers to the world of cyber forensics and its critical concepts. The text was written to fulfil the need for a book that introduces forensic methodology and sound forensic thinking, combined with case studies and some new dimensions of cyber forensics, such as cloud forensics and machine learning problem-solving approach. Starting with the basic concepts of computer forensics, each of the 15 chapters of the book focuses on a particular forensic topic composed of two parts: background knowledge and hands-on experience through case studies.

Critical Concepts, Standards, and Techniques in Cyber Forensics is intended for students who want to understand the fundamentals of computer forensics and the book can also be used as a set of guidelines for setting up of forensic laboratories. The broad aim of this book is to describe and explain the steps taken during forensic examination, with the intent of making the reader aware of the constraints and considerations that apply during a forensic examination in law enforcement and private sector. Upon reading this book, the reader will gain an insight to the field of cyber forensics and also would help him/her to start their journey of becoming a computer forensics expert.

This book is intended for upper-undergraduate and graduate-level students who are taking cyber forensic courses or working on digital forensics research. This book can also be used as a ready reference by digital forensics practitioners, IT security analysts, and security engineers working in the IT security industry, particularly IT professionals responsible for digital investigation and incident handling or researchers working in the related fields.

M. Akheela Khanum
Department of Computer Science and Engineering, Integral University, India

M. Akheela Khanum *is an Associate Professor and also serving as the head of the Department of Computer Science & Engineering in Integral University, Lucknow, India. She has around 16 years of experience in research and academics. Her research interests includes HCI, software engineering, cyber laws, artificial intelligence, and deep learning.*

Preface

This is a book about Cyber Forensics. By "Cyber Forensics" we mean scientific processes of extracting, analysing and preserving the data from electronic devices to support crime investigation. The advancement of computational technologies at brisk pace has opened a new frontier for cyber-crime. The goal of cyber forensics is to perform a structured investigation while maintaining a documented chain of evidence to find out exactly what happened on a computing device or on a network and who was responsible for it. As a Cyber forensics expert one has to identify, acquire, preserve and analyse data without compromising with integrity and confidentiality so that it can be used as evidences in legal proceeding. They also need to be aware and abide by the jurisdiction and legal regulations.

Until recently, organizations have not taken the cybercrime very seriously. However latest trends in cybercrime like remote access attacks, use of artificial intelligence in social engineering, Vulnerability of emerging IoT systems, use of smart phones and cloud computing environment has forced the need of cyber forensics expert and standard which can assist the crime investigations in digital world.

GROWING PROBLEM

Cyber-attacks know no borders and evolve at a fast pace with the advancement in computing technologies. Based on the reports published by Ana Bera (Bera, 2019) and Jack Foster (Foster, 2018), the statistics are very terrifying. Some of the key points of these reports are:

- In 2018, almost 700 million people were victims of some type of cybercrime.
- A hack occurs every 39 seconds.
- 60% of fraud goes through mobile devices, 80% of which are generated from mobile applications.
- Almost 38% frauds are credit or debit card fraud.
- 53% systems are getting infected by a virus or some other security threat.

- 34% attacks are email or social media hacking.
- 33% frauds are through online shopping scams.
- 780,000 records were lost per day in 2017.
- Two billion data records were compromised in 2017 (privacyrights, 2019) and more than 4.5 billion records were breached in the first half of 2018 alone (dickson, 2019).
- By 2020, cso online predicts healthcare industry ransomware attacks will be quadruple (morgan, cybersecurity business report, 2017).
- It is estimated that cyber-crime to cost $6 trillion by 2021 (morgan, cybercrime damages $6 trillion by 2021, 2019).
- 57.24% of computers in china and 49.19% computers in taiwan are infected by malware.
- Advancement in the field of iot has opened new frontiers in cyber crime

EMERGING NEED OF FORENSICS EXPERTS

The good news is that federal, state and local law enforcement authorities are becoming more sophisticated about cybercrime and are devoting more resources to responding to these threats. However most of the law enforcement agencies are understaffed when it comes to having trained cyber forensics experts. Another problem is shortage of effective communication and collaboration between forensics experts, technologists, law enforcement agencies and academicians. One of the major reasons for lack of cyber forensics experts, who have a working knowledge of cyber forensics, is the exposure. Academics are teaching the subjects, but most lack real-world experience, which is critical when training students. Also, many academics are not current with forensics trends and tools.

SCOPE OF CYBER FORENSICS

Cyber forensics is an emerging field. Fields like cloud computing, data analytics, machine learning and web mining has opened new avenues for forensics experts. Not only technologists are concentrating on cyber forensics, but also professionals from law enforcement agencies are also taking courses in the subject. Learning forensics basics will help attorneys especially to determine the kinds of evidence that can be found by examining digital devices and what techniques can be used to legally obtain it. On the academic front, full-fledged degree courses in cyber forensics are being developed and implemented by various academic institutes globally. Apart from this various Certification programs are already exist.

Experts as well as fresher's in the field of cyber forensics have a lot of job opportunities. Government departments, State and local law enforcement agencies are hiring computer forensics specialists. On the corporate front, all companies (especially large and mid-size having cloud/ distributed environment or even having web applications) will have serious need of cyber forensics experts.

PURPOSE

The purpose of this book is to provide information and critical knowledge to the cyber forensics, security, and law enforcement professionals how to acquire and analyse the critical data while preserving its integrity and maintain the confidentiality requirements. The book also guides how to conduct a cyber-forensics investigation and report the findings as legal evidence. This book also provides the fundamental knowledge you need to perform different phases of investigation. It discusses about cyber threats like malware, steganography and financial frauds and how we can prevent them. It also provides the insights about the role of different entities involved in an investigation and how much important it is for investigators to collaborate and communicate with them. The book also discusses the issue of legal aspects of multiple jurisdictions and the need of common law enforcement agencies across the globe. Finally, through case studies, you will gain the knowledge and skills required to master the deployment of countermeasures to thwart potential cyber-attacks.

AUDIENCE

This book focuses on providing in-depth knowledge about online forensic practices and methods. Highlighting a range of topics such as data mining, digital evidence, and fraud investigation, this book is ideal for security analysts, IT specialists, software engineers, researchers, security professionals, criminal science professionals, policymakers, academicians, and students.

EMPHASIS

This book is an introduction to critical concepts and techniques of cyber forensics. You will learn the concepts, definitions and characteristics of cyber forensics which make it complex in comparison with traditional forensics. This book discusses the steps involved in a cyber-forensics investigation, the parties involved which can affect results of the case and different considerations investigator has to focus on while investigation a case. It also guides you in setting up a forensic lab.

This book also deals with latest trends like mobile forensics, cloud forensics, e-mail forensics, web forensics and data mining techniques to assist investigators.

WHAT YOU WILL LEARN

By going through the material presented in this book, you will learn:

- The concept of cyber forensics, how it is different from the traditional process of forensics investigation.
- What are the steps involved in a forensics case investigation.
- Different parties involved in an investigation and how their support is necessary for an effective investigation.
- What are the requirement and process to setup a forensic lab?
- What are the latest trends in cyber forensics?
- How you can apply machine learning approaches and data mining techniques for effective forensics investigation.

Depending on your background, and your motivation for being interested in Cyber forensic, you will gain different kinds of skills and knowledge from this book, as set out in following Table.

Skills and knowledge to be gained from reading this book, depending on readers' goals and background

- Background concepts of cyber forensics
- Evolution and Goals of cyber forensics
- The challenges forensics experts has to face during investigation
- Phases of cyber forensics investigation
- Parties involved in the investigation and how we can effectively communicate and collaborate
- Traditional issues like malware attack, digital stenography, cyber terrorism
- Latest trends like mobile forensics, web forensics, cloud forensics
- Using machine learning techniques to counter cyber attacks
- Application of data mining and knowledge discovery to assist forensics experts

BOOK ORGANIZATION

The early chapters are organized in order of providing conceptual background, starting with an introduction to cyber forensics and its importance, the goals of cyber forensics, how it is evolving and the current challenges (Chapters 1–3). This is followed by chapters on two important issues, malware attacks and digital terrorism attacks (Chapter 4-5), that provides the insight about malware attacks and other cyber terrorism attacks and how we can prevent them. After this we discussed one of the important aspects of investigation, i.e. how investigator can acquire, preserve and analyse data to produce legal evidence (Chapter 6). In the following chapters, the book provides insight about the process and requirements of setting up a forensics lab and details about digital crime evidence (Chapter 7-8). Then we move on to a series of chapters covering fundamental topics in cyber-crime: digital steganography, email forensics, web forensics, message forensics, and financial fraud detection (Chapter 9-11). The next three chapters look at latest trend in cyber forensics, i.e. cloud forensics and how machine learning and data mining approaches can assist to forensics experts in countering sophisticated cyber-crimes and investigating the cases (Chapters 12–14). The final chapter is devoted to the forensics case studies (Chapter 15).

REFERENCES

Bera, A. (2019). *Terrifying Cybercrime Statistics*. Retrieved from safeatlast.co: https://safeatlast.co/blog/cybercrime-statistics/#gref

Dickson, F. (2019). *2019 Thales Data Threat Report – Global Edition*. Retrieved from thalesesecurity.com: https://www.thalesesecurity.com/2019/data-threat-report

Foster, J. (2018). *21 terrifying cyber crime statistics*. Retrieved from dataconnectors. com: https://www.dataconnectors.com/technews/21-terrifying-cyber-crime-statistics/

Gravrock, E. v. (2019). *Here are the biggest cybercrime trends of 2019*. Retrieved from weforum.org: https://www.weforum.org/agenda/2019/03/here-are-the-biggest-cybercrime-trends-of-2019/

Milkovich, D. (2019). *15 Alarming Cyber Security Facts and Stats*. Retrieved from cybintsolutions.com: https://www.cybintsolutions.com/cyber-security-facts-stats/

Morgan, S. (2017). *Cybersecurity Business Report*. Retrieved from csoonline.com: https://www.csoonline.com/article/3237674/ransomware-damage-costs-predicted-to-hit-115b-by-2019.html

Morgan, S. (2019). *Cybercrime Damages $6 Trillion By 2021*. Retrieved from cybersecurityventures.com: https://cybersecurityventures.com/hackerpocalypse-cybercrime-report-2016/

privacyrights. (2019). *Data Breaches*. Retrieved from privacyrights.org: https://privacyrights.org/data-breaches

Vojinovic, I. (2019). *30+ Fear-Inducing Cyber Security Statistics*. Retrieved from smallbizgenius.net: https://www.smallbizgenius.net/by-the-numbers/cyber-security-statistics/#gref

Acknowledgment

This work was a great experience for us into the domain of forensic science. There are lots of people who helped us directly and indirectly to make this book reality. We would like to acknowledge the contribution of each individual who helped us in the conception and completion of this book.

We want to take this opportunity to offer our sincere gratitude to them. A very special thanks to IGI publication team, particularly Jan Travers, Courtney Tychinski and Miss Halle N. Frisco without their continuous encouragement and support this book would not have been possible. We also thank our editorial advisory board members Dr. T J Siddiqui, Dr. M Akheela, Dr. Rashid Ali, Fahad U Khan, Prof. Ubaidullah Bokhari, Adil Kaleem, Dr. Arif Siddiqui and IGI book development team for their guidance and valuable suggestions during the entire journey of book publication.

Thanks to our reviewers, their efforts in time constrained impartial and critical review are essential to finish the book in time.

We would like to express our deep gratitude to Dr. M A Khanum, who wrote the Foreword for this book.

Thanks to our friends and colleagues for providing help wherever and whenever necessary.

This acknowledgement will not be complete until we pay our gratitude and regards to our parents and family members for their unflinching and encouragement to us in all our pursuits. It's the confidence of our family members in us that has made us the person that we are today. We dedicate this book to them.

Finally, we wish to thank the organizations and individuals who granted me permission to use the research material and information necessary for the completion of this book.

Last but not the least we are heartily thankful to almighty God for showering His blessings forever during our entire life.

Chapter 1
Cyber Forensics:
Its Importance, Cyber Forensics Techniques, and Tools

Sonali Yadav
Integral University, India

ABSTRACT

Today one of the major difficulties facing all organizations is cybercrime. Cybercrime is any crime related to computers or the internet. Cybercrimes cover a vast range, from sending fake emails to downloading and distributing copyrighted material. Cyber forensics is among one of the important branches of computer science. It deals with cybercrime investigation. In this chapter, the author provides an overview of cyber forensics. The chapter focuses on its importance and some of the techniques and tools used by cyber forensic investigators.

INTRODUCTION

Day-by-day the number of internet users is increasing and so is the Cybercrime. No one realised that internet can be used to harm mankind. Whenever an organization found that there are some loopholes in their security system, it has led to a compromise in protecting their vital data. Then the questions arise: How did this happen and how early can it be prevented from happening? This is where the role of forensics comes into play. The goal of Cyber forensics is to perform crime investigations by using evidence from digital data to find who was responsible for that particular crime said by (prabhu490730, 2015). The cyber forensic investigator collects and examines all

DOI: 10.4018/978-1-7998-1558-7.ch001

the bits and pieces of information and evidence left behind the crime scene. Then the forensic investigator is liable to answer the question of who and what.

It is important to keep in mind that the area of forensics is very broad in nature as it is related to IT. It is very broad in nature, and involves many sub-specialties. Here we will focus on Cyber forensics. Cyber Forensics, Computer Forensics or Digital forensics, more or less, mean the same. In this article, we will use the term cyber forensics and computer forensics interchangeably.

CYBER FORENSICS

Cyber is a prefix used to describe, a person, a thing or any idea related to computers and the internet. Forensics means using some sort of scientific process for the collection, analysis, and presentation of the evidence which has been collected. Forensics deals primarily with the recovery and examination of latent evidence. Latent evidence can take many forms, from fingerprints left on a window to DNA evidence recovered from blood stains to the files on a hard drive as per An Introduction to Computer Forensics-Infosec Resource. Thus, a formal definition of cyber forensics is:

Cyber Forensics is the science of examining, analysing and reporting electronic evidence collected from computers, networks, wireless communication and storage devices." or in other words "We define cyber forensics as the discipline that combines elements of law and computer science to collect and analyse data from computer systems, networks, wireless communications, and storage devices in a way that is admissible as evidence in a court of law by .

Mostly, the data collected during a cyber-forensic investigation is not easily available or seen by a common computer user. This may comprise items like fragments of data that can be found in the space allocated for existing files and deleted files from the computer system, which can only be known by a cyber-forensics expert. Special skill, practice, and tools are essential for obtaining this type of evidence. In a crime scene cyber forensics is mainly concerned with three types of data and they are as follows (as said by (New York Computer Forensics).

1. **Active Data:** Active data is the data available on the computer system. This type of data is easily noticeable and can be obtained without using any restoration process. The data or information readily accessible to users includes word files, spread sheets, images, databases, email-messages, program files, system files or files used by the operating system. This is the easiest type of data.

2. **Archival Data:** Archival data is a collection of data that has been moved to a storage media (Like cloud) for backup and storage. This type of data includes chats, a simple list of files, files organized under directory or catalogue structure, backup tapes, entire hard drives.

3. **Latent Data:** Latent data, also known as ambient data, is not easily seen or accessible upon first glance at the scene of a Cyber-crime by an expert. It takes a much deeper level of investigation by the cyber forensic experts to unearth them. Specialized software is needed to access this type of data. Obtaining latent data is time-consuming and costly compared to the other two types of data. Some example of Latent data includes:

    a) Deleted files or partially overwritten files.

    b) The information which is in computer storage but is not readily referenced in the file allocation tables;

    c) The information which cannot be viewed readily by the operating system or commonly used software applications;

    d) Data which has been purposely deleted and is now located in: Unallocated spaces in the hard drive; Swap files; Print spooler files; Memory dumps;

    e) The slack space between the existing files and the temporary cache.

Cyber forensics is all about collecting data and analysing them to prove the crime or breach of policy. It focuses on obtaining evidence of illegal misuse of computers in a way that could lead to the trial of the guilty. A Cyber Forensics investigation could involve looking at all three types of data mentioned above, depending on the circumstances. However, they are particularly interested in latent data. Software developers often build program applications to combat and capture online criminals. These applications are the heart of cyber forensics.

IMPORTANCE OF CYBER FORENSICS

The digital era in which we are living today is prone to cyber threats and it would be very difficult to extract the kind of evidence required to solve many of the cases brought forth to the court. Cyber forensic science is an enormously trustworthy and helpful recourse needed to try such cases in court. To be able to carefully examine cybercrime, cyber forensics is needed to access the type of encrypted and buried information that is stored in hard drive of computer system and other storage Medias. In the world of professional hackers and hacking techniques, it would be impossible to uncover needed evidence for cyber or non-cybercrimes, without this system of forensic science. Evidence revealed through cyber forensics is subject to the same legal guidelines as all other criminal evidence. It must be legally obtained to be admissible in court. Each country has its own set of unique guidelines for the use of cyber forensic evidence, and this science has been utilized in some major criminal court cases since the mid 1980's (Emiliogarcia, 2014).

Cyber forensics can be helpful to all types of organizations (for example corporation as well as law firms). For example, if a company has reason to believe that an employee is distributing business secrets or storing illegal contents, they might employ a forensic investigator to help build a case against that employee. Sometime employee might erase their local data and have unauthorized access to the office servers. If one has doubt that computer device contains evidence that may be important to their case, it is best to obtain that evidence through a licensed and experienced investigator who is highly qualified in cyber forensics. If one hires a skilled investigator, it means that the information collected is legally defensible and uncorrupted. All investigators must have great qualifications and extensive experience on the stand. This is important because your investigator will be called to testify about what they did; their justification for doing it, and the methods they used. A good forensic investigator not only delivers the evidence, but knows how to manage their vocal inflection. They also know how to present themselves in front of judge and jury. Small details like this can profoundly impact your case, making it crucial that you partner with investigators who know how to testify given in (News Team, 2017).

CYBER FORENSIC TECHNIQUES

For all cyber forensics experts, it is very important to gain knowledge of as many forensics techniques as possible. This will not only help them to maximize their chances of dealing with a broad spectrum of the situation but also useful in finding solutions very quickly. In short, with the knowledge of multiple forensics techniques, there are fewer chances to trap in a problem. Some of the most popular cyber forensic techniques used by cyber forensic experts as per (Shankdhar, 2019) are:

Live Forensics

Traditionally cyber forensics experts used to take a snapshot of memory and storage media as images, and perform analysis on these images in an inaccessible environment. This can, of course, stop the analysis pipeline, as imaging is not a time-efficient process. In contrast to traditional cyber forensic techniques, live forensic deals with active threats and attacks at runtime. Live Forensic or Live Response tries to discover, control and remove threats in a live, running system environment. Live forensics believes in active response compared to the passive response of traditional forensics. Thus it is useful for dealing with a threat on the spot. Live as well as traditional forensics follows the same steps of identification, Analysis and eliminating the threat but the only difference is in the response time. Live forensics scenarios are short-lived. So, to be successful, one has to be focused on narrowing down the source of the threat. This means, that instead of brute-forcing your way into the identification of the problem, you should look for "usual suspects" files in the system, such as TEMP directories. On Windows, a good way of initiating live forensics is by peaking at the active user's APPDATA directory, especially its ROAMING folder is written in (Ryan Fahey, 2019).

Data Recovery

Our lives have become more and more data-driven. This can include personal data (i.e. photos, videos or personal documents) or professional data (such as documents, sensitive and important company information). We cannot afford to lose any of these data for good. Data recovery is a technique through which a cyber-forensic expert recovers or restores the data or information that has been deleted, damaged or lost. Sometimes we intentionally or unintentionally delete some of the files. But these files hardly ever get erased permanently. The system keeps them in the drive until it requires space for a new file. Thus, we can recover the deleted file in a certain time frame. Data recovery is commonly done in two ways:

1. In-place recovery: where tools can be used to recover data by remediating disk drive errors;
2. Read-only recovery: this scheme does not restore errors on the actual point of failure. instead of storing the recovered files someplace else on the disk.

Password Recovery

In this digital world, password provides strong protection to all type of data or information (i.e. personal or professional). During crime investigations, a common issue faced by law enforcement is password protected files on the suspect's system. In such a scenario password recovery is our only and best option left to recover or access our files. Password recovery can be achieved by cracking the password through brute force, which attempts all possible combinations allowed for that password. Brute force techniques are very time-consuming in many cases. A smarter approach can be employed to significantly decrease the number of possible passwords. The problem can be compounded if the files are also encrypted. Passware is one of the tools used by law enforcement agencies in the U.S. to crack password-protected files. Without password recovery, these password protected files are of no use.

File Carving

File Carving is a forensic technique that uses file contents rather than file metadata, to find or restore the file. As we know, that whenever a file is deleted from a drive it was not removed from that drive. Usually, the operating System merely loses its handle on the file. Thus, we cannot access the file through our file system, as it is now oblivious to the file's existence itself. But we can still restore such files based on their content. File carving extracts meaningful, structured data from a structure less, unallocated portion of the drive. It is most useful when file or directory entries are either corrupt or missing. An eminent case of file carving was when the U.S. Navy Seals raided Osama bin Laden's compound and took away all storage drives found inside. The carving was employed to dissect those drives, and the information acquired thereafter aided in tightening national security written in (Ryan Fahey, 2019).

Known File Filtering

During the investigation of a crime, cyber forensic experts encounter with a large amount of data. Among these, most of the data are completely irrelevant. Most of the time Investigator are, often, searching for a specific type of data or file, which become difficult to filter through tons of unrelated artefacts. File filtering technique make this simple; rather than excluding all the irrelevant files, expert start with some known data of the relevant file. This makes the process of exclusion much faster. Known file filtering is a common forensics technique used to locate only relevant files by filtering out irrelevant artefacts. Known file filtering makes use of popular cryptographic hashes MD5 or SHA1, in tandem with hash values of application installation files. It then looks for a matching hash in the file system. A major drawback of Known File Filtering is that it can only work if the hashes match perfectly. This means that, if the relevant files are even slightly corrupted, this technique becomes powerless given in (Ryan Fahey, 2019).

String and Keyword Searching

Long before digital files were considered as legal evidence, forensic experts used to look in every paper document to find special phrases or words that were relevant to their inquiry. Today we call these special phrases or words as strings and keywords respectively. Searching for these strings can greatly fasten forensic investigations, especially if the data-set is quite large. In cyber forensics, string and keyword searching can help identify relevant data, as well as the source of potential threats. The key point here is to identify good keywords and strings. For instance, if you want to look for a file that contains instructions on painting portraits, avoid using the term "instructions" in your search; instead, focus on "portrait," as you might have other files containing the word "instructions," while very few files include "portrait."

CYBER FORENSIC TOOLS

Computers and electronic devices have evolved much faster, and are being used in modern crimes both as target or weapon. The art of investigating a crime conducted with or involving computers is called cyber forensics or computer forensics. Attackers have evolved; they are using sophisticated computer systems to commit terrible crimes. The target can be a home system, corporate network or even all the computers that they can connect to it. With this increasing rate of crime involving computers, evidence collection has become a vital part. Programmers developed tools that help in collecting digital evidence. These tools have evolved and can carry out all kinds of actions– from basic to advance level.

Based on the task performed, tools can be categorized as Network Forensic tools, Database Analysis tools, File Analysis tools, Registry Analysis tools, Email Analysis tools, OS Analysis tools, Disk and data capture. There are many tools available outside but this article covered some of the popular tools like:

1. Volatility
2. EnCase
3. Forensic Tool Kit (FTK)
4. XWF (X-Ways)
5. Oxygen Forensic Suite
6. CAINE
7. MailXaminer
8. Autopsy

Volatility

Volatility is an open-source framework used to perform volatile memory forensics. It is written in Python and supports almost all 32 bit and 64-bit machines. It can perform reconnaissance on process lists, ports, network connections, registry files, DLLs, crash dumps and cached sectors. It can also analyse system hibernation files and can check for rootkit presence as well. In Kali Linux, the Volatility framework is by default present in the forensic section. Below is a snapshot of volatility written by (Harpreet Passi, 2018).

Figure 1. Snapshot of Volatility (Harpreet Passi, 2018)

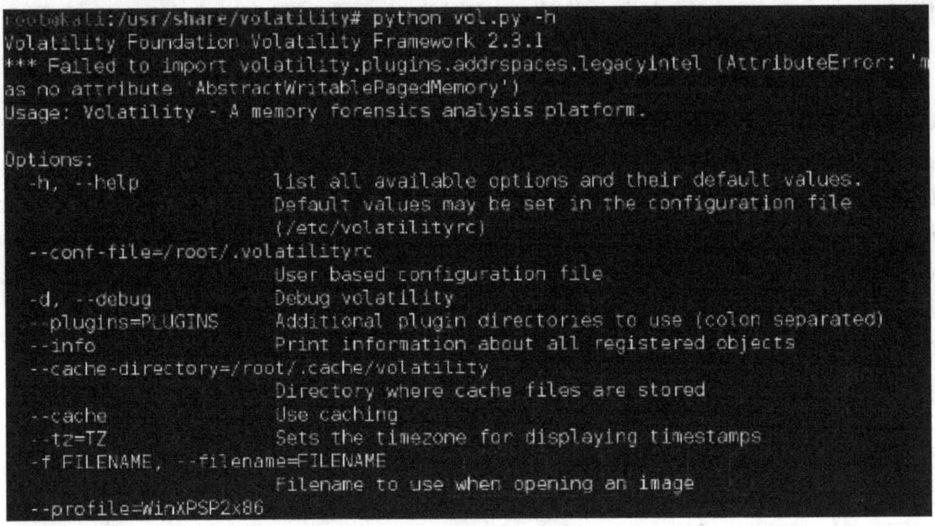

```
root@kali:/usr/share/volatility# python vol.py -h
Volatility Foundation Volatility Framework 2.3.1
*** Failed to import volatility.plugins.addrspaces.legacyintel (AttributeError: 'm
as no attribute 'AbstractWritablePagedMemory')
Usage: Volatility - A memory forensics analysis platform.

Options:
  -h, --help              list all available options and their default values.
                          Default values may be set in the configuration file
                          (/etc/volatilityrc)
  --conf-file=/root/.volatilityrc
                          User based configuration file
  -d, --debug             Debug volatility
  --plugins=PLUGINS       Additional plugin directories to use (colon separated)
  --info                  Print information about all registered objects
  --cache-directory=/root/.cache/volatility
                          Directory where cache files are stored
  --cache                 Use caching
  --tz=TZ                 Sets the timezone for displaying timestamps
  -f FILENAME, --filename=FILENAME
                          Filename to use when opening an image
  --profile=WinXPSP2x86
```

EnCase

EnCase is a product that has been designed for forensics, digital security, security investigation and e-discovery use. Thus EnCase is a multipurpose forensic investigation tool. EnCase is customarily utilized to recover proof from seized hard drives. EnCase allows the specialist to direct a top to bottom investigation of client records to gather digital evidence which can eventually be used in a court of law. It can help forensic investigators across the investigation life cycle: (Harpreet Passi, 2018)

1. Forensic triage: Prioritizing the files for investigation based on volatility and other parameters.
2. Collect: The gathering of digital data without compromising integrity.
3. Decrypt: Examining encrypted data files by decrypting them. This can be done using any password recovery technique.
4. Process: Aid in indexing the evidence and in automating common jobs so that time can be efficiently used. Hence spending time on investigation rather than the process.
5. Investigate: It can perform an investigation for almost all windows and mobile operating systems.
6. Report: Create a report that will serve all spectators. The report must have templates with various format options.

Feature of EnCase as given by (Ravi Das, 2019):

1. It is a very user-friendly but expensive tool.
2. With the paid version of EnCase which supports all utilities, it also has a free version that can be used for evidence acquisition which is very easy to use. This tool is known as the EnCase Imager.
3. With the increase in cyber threats, encryption plays a significant role in securing data in any type of system. EnCase has built-in support for almost all types of encryption including Bitlocker, MacAfee, Symantec, Sophos, etc.
4. Good keyword searching capabilities and scripting features are available.
5. The latest versions of EnCase sometimes are not compatible with other forensic based tools.
6. There is more usage of Encase for mobile forensics.

Forensic Tool Kit (FTK)

The Forensic Toolkit, or FTK, is a computer forensic investigation software package created by Access Data. It examines a hard drive by searching for different information. It can, for instance, find deleted emails and can also scan the disk for content strings. These can then be used as a secret keyword reference to breaking any encryption. The toolbox incorporates an independent disk imaging program called the FTK Imager. It saves an image of a hard disk in one document or in different segments which can then be recreated later. It computes MD5 hash values and affirms the integrity of the information before the closing of the documents. The outcome is an image file(s) that can be saved in several formats as per given in (Ravi Das, 2019).

Features of Forensic Tool Kit

1. It has a simple user interface and advanced searching capabilities.
2. FTK supports EFS decryption.
3. It produces a case log file.
4. It has significant bookmarking and salient reporting features.
5. FTK Imager is free
6. FTK does not support scripting features.
7. It does not have multitasking capabilities.
8. There is no progress bar to estimate the time remaining.
9. FTK does not have a timeline view.

XWF (X-Ways)

X Ways Forensics is a powerful, commercial Computer Forensic Tool. It is Windows-based licensed software that offers ample functionality about computer forensics. One of the best advantages of this software is that it can be used in a portable mode (Ravi Das, 2019).

Features of XWF(X-Ways Forensics) given in (**X-Ways Software Technology**)

1. Disk cloning and imaging.
2. Ability to read partitioning and file system structures inside raw (.dd) image files, ISO, VHD, and VMDK images
3. Complete access to disks, RAIDs, and images more than 2 TB in size (more than 232 sectors) with sector sizes up to 8 KB
4. Built-in interpretation of JBOD, RAID 0, RAID 5, RAID 5EE, and RAID 6 systems, Linux software RAIDs, Windows dynamic disks, and LVM2
5. Automatic identification of lost/deleted partitions
6. Native support for FAT12, FAT16, FAT32, exFAT, TFAT, NTFS, Ext2, Ext3, Ext4 etc.
7. Superimposition of sectors, e.g. with corrected partition tables or file system data structures to parsing file systems completely despite data corruption, without altering the original disk or image
8. Access to logical memory of running processes
9. Various data recovery techniques, lightning-fast and powerful file carving
10. Well maintained file header signature database based on GREP notation
11. Data interpreter, knowing 20 variable types

Oxygen Forensic Suite

The Oxygen Forensics package is mobile forensic software for the logical examination of smartphones, cell phones, and PDAs. The suite can extract device information, contacts, calendar events, SMS messages, occasion logs, and records. Oxygen Forensic Suite is also used to gather digital evidence from cloud services used on Smartphones. It can also extract various types of metadata which is important in any digital forensic investigation. The suite gets to the device by utilizing proprietary protocols given (Ravi Das, 2019).

Features of Oxygen Forensic Suite given in (Oxygen Forensics)

1. Oxygen allows for physical extraction information and data from Android devices while bypassing device security.
2. The user interface and options are very simple and clear to understand.

3. The final report can be saved in multiple readable formats such as .xls, .xlsx, .pdf, etc.
4. It is an economically better option when compared to other mobile forensic tools.
5. It has built-in functionality that can be used to crack passwords for encrypted iTunes, locked iPhones or android backups.
6. Its support for a range of mobile devices is limited.
7. Since the tool is computer-based, there is a higher statistical probability of virus/malware entering inside the phone that is being examined.
8. It uses a brute force technique which incurs a lot of time to complete the process.

CAINE

CAINE is an acronym for COMPUTER Aided Investigative Environment. It is an Italian GNU/Linux live distribution created as a Digital Forensic Project. CAINE is an open-source Linux distribution that has been developed specifically for digital forensics. CAINE offers an entire forensic environment that is structured to integrate existing software tools like software and to provide a friendly graphic interface. Below is the snapshot of CAINE.10.0 "Infinity".

The main design objectives of CAINE as given in (CAINE, 2018)

1. an interoperable environment that supports the digital investigator during the four phases of digital investigation
2. a user-friendly graphical interface
3. user-friendly tools

MailXaminer

MailXaminer is preferred by many investigators who belong to reputed and significant law enforcement agencies. MailXaminer performs email analysis. It examines emails from both application and web-based mail clients. It helps the investigator in-collecting email evidence, arranging the evidence, searching the emails using various advanced options like Regex. It can detect and report obscene image attachments by using skin tone analysis said by (Harpreet Passi, 2018).

Features of MailXaminer given by (Inc SysTools, 2019)

Figure 2. Snapshot of CAINE 10.0 by (CAINE, 2018)

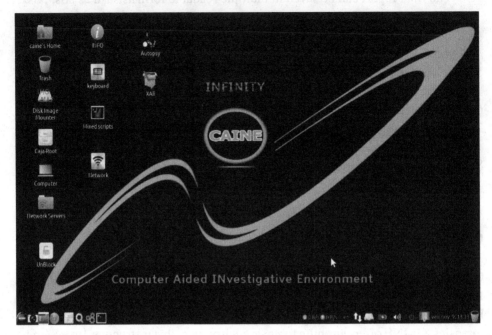

1. Support 20+ email formats: Extensive list of email formats helping in view any email anytime.
2. One Case, Multiple Investigators: multiple users can investigate a case through the user management dashboard.
3. Flexible Evidence Report Formats: Get evidence files in formats with universal acceptability & approval Email formats
4. Control User Permissions: Give full or restricted case access to users depending on their role and complexity

Autopsy

An autopsy is a GUI based open source software that allows efficient analysis of hard drives and smartphones. It is used by different law enforcement agencies, military, and corporate investigators to conduct digital investigations. It is available for both Windows and Linux and is pre-installed in Kali Linux, given in (Carrier Brian, 2019).

Table 1. Comparison between different tools of Cyber Forencise

S. No	Tool Name	Open Source(Free)	Closed Source (Not-free)	Design Objective
1	Volatility	YES		To perform volatile memory forensics
2	EnCase	YES		Usually utilized to recover proof from seized hard drives
3	Forensic Tool Kit (FTK)	YES		To scan the hard drive and look for evidence
4	XWF(X-Ways)		YES	Used for- disk imaging and analysis, analysis of various disk formats, case management, registry view, metadata extraction, etc.
5	Oxygen Forensic Suite		YES	To gather digital evidence from mobile phones and cloud services used on phones.
6	CAINE	YES		An interoperable environment that supports the digital investigator during the four phases of the digital investigation
7	MailXaminer		YES	To Perform Email Analysis.
8	Autopsy	YES		Used to efficiently analyze hard drives and smartphones

Features of Autopsy given in (Carrier Brian, 2019)

1. Collaborate with fellow examiners on large cases.
2. Displays system events in a graphical interface to help identify activity.
3. Text extraction and index searched modules enable you to find files that mention accurate terms and find regular expression patterns.
4. Extract web activity from common browsers to help identify user activity.
5. Uses RegRipper to identify recently accessed documents and USB devices.
6. Identifies short cuts and accessed documents
7. Parses MBOX format messages, such as Thunderbird.
8. Thumbnail viewer: Displays thumbnail of images to help quick view pictures.

CONCLUSION

This article gives a brief about cyber forensics and its importance. It also explains some of the popular forensic techniques and tools. The techniques and tools are not arranged according to priority and popularity. Some tools are exclusively designed for hard disk analysis, while some for mobile investigations and so on. If you are new to cyber forensics than this article helps you understand cyber forensics, why it is so important in this digital era, what are the different techniques followed by experts to find the revenant evidences concerning the crime and by using what type of the tools? Many of the tools available today are open source, so you can start with these tools, taking a deep dive into each one.

One can also begin with the pre-built Virtual machine (VM) and distributions like CAINE so that one can utilize time efficiently and learn in deep. Be sure that identifying related information and comparing it with real-world scenarios is important.

As the author discussed only some of the techniques and tools, you may also search for more forensic techniques, tools, and experiments. As attackers are getting evolved and advanced with each crime; software development companies are trying to develop more sophisticated tools that can speed up the investigation, whenever used by experts. The point to be remembered here is that no matter how advanced the tool becomes; it requires an expert eye to identify the logic and correlate the fact and figures.

REFERENCES

BrianC. (2019). *Autopsy Features*. Retrieved from https://sleuthkit.org/autopsy/features.php

CAINE. (2018). *CAINE 10.0 "Infinity" Computer Aided Investigative Environment*. Retrieved from https://www.caine-live.net/

Das, R. (2019). *tool-comparison*. Retrieved from https://resources.infosecinstitute.com/category/computerforensics/introduction/commercial-computer-forensics-tools/tool-comparison/

Das, R. (n.d.). *An Introduction to computer forensics*. Retrieved 2019, from infosecinstitute.com: https://resources.infosecinstitute.com/category/computerforensics/introduction/#gref

Emiliogarcia. (2014). *The Importance of Computer Forensic Investigations*. Retrieved from https://www.smgconsultingservices.com/the-importance-of-computer-forensic-investigations/

Fahey, R. (2019). *forensic-techniques-part-1*. Retrieved from https://resources.infosecinstitute.com/category/computerforensics/introduction/areas-of-study/digital-forensics/forensic-techniques-part-1/#gref

Forensics, O. (n.d.). *Oxygen forensic® detective features*. Retrieved from https://www.oxygen-forensic.com/en/products/oxygen-forensic-detective

Inc SysTools. (2019). *Mailxaminer: Email forensic redefined*. Retrieved from https://www.mailxaminer.com/: https://www.mailxaminer.com/features.html

New, Y. C. F. (n.d.). *The Computer Forensics Process*. Retrieved from https://newyorkcomputerforensics.com/computer-forensics-process

News Team. (2017). *What is digital forensics and why is it important?* Retrieved from https://www.firstlegal.com/what-is-digital-forensics-and-why-is-it-important

Passi, H. (2018). *Top 20 Trending Computer Forensics Tools of 2018*. Retrieved from https://www.greycampus.com/blog/information-security/top-twenty-trending-computer-forensics-tools

prabhu490730. (2015, March). Retrieved from https://prabhurockstar.wordpress.com/

Shankdhar, P. (2019). *Popular Computer Forensics Top 21 Tools*. Retrieved from https://resources.infosecinstitute.com/computer-forensics-tools/

US-CERT. a. g. (2008). Retrieved from https://www.us-cert.gov/sites/default/files/publications/forensics.pdf

X-Ways Software Technology. (n.d.). *X-Ways Forensics: Integrated Computer Forensics Software*. Retrieved from www.x-ways.net/forensics

KEY TERMS AND DEFINITIONS

Cyber Forensics: Cybercrime investigation methods.
Cyber Forensics Techniques: To collect and preserve evidence.
Cybercrime: It is also known as digital crime.
Forensics Tools: Supporting tools for cyber forensics and digital forensics.

Chapter 2
Cyber Forensics Evolution and Its Goals

Mohammad Zunnun Khan
Integral University, India

Anshul Mishra
City College, Lucknow, India

Mahmoodul Hasan Khan
Institute of Engineering and Technology, Lucknow, India

ABSTRACT

This chapter includes the evolution of cyber forensics from the 1980s to the current era. It was the era when computer forensics came into existence after a personal computer became a viable option for consumers. The formation of digital forensics is also discussed here. This chapter also includes the formation of cyber forensic investigation agencies. Cyber forensic life cycle and related phases are discussed in detail. Role of international organizations on computer evidence is discussed with the emphasize on Digital Forensic Research Workshop (DFRWS), Scientific Working Group on Digital Evidence (SWDGE), chief police officers' involvement. Authenticity-, accuracy-, and completeness-related pieces of evidence are also discussed. The most important thing that is discussed here is the cyber forensics data.

EVOLUTION OF CYBER FORENSICS

The 1980s was the era when computer forensics came into existence after personal computers became a viable option for consumers. FBI had created a program in 1984 named as the 'Magnetic Media Program', in the current era, it is known as the

DOI: 10.4018/978-1-7998-1558-7.ch002

Computer Analysis and Response Team (CART). Michael Anderson was known as the father of computer forensics because he had started developing measures in this field. He was a special agent in criminal investigation division. He had served the American government until the mid-1990s, after which he founded New Technologies, Inc., a leading computer forensics firm (H. Armstrong, 2004).

Until the late 1990s, what became known as digital forensics was commonly termed 'computer forensics. At first, computer forensic technicians were law enforcement officers who were also computer hobbyists. In the USA in 1984, work began in the FBI Computer Analysis and Response Team (CART). One year later, in the UK, the Metropolitan Police set up a computer crime unit under John Austen within what was then called the Fraud Squad.

A major change took place at the beginning of the 1990s. Investigators and technical support operatives within the UK law enforcement agencies, along with outside specialists, realized that digital forensics (as with other fields) required standard techniques, protocols, and procedures. Apart from informal guidelines, these standard tools and techniques did not exist and urgently needed to be developed. A series of conferences, initially convened by the Serious Fraud Office and the Inland Revenue, took place at the Police Staff College at Bramshill in 1994 and 1995, during which the modern British digital forensic methodology was established.

In the UK in 1998 the Association of Chief Police Officers (ACPO) produced the first version of its Good Practice Guide for Digital Evidence (Association of Chief Police Officers, 2012). The ACPO guidelines detail the main principles applicable to all digital forensics for law enforcement in the UK.

As the science of digital forensics had matured, these guidelines and best practices have slowly evolved into standards and the field has come under the auspices of the Forensic Science Regulator in the UK.

Formation of Cyber Forensic Investigation Agencies

In the year 1988, a meeting was organized in Oregon that led to the formation of the International Association of Computer Investigative Specialists (IACIS). Soon after that, the first module was designed to teach SCERS (Seized Computer Evidence Recovery Specialists) (M. Meyers, M. Rogers, 2006).

Computer Forensic Timeline is illustrated in Fig.1 and it represents the evolution of the digital forensics domain as such.

Figure 1. Computer Forensics Timeline

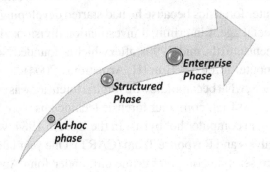

Computer Forensics Timeline is:

- *Ad-hoc phase*

In this phase, the lack of structure, lack of clear goals, lack of adequate tools, processes & procedures and further major legal issues on how to proceed with digital evidence was seen.

- *Structured Phase*

It is a complex solution for computer forensic in which from accepted procedures, special tools have been developed and most importantly enabling criminal legislation to the wide use of digital evidence.

- *Enterprise Phase*

Three areas of this phase are real-time collection of evidence, developing field collection tools and forensic becoming a service in companies.

Figure 2. computer forensic investigatory method

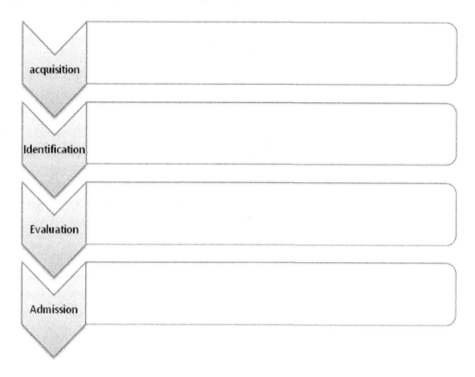

DIFFERENT COMPUTER FORENSICS MODELS SINCE 1984 TILL DATE

Computer Forensic Investigative Process (1984)

Pollitt (M. M. Pollitt, 1995), (M. M. Pollitt, 2007) has projected a technique for managing digital proof investigation so that the results will be scientifically reliable and lawfully acceptable. It contains four distinct phases.

In the Acquisition phase, the data for proof was acquired with approval from the authority. It's followed by the Identification phase whereby the tasks to spot the digital elements from the non-inheritable proof and changing it to the format understood by a human. The analysis part comprises of the task to work out whether or not the elements identified within the previous section, is so relevant to the case being investigated and may be thought-about as a legitimate proof. Within the final section, Admission, the non-inheritable & the extracted proof is conferred within the court of law.

Figure 3. DFRWS model

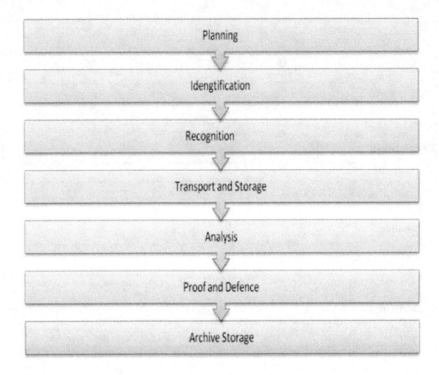

DFRWS Investigatory Model (2001)

In 2001, the first Digital Forensics Analysis Workshop (DFRWS) (G. Palmer, 2001) proposed a general-purpose digital forensics investigation method. It includes six phases.

DFRWS investigatory model started with an Identification section, during which profile detection, system observance, audit analysis, etc., were performed. It's forthwith followed by the Preservation section, involving tasks like putting in place correct case management and guaranteeing an appropriate chain of custody. This section is crucial, therefore, make sure that the information collected is free from contamination. the consecutive section is understood as assortment, during which relevant knowledge area unit being collected utilizing numerous recovery techniques which are approved. Following this section, we have 2 crucial phases, namely, Examination section and Analysis section. In these 2 phases, tasks like proof tracing, proof validation, recovery of hidden/encrypted knowledge, data processing, timeline, etc., were performed. The last section is the Presentation. Tasks associated with this section area are unit documentation, knowledgeable testimony, etc.

Figure 4. Abstract Digital Forensics Model

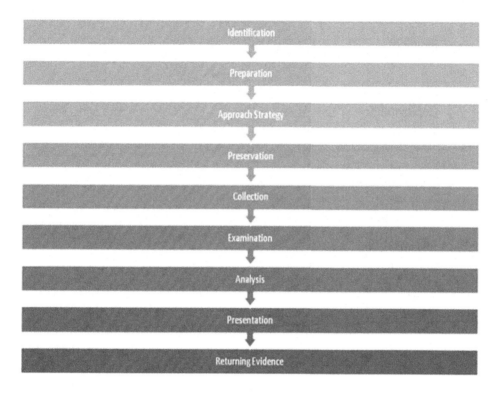

Abstract Digital Forensics Model (ADFM) (2002)

Galvanized by DFRWS inquiring model, Reith, Carr & Gunsch M. (Reith, C. Carr & G. Gunsh, 2002), planned an enhanced model referred to as Abstract Digital rhetorical Model. In this model, the author introduced 3 further phases, so increasing the number of phases to 9.

The 3 important phases introduced in this model were Preparation, Approach Strategy and Returning proof. In the Preparation section, an activity like getting ready tools, establish techniques and obtaining management support, were done. Approach Strategy was introduced with the target to maximize the acquisition of unblemished proof and at the same time to reduce any negative impact on the victim and encompassing individuals. To confirm that evidence safely comes back to the rightful owner or properly disposed of, the Returning proof part was additionally introduced. The first phase in ADFM is the Identification section. During this part, the task to acknowledge and confirm the form of an incident is performed. Once the incident sort was observed, consecutive part, Preparation, is conducted, and followed by Approach Strategy part. Physical and digital knowledge which is non-inheritable

Figure 5. Integrated Digital Investigation method

should be properly isolated, secured and preserved. There's additionally a necessity to concentrate on a correct chain of custody. All of those tasks are performed beneath the Preservation part. Next is the Assortment part, whereby, knowledge extraction and duplication were done. Identification and locating the potential proof from the collected knowledge, employing a systematic approach area unit conducted within the next following part, referred to as the Examination part. The task of forming many proofs and drawing conclusions supported the proof foundation is completed in the Analysis part. During the following phase, the Presentation part, the findings are summarized and conferred. The investigation processes are completed with the polishing off of the Returning proof part.

Integrated Digital Investigation method (IDIP) (2003)

This investigation method was planned by Carrier & Spafford (B. Carrier & E. H. Spafford, 2003) in 2003, to mix the varied accessible inquiring processes into one integrated model. The author introduces to the construction of the digital crime scene that refers to the virtual environment, created by the software and hardware system wherever the digital proof of against the law or incident exists.

Figure 6. Increased Digital Investigation method Model

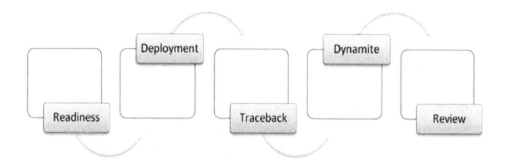

The process started with a section that needs the physical and operational infrastructure to be able to support any future investigation. During this Readiness section, the types of equipment should always be prepared and therefore the person should be capable of using it effectively. This section is so important that it is associated throughout the lifecycle of a company. It additionally consists of two sub-phases particularly - Operation Readiness and Infrastructure Readiness. Forthwith following the Readiness part, is the deployment section that offers a mechanism for a happening to be detected and confirmed. Two more sub-phases are introduced, namely, Detection & Notification and Confirmation & Authorization. Collection and analysing physical proofs are exhaustively done in Physical Crime Scene Investigation part. The sub-phases introduced area unit Preservation, Survey, Documentation, Search, Reconstruction, and Presentation. Digital Crime Scene Investigation is analogous to Physical Crime Scene Investigation with the exception that it's currently focusing on digital proof in the digital environment. The last part is the Review part. The full Digital Crime Investigation Readiness, Deployment, Physical Crime Investigation are reviewed in Review Investigation processes part to spot areas of improvement that will end up in new procedures or new training requirements.

Increased Digital Investigation Method Model (EDIP) (2004)

As the name implies, this inquiring model is developed on the previous model, the Integrated Digital Investigation method (IDIP), as planned by Carrier & Spafford. The improved Digital Investigation Method Model, additionally referred to as EDIP (V. Baryamereeba & F. Tushabe, 2004) introduces one important section referred to

Figure 7. DFMMIP model

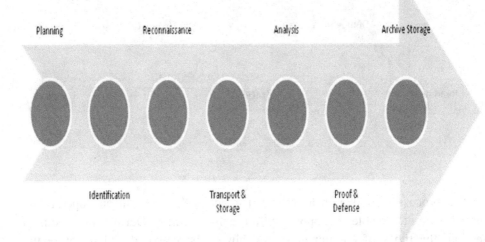

as the Traceback section. This module helps investigators to trace back the original crime scene like we can determine the actual origin of the IP Packets.

The investigation method started with the Readiness section and therefore the tasks performed in this phase are identical as in IDIP. The second section, readying part, provides a mechanism for a happening to be detected and confirmed. It consists of five sub-phases particularly Detection & Notification, Physical Crime Scene Investigation, Digital Crime Scene Investigation, Confirmation and finally, Submission. Unlike DIP, this part includes each physical and digital crime scene investigations and presentation of findings to legal entities (via the Submission phase). In Trackback part, the main objective is tracking down the source crime scene, together with the devices and site. it's supported by 2 sub-phases particularly, Digital Crime Scene Investigation and Authorization (obtaining approval to perform investigation and accessing information). Following Traceback, is the Dynamite part. During this part, the investigation is conducted at the main crime scene, to distinguish the potential culprit(s). It contains four sub phases, namely, Physical Crime Scene Investigation, Digital Crime Scene Investigation, Reconstruction and Communication. In Reconstruction sub-phase, items of knowledge collected area unit, place along to construct a series of potential events that might have happened. The Communication sub-phase is analogous to the previous Submission part.

Digital Forensics Model Supported Malaysian Investigation Method (DFMMIP) (2009)

In 2009, (Perumal, S. P. Sundresan, 2009) planned yet one more digital rhetorical investigation model that is established on the Malaysian investigation processes. The DFMMIP model contains seven phases. The first phase is planning, where the investigators plan out the activities to be performed systematically in order to carry out the investigation.

Upon completion of the first section, the planning, Identification part is followed. After that, the Inspection activity section is conducted. This section deals with investigating the media while the devices are still running (in operation) that is analogous to live forensics. The author argued that the presence of live information acquisition that focuses on fragile proof will increase the possibilities of positive prosecution. Before acquired data is analysed, it has to be securely transported to the investigation web site and be stored safely. This activity is carried out in Transport & Storage part. Once the data is prepared, the Analysis part is invoked and the facts are going to be analysed and examined using the acceptable tools and techniques. Just like the Presentation phase in the previous models, the investigators are needed to submit the reports of investigation to support the conferred case in the court of law. This activity is carried out in Proof & Defence part. Finally, the Archive Storage section is performed, whereby relevant evidences are properly stored for future references and training purposes.

INTERNATIONAL ORGANIZATION ON COMPUTER EVIDENCE

The discipline continued to grow in the 1990s, with the first conference on collecting evidence from computers held in 1993. Two years later, the International Organization on Computer Evidence (IOCE) was established (Willer L, 2006) & (NCJ 187736, 2001).

Digital Forensic Research Workshop (DFRWS)

IOCE works voluntarily and it is a non-profit organization. It takes research initiatives based on knowledge and idea-sharing about digital forensics research. It also organizes yearly conferences and sponsors technical working groups as well.

Scientific Working Group on Digital Evidence (SWDGE)

The federal Crime Laboratory Directors group formed (Scientific Working Group on Digital Evidence) SWGDE in 1998. It includes the traditional process of examining audio-video and with the development in digital technologies, methods for examining digital still photography was added with computer forensics. As an outcome, they formed a cluster to explore digital evidence as a part of the main forensic discipline. This group comprised of members from prominent organizations such as the American Association of Forensic Science, International Organization on Computer Evidence, High Technology CrimeInvestigation Association & International Association of Computer Investigative Specialist. SWGDE was focused on the practice of digital evidence forensics primarily in the laboratory setting (H. Armstrong, 2004) & (J. Giordano, 2002).

Chief Police Officers Involvement

Association of Chief Police Officers (ACPO) was established in 1948. It was a non-profit organization, functioning in England, Wales, and Northern Ireland. It was responsible for development of policing practices and has designed and published a guide with procedures to be followed while collecting computer-based evidence to ensure good field practice (M. Gregg, 2004).

DEVELOPMENT OF CYBER FORENSICS

Computer forensics is the study of evidence by extracting, analysing and documenting them from a computer system or its associated network. It is regularly used by law officials to seek out evidence for a criminal trial. Officers of Government agencies and business organizations may also require specialist computer forensic techniques. The discipline of computer forensics seems to be new and has been founded around the 1980s.

The investigators have to submit proof in the court to support legal proceedings with respect to a crime. This digital evidence consists of data from storage media like hard disk, floppy disks, zip disks, Compact discs, DVDs, emails, data transmitted over communication links (wired and wireless), log files generated by the operating system, logs from perimeter devices like routers and switch, PDA, Mobile Phones, MP3 players, USB devices, and even plethora of devices which do not fit into the original concept of computers like the washing machines, engine management system in cars, GPS devices (W. Jansen, R. Ayers, 2004) & (C. Marsico, M. Rogers, 2005).

For evaluation and acceptance of Digital evidence (a new type of evidence, previously not considered by courts), certain basic principles are suggested by research scholars and these are given below:

- *Authenticity* – the evidence should be authentic that is "it should specifically be linked to the circumstances and persons alleged – and produced by someone who can answer questions about such links"
- *Accuracy* – the digital data produced as evidence should be accurate that is the evidential data should be free from any reasonable doubt about the quality of procedures used to collect the material, and analysed with the help of appropriate techniques and quality processes . In the case of exhibits which themselves contain statements 'accuracy' must also encompass accuracy of the content and that normally requires the document's originator to make a witness statement and be available for cross-examination"
- *Completeness* - "tells within its terms a complete story of a particular set of circumstances or events". There should not be any missing data.

In addition to these considerations, forensic evidence must exhibit the following properties:

- Chain of custody, transparency and explainable are the other basic principles they need to be followed among the other principles.

Unlike the physical evidence, the digital evidence, by itself has no informational value. It requires skill and talent in interpreting the latent information which is dependent on the process by which it is unraveled and the process, in turn, depends on the basic principles of computer science. To be legally acceptable in the court, it requires a motivated skilled expert who will apply appropriate tools to achieve, efficiency and reliability.

CYBER FORENSICS DATA

Cyber Forensics focuses on three kinds of data namely active data, latent data, and archival data.

Active Data

An active data is one that is currently available, visible and that which can be understood using an application within a computer. Active data might also be protected using passwords or some means of encryption. Some of the active data are word processor files, spreadsheets, files and directories, email content, database programs, system files, history files, temporary internet files, cookies, recycle bin and the like.

Latent Data

Latent data also called ambient data is volatile in nature. These types of data may be in the form of deleted files, memory dumps and similar data which reside in swap files, temporary files, printer spool files, metadata, and shadow files. It requires an expert talent to bring to light the latent data using specialized tools and techniques.

Archival data

Data that has been stored or backed up to external storage media such as tapes, CDs, DVDs, external hard disks, pen drive, zip disks, network servers on the internet is archival data. Necessary precautions have to be taken while performing forensic examination since the backup peripheral devices do not have all the information. Hence, it is always better to perform a forensic examination on source media because backups do not store latent data.

CARDINAL RULES IN CYBER FORENSICS

Set of five 'A's can express the rules of computer forensics:

1. Admissibility must guide actions: everything should be documented.
2. Acquire the evidence in the original alteration or damaging is not allowed.
3. Authenticate your copy identical to the source data
4. Analyze while retaining the data its integrity should be maintained.
5. Anticipate the unexpected.

These rules are meant to assist a forensically perfect examination of computer-related media and can be testified in a court of law by forensic examiners while handling of a particular piece of evidence. A forensically perfect examination is conducted under inhibited conditions, such that it has proper documentation, replication of evidence is possible, and these are able to verify.

A forensically perfect methodology follows no data modification on the original evidence, a pristine condition should be preserved. If the same set of tools and procedures are followed by any other expert then the results must be replicable, i.e. the same results are extracted by that expert also.

CONCLUSION

This chapter focuses on the evolution process and also discussed different phases of cyber forensics, in this chapter credential rules, were given for the cyber forensics. It also discusses the data lifecycle of Cyber Forensics.

REFERENCES

Armstrong, H., & Russo, P. (2004). *Electronic forensics education needs of law enforcement*. Available from http://www.ncisse.org/publications/cissecd/Papers/S4P02.pdf

Baryamereeba, V., & Tushabe, F. (2004). The Enhanced Digital Investigation Process Model. *Proceeding of Digital Forensic Research Workshop*.

Carrier & Spafford. (2003). Getting Physical with the Digital Investigation Process. *International Journal of Digital Evidence, 2*(2).

Giordano, J. C. (2002). *Maciag Cyber forensics: a military operations perspective*. Available from: http://www.utica.edu/academic/institutes/ecii/publications/articles/A04843F3-99E5-632B-FF420389C0633B1B.pdf

Gregg, M. (2004). *The certified computer examiner certification*. Available from: http://www.gocertify.com/article/certifiedcomputerexaminer.shtml

Jansen, W., & Ayers, R. (2004). *Guidelines on PDA forensics* [NIST 800-72]. Gaithersburg, MD: National Institute of Standards and Technology. doi:10.6028/NIST.SP.800-72

Marsico, C. M. (2005). *Rogers iPod forensics*. Available from: https://www.cerias.purdue.edu/tools_and_resources/bibtex_archive/archive/2005-13.pdf

Meyers, M. M. (2004). *Rogers Computer forensics: the need for standardization and certification*. Available from: http://www2.tech.purdue.edu/cpt/courses/CPT499S/meyersrogers_ijde.pdf

National Institute of Justice Electronic Crime Scene Investigation: A Guide for First Responders (NCJ 187736). (2001). Washington, DC: Office of Justice Programs.

Palmer, G. (2001). DTR-T001-01 Technical Report. A Road Map for Digital Forensic Research. *Digital Forensics Workshop (DFRWS)*, Utica, NY.

Pollitt, M. M. (1995). Computer Forensics: An Approach to Evidence in Cyberspace. *Proceeding of the National Information Systems Security Conference, 2*, 487-491.

Pollitt, M. M. (2007). An Ad Hoc Review of Digital Forensic Models. *Proceeding of the Second International Workshop on Systematic Approaches to Digital Forensic Engineering (SADFE'07)*. 10.1109/SADFE.2007.3

Reith, Carr, & Gunsh. (2002). An Examination of Digital Forensics Models. *International Journal of Digital Evidence, 1*(3).

Rogers, M. K., Goldman, J., Mislan, R., Wedge, T., & Debrota, S. (2006). Computer Forensics Field Triage Process Model. *Conference on Digital Forensics, Security and Law*, 27-40.

Sundresan. (2009). Digital Forensic Model based on Malaysian Investigation Process. *International Journal of Computer Science and Network Security, 9*(8).

Willer, L. (2006). *Computer forensics*. Available from: http://www.giac.org/certified_professionals/practicals/gsec/0854.php

KEY TERMS AND DEFINITIONS

Cardinal Rules in Cyber Forensics: Ethics and cardinal rules to be followed.

Computer Forensics Timeline: Computer forensics is mainly about investigating crime where computers have been involved.

Cyber Forensics: Cyber forensics is the scientific processes of identification, seizure, acquisition, authentication, analysis, documentation, and preservation of digital evidence.

Digital Evidence: Digital evidence is defined as information and data of value to an investigation that is stored on, received, or transmitted by an electronic device.

Evolution of Cyber Forensics: Explores the ways of emerging requirements of the cyber forensics.

Investigation Agencies: An agency authorized by law or regulation to conduct a counterintelligence investigation.

Chapter 3
Current Challenges of Digital Forensics in Cyber Security

Abhishek Kumar Pandey
*Babasaheb Bhimrao Ambedkar
University, India*

Ashutosh Kumar Tripathi
https://orcid.org/0000-0003-4021-9819
*Babasaheb Bhimrao Ambedkar
University, India*

Gayatri Kapil
*Babasaheb Bhimrao Ambedkar
University, India*

Virendra Singh
*Babasaheb Bhimrao Ambedkar
University, India*

Mohd. Waris Khan
*Babasaheb Bhimrao Ambedkar
University, India*

Alka Agrawal
*Babasaheb Bhimrao Ambedkar
University, India*

Rajeev Kumar
https://orcid.org/0000-0002-1813-1362
*Babasaheb Bhimrao Ambedkar
University, India*

Raees Ahmad Khan
*Babasaheb Bhimrao Ambedkar
University, India*

ABSTRACT

The digital age has undoubtedly revolutionized the life and work of people. However, this sheen of digital technology remains challenged by the spate of cybercrimes that imperil the privacy and data of the end-users. The alarming rise in cybercrimes has become a major concern for cyber specialists. In this grim context, digital forensics has emerged as a boon for cyber specialists because it has proven to be an effective means for investigating cyber-attacks. This chapter reviews the existing tools and approaches in the field of digital forensics in cybersecurity. This chapter also discusses the current challenges and problems that are faced by a forensic investigator. In addition, it enlists the different categories of digital forensics. The study concludes by underlining the importance and the need for extensive research in digital forensic tools.

DOI: 10.4018/978-1-7998-1558-7.ch003

INTRODUCTION

The use of computers in business, home, office and many other places is very popular and necessary nowadays. The world of the digital era is expanding rapidly as more and more users become a part of the cyber world and benefit from it. However, not all the users of internet adhere to the standard and valid use of computers. This era has witnessed a steep increase in what is termed as negative computing which is the use of computers and the internet for illegal and unauthorized work. The negative use of computers creates many subdomains that must be prevented. Digital forensics plays an important role in detecting and examining these subdomains and thus becomes a deterrent in containing cyber attacks. Digital forensics techniques and tools are being used by cyber specialists to collect and relate digital evidence to find the truth behind any cybercrime.

A survey by India Times in early 2019 stated that *"58% of data breach victims are the persons or organizations who have a small type of business at very low or medium-level"* (C.R. Srinivasan, 2019). Moreover, with the voluminous increase in the use of mobile devices, tabs, laptops, etc., the implementation of cyber-attacks is very easy for the attackers. Hence, the examination and analysis of cyber-attacks and security exploits have become imperative. In this paper, the first section is about different perspectives of digital forensics and their examination tools. In the second section, the authors discuss different challenges & issues and their importance. Then the paper talks about future research topics in digital forensic. The final section profiles the recommendations and the conclusion.

DIGITAL FORENSICS IN DIFFERENT PERSPECTIVE

Digital forensic has different domains and types for a different kind of analysis and identification procedure. Some are described below:-

Data Forensics

It deals with digital data. Data forensic is about the process of how to use the data or Metadata for investigation and find real evidence or truth. Data carving is a technique that is used in data forensic. Data carving is a process of retrieving data or files from the raw fragments. (Nadeem Alherbawi, 2013) Gave a detailed description of data carving and proposed a method of data craving to handle the fragmentation issue in the examination of data. Some standard tools for data forensics are shown in figure 1.

Figure 1. Tree Structure of the Standard Tools

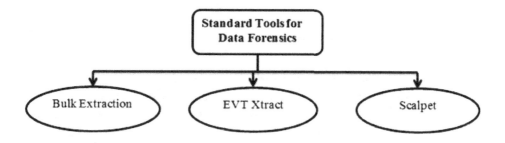

Figure 1 shows some commonly used data for forensic tools including Bulk Extraction, EVTXtract, and Scalpet. Further, Bulk Extraction, EVTXtract, and Scalpet are used to analyze disk image, a file or a directory and extract any relevant data without changing the file system structure.

Cloud Forensics

Cloud forensics is a subpart of network forensics or in other words cloud forensic is a type of forensic which deals with the huge networks and is related to the investigation of the incident that is done by or over the cloud. The crimes done on the cloud are very difficult to examine because some classical and basic techniques of digital forensic examination do not work on the cloud environment and that's why cloud forensic is gaining more significance (Sonamjain, 2014). But there are limitations in cloud forensic examination. When the cloud is public, the physical access to the cloud is denied for the investigation team because of privacy issues (Burney A., 2016). This becomes a very tough task for the examiners as they cannot investigate the scene without physical accessibility. Some standard tools for cloud forensics which are used during the investigation have been shown in figure 2.

Figure 2 shows some commonly used data for forensic tools including Frost and UFED Cloud Analyzer. Further, both Frost and UFED Cloud Analyzer tools are very valuable in cloud forensic examination. The basic works of tools are data acquired from API logs, Virtual Disk and gust firewall logs. These procedures of examination facilitate the tasks of the examiners.

Figure 2. Tree Structure of the Standard tools for Cloud Forensic

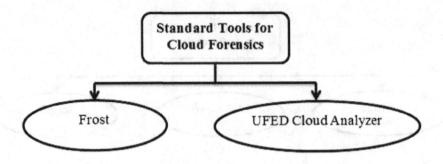

Figure 3. Tree Structure of the Standard tools Android/Mobile Forensic

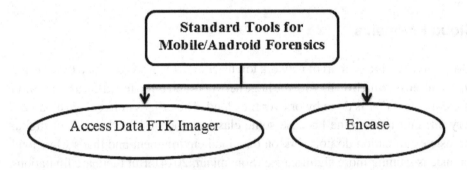

Android/Mobile Forensics

It is a type of forensics that is growing rapidly since the last decade as the use of mobile phones has increased tremendously. So, the attacks and crimes have accelerated at the same speed. Hence, the mobile/android forensics is a very important subdomain of digital forensics nowadays. In this type of forensic technique, the examiner inspects all kind of ways related to mobile phones to find Metadata or information related to the incident that has happened. Some standard tools for android/mobile forensics are shown in figure 3.

Figure 4. Tree Structure of the Standard Tools Memory Forensic

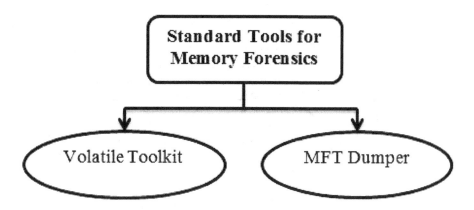

Figure 3 shows some commonly used data forensic tools including Access Data FTK Imager and Encase. Further, both tools can find and record digital evidence from Phone to validate it but it has some limitations. The tools can only access the phone data, not the SIM and this creates a gap between phone data access and SIM data access because that there are huge importance and scope of research in Mobile/Android Forensic.

Memory Forensics

In this type of forensics, the examiner investigates and analyzes the data that is deleted or removed or moved from the system with the help of tools and techniques and finds the possible metadata to find complete evidence. Some common tools used to examine memory forensics are Volatile Toolkit, MFT Dumper, etc. Memory forensics is a field of digital forensic that has many key and fundamental factors. This gives more prominence to memory forensic in the digital forensic examination because at the memory level nothing is encrypted and nothing can be hidden. But there are ways to bypass and be anonymous from the analysis phase also. A famous way of bypassing is by using TOR Browser. It is very difficult to trace out the evidence or any kind of relevant data on *the tor browser* network. According to Divya Dayalmurthy (2013), the research references are available only for General memory dump analysis and monitoring the tor traffic on the network. Even this research is not of much use in preventing the TOR connection and analyzing it (Dayalamurthy, 2013). The author says that there is a massive need for research on TOR dump memory analysis because with the help of that any examiner can find

Figure 5. Tree Structure of the Standard Tools Network Forensic

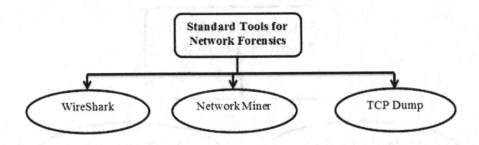

the metadata related to the incident and analyze it. Some standard tools for memory forensics are shown in figure 4.

Figure 4 shows some commonly used data forensic tools including Volatile Toolkit and MFT Dumper. Further, both tools are commonly used for Memory forensic. The volatile toolkit is a command-line toolkit to scan and analyze the volatile memory. Some researchers and examiners also refer to it as the volatool. Volatool can examine the date and time, running processes, open ports, the process to port mapping, etc. (Walters A., 2007).

Network Forensics

In this forensic domain, analysts examine and collect the evidence from network and network layer. This is a vast kind of forensic domain and cloud forensics is a subpart of this domain of digital forensics. Some common tools used to examine network forensics are WireShark, Network Miner, TCP Dump, etc. The basic functionality is the same for every Network forensic tool. Functionality of these tools is written as follows:

- **Collection of data:** Every Network forensic analysis tool has this functionality to collect the data and save it for future use.
- **No Manipulation in data:** Every Network forensic analysis tool needs to follow this rule so that no data manipulation is allowed in any kind of data.
- **Reply feature:** Network analysis tools can reply to the incident and warn the user of the danger (Shrivastava G, 2016).

(Chhabra G. S., 2015) gave a distributed framework for network forensic analysis and talked about the importance of the distributed system. According to the study, there are many issues with network forensics like storage space, effective attack attribution, etc., so the authors suggest a distributed framework in which the writer shows different levels of network forensic examination very briefly. Some standard tools for network forensics are shown in figure 5.

Figure 5 shows some commonly used data forensic tools including WireShark, Network Miner and TCP Dump. These tools are used to analyze network traffic, data transportation, Packets, etc., on Network.

Metadata is a type of small data or information from which an examiner or analyzer can find or analyze some sensitive data related to the incident and find the desired information. Every file, image, document, webpage that is digital has metadata related to that file. Metadata contains images that are captured, it specifies the latitude & longitude of the place where the image was captured and more such related information. In case of any incident of cybercrime, the meta-information or metadata is used for the investigation purpose by the forensic examiners. Metadata has become a massive issue in the recent past drawing a lot of focus from the researchers too.

CURRENT ISSUES & CHALLENGES

In the present scenario, cyber crimes have inundated the cyber world creating several challenges for cybersecurity experts. Since a lack of awareness among the end-users creates a path for attackers to exploit them or their organizations, digital forensic has gained enormous significance in the investigation process of an incident related to cybercrime. But this has also created lots of issues and challenges for the experts and examiners, some related to technology or advancement, some related to standards and rules and some related to the basic functionality of investigation. The main issues and challenges of digital forensics can be classified mainly in three major parts -

I.   Source Related Issues & Challenges
II. Law Related Issues & Challenges
III. Scientific Issues & Challenges (Christa Miller, 2019)

Source Related Issues & Challenges

These types of challenges and issues come in digital forensics because of the problem of functional issues, functional issues are related to the basic environment or plan of action that is taken by the experts and examiners to investigate the incident. Some of the major issues are mentioned below:

Figure 6. Tree Structure of the Issues and Challenges of Digital Forensic

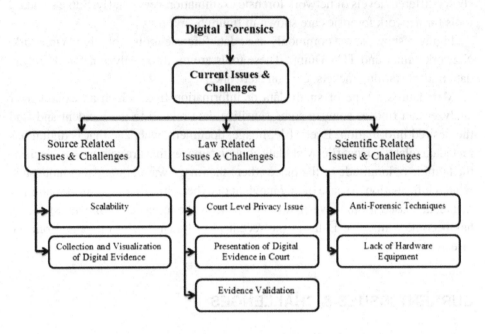

Scalability

This is a crucial problem and a burning area of digital forensics. Scalability is related to the volume issue of digital investigation. In the volume issue, the examiners talk about the quantity of the metadata or sensitive information found on the crime scene. Sometimes, it is a very composite work for an examiner or expert to collect and use the collected data to find the desired information. Some researchers have found the main problems of this issue to be:

- The volume and complexity of a victim's data or system are increasing rapidly.
- According to digital harm or data growth, the experts will neither update themselves nor adopt new technology very often.
- The proportion of cybercrime incidents is much high as compared to examiners that are present in the industry nowadays. So, this creates a misbalanced situation. Hence, it requires an in-depth investigation for every expert or examiner (Roussev V., 2016).

So, to mitigate this type of issue and challenge, we need to create a structured time-stamped forensic examination process that aligns with the current scenario of Cybercrime and investigation.

Collection and Visualization of Digital Evidence

This is another important challenge of digital forensics which the examiners are facing at present. It is different from scalability. Scalability is about the volume of data at the evidence collection and analysis time but in this, the examiners focus on the time that is taken to collect and visualize the evidence in a readable manner in front of the affected parties and jurisdictions. Because of the scientific issues like data encryption, steganography, data hiding, defragmentation and, etc., the examiners take more time than normal. This creates a massive issue in digital forensics and sometimes the retrieval of data is too critical and complex. This also leads to the risk of corrupted data. So all these technical issues make the collection and visualization of sensitive data a time taking process because of which further non-technical investigation also gets delayed. To reduce this type of issue the mitigation strategies are very confusing because if the examiner creates a fast collection strategy, then the risk of data corruption increases. So, the researcher Roussev (2016) has suggested that *"A good solution of the issue is to make an embedded help team for a forensic examiner in the large investigation"* (Roussev V., 2016).

Law-Related Issues and Challenges

In this type of issue different countries have different laws and some countries don't even have a law or established standards for cyber and forensic examinations. So, there are several ambiguities and issues related to digital forensics and cybersecurity laws. For instance, if an examiner finds that the incident has been done by a system that is located in a foreign country and that country does not have any cyber law, then the examiner can't do anything and this creates an enormous challenge for the experts and examiners. There are many other law-related issues. Some of the major issues are mentioned below:

Court Level Privacy Issue

The main focus of this type of issue is privacy. In simple words, in most cases, experts need to disclose the private data or information related to an organization and a person to found the real truth. 60% of the individual users and 77% of the enterprises (medium, small & big) produce private confidential information and data in their daily uses and this type of information may be risky for them if the information or data gets disclosed publicly or to attackers. So, this is an issue for forensic examiners and court because it is very difficult to maintain privacy.

Presentation of Digital Evidence In Court

This is a very common issue faced by every examiner because the presentation of evidence in the courtroom is very difficult in a readable form. And sometimes the opposition party questions the format of sensitive data in which the data is represented in the front of the court and common in many cases opposition questions on the validation of tools that are used in the collection and analysis phase of Forensic investigation.

Evidence Validation

Evidence validation is the heart of digital forensic and plays a crucial role in resolving any kind of digital or cybercrime. There are many cases in court in which the opposition lawyer challenges the tool used in the examination of evidence and it creates a major issue in digital forensics because every tool has its pros & cons. So it's difficult for an examiner to find which tool is perfect for which task. Many countries have their legal valid tool list after this issue but these tools also have vulnerabilities. There is no 100% perfect tool for any task and this issue continues to be a dilemma in digital forensics.

Scientific Issues and Challenges

Scientific or technical issues are very critical in today's era because the use of technology is present in both a good and bad way. Like examiners and investigators use the computers and technologies in a good manner to examine the evidence and crime scene, some persons use the technology and computer in a nugatory manner to do some illegal, unauthorized activity and to be anonymous. This type of use of technology and computers scientifically create an issue and this is both the most dangerous and most effective issue in today's era. There are mainly two types of challenges that are described as follows:-

Anti-Forensic Techniques

According to Simson L. (2007) anti-forensic techniques and tools are used to interrupt or damage or frustrate the forensic analysis or examination tools or examiners (Garfinkel S., 2007). This is very harmful to any investigation process

Figure 7. Encryption (What Is Encryption?)

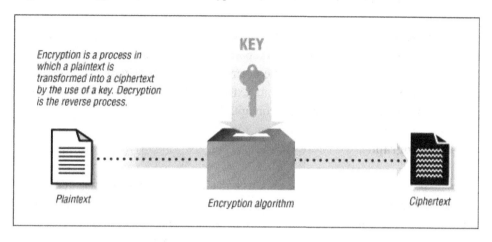

and there is still no foolproof solution for this issue in the digital forensic world. Some common and famous anti-forensic techniques are as follows:

- Data Encryption

Encryption is the process of encoding your data with the help of some keys. This is a very legal process that is used by standard users but intruders and illegal persons also use this technique for hiding their data and information from the forensic examiners. There are a variety of free tools available to encrypt the data and that's why this is a very common problem that a forensic examiner faces. Sometimes it's easy to decrypt the data encrypted by common tools, but the decryption of data is very crucial and complex for a forensic examiner because there are a variety of encryption algorithms present and some are very complex, so it takes more time to identify and decode the algorithm for a forensic examiner. Microsoft has created a tool that helps the forensic examiners a lot but it has some limitations. The name of the tool is MICROSOFT COMPUTER ONLINE FORENSICS EVIDENCE EXTRACTOR (MCOFEE). MCOFEE has many types of options like password decryptor, internet history recovery, and other data extraction options. This tool and many others like this help the forensic examiners to mitigate this issue to some extent, but that's not fully sufficient.

Figure 7 shows that there is Plain text on the left side which the sender needs to convert into cipher text so when the system uses the encryption algorithm with suitable key, the plain text is converted into cipher text.

- **Data Hiding in Storage Space**

Sometimes an intruder tries to hide information or data so intruders hide files or data to a storage medium or contiguous space. Intruders hide this type of data with some special kind of technique, so the normal or classical memory forensic tools can't find them out. Sometimes the data extraction from unknown storage is very complex and risky and the data gets corrupted.

- **Steganography**

In the present context, the most famous and challenging anti-forensic technique is steganography. Steganography is the process of hiding some data in a file, video or any kind of multimedia. In simple words, "**data into a data**". Steganography is a very widely used technique because there are many tools available on the internet for steganography which are free of cost like CryptApp, Shadow, Crypsis, etc. The tool of Microsoft MCOFEE is also used for identifying steganographic multimedia and it is helpful but there are no 100% perfect tools or non-vulnerable or non-limited tools for any anti-forensic technique.

There is another technique for identifying steganography for normal technical persons if they know machine level language, i.e., bit values. In such a case the examiner can find classical or weak steganographic multimedia. The analyzer only needs to use a hex converter to convert the file into the bit values and then analyze the header part and full bit value. Here the examiner will find some different data than 00 or 11 and after a little amount of deep learning, the examiner can find classical steganography multimedia.

Attack against Cyber Forensic Tools (CFT)

The intruders in this scenario are very friendly with the forensic examiner's tools. Because of this they easily find the vulnerabilities of the tools because there is a fully documented explanation of most tools that are present on the internet and that is a master key for an intruder and that's why they easily exploit or crack the examiner's tools and bypass the analysis process. Most popular attacks against CFTs are the following.

- Failure to validate data.
- Denial of service attack

Figure 8. DDosAttack (Juliana De Groot, 2019)

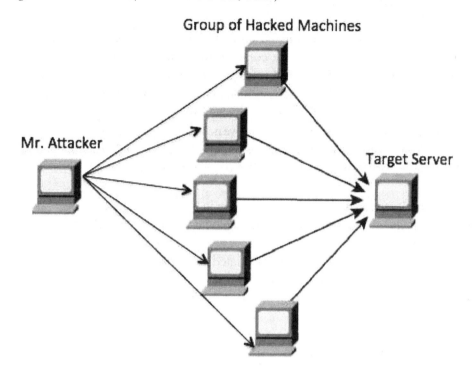

Figure 8 describes the basic functionality used in modern distributed denial of service attacks. In this type of attack, the attacker hijacks many other systems and servers with the help of botnet (a type of hidden malware) and remotely or manually requests the desired servers at the same time with all hijacked system for better and effective results.

Lack of Hardware Equipment

This is a very important issue in digital forensics because there is a major lack of hardware equipment in the forensic investigation process. Sometimes the case is not too big to afford or use high embedded hardware. There are also some fields of digital forensics for which the hardware has not been manufactured yet. Hardware plays a vital role in the digital forensic investigation because, with the help of hardware, the examiner works properly without any delay in time. And in the phase where an examiner collects the evidence, the hardware can play a master role because with the help of hardware and examiner's doesn't need a large team to get the result. The lengthy-time duration that an examiner takes in the collection phase also gets reduced.

RECOMMENDATION AND FUTURE WORK

This research paper focused on the current challenges of Digital Forensic in Cybersecurity and discussed some common tools that are used by the forensic examiners. This paper has also enlightened the aspects that need further development in digital forensic to confront the issues and challenges posed by cybercrimes. It also discusses the techniques that are involved to spoof or confuse the forensic examination tools. There is also an imperative need for tools and hardware equipment in Digital Forensic. Furthermore, lawmakers need to effectual is common laws for cybersecurity. Followings are some areas for research in the future:

- To mitigate the problem of data volume in forensic examination.
- To analyze and propose an international Standard for Digital Forensic examination.
- To provide impetus to projects related to hardware embedded system to examine the Cybercrime investigation.
- New Systematic examination process for cloud forensic.

CONCLUSION

It is evident from this paper's analysis that digital forensics in cybersecurity calls for more extensive and exhaustive research which should be academic as well as industry-centric. The present context also demands established and defined international laws and standards for cybersecurity and forensic investigation because there is too much confusion between the laws and jurisdiction processes. Digital forensic is a very wide and broad topic in itself, hence, the international authorities need to encourage the research in this field and also in hardware development to identify and mitigate the technical and functional issues and challenges.

ACKNOWLEDGMENT

This work is sponsored by the Council of Science and Technology, Uttar Pradesh, India.

REFERENCES

Burney A., A. M. (2016). Forensics Issues in Cloud Computing. *Journal of Computer and Communications*, 63-69.

Chhabra, G. S., &. S. (2015). Distributed Network Forensics Framework: A Systematic Review. *International Journal of Computers and Applications*.

Christa Miller. (2019). *Career Paths In Digital Forensics: Practical Applications*. Retrieved from https://articles.forensicfocus.com/2019/07/31/career-paths-in-digital-forensics-practical-applications/

Dayalamurthy, D. (2013). Forensic Memory Dump Analysis And Recovery Of The Artifacts Of Using Tor Bundle Browser- The Need. *Australian Digital Forensics Conference*.

Garfinkel, S. (2007). Anti-forensics: Techniques, detection and countermeasures. *2nd International Conference on i-Warfare and Security*, 77-84.

Juliana De Groot. (2019). *A History of Ransomware Attacks: The Biggest and Worst Ransomware Attacks of All Time*. Retrieved from https://digitalguardian.com/blog/history-ransomware-attacks-biggest-and-worst-ransomware-attacks-all-time

Nadeem Alherbawi, Z. S. (2013). Systematic Literature Review on Data Carving in Digital Forensic. *Procedia Technology*. Retrieved from https://www.sciencedirect.com/science/article/pii/S2212017313003198

Roussev, V. (2016). *Digital forensic science: issues, methods, and challenges*. Synthesis Lectures on Information Security, Privacy, & Trust.

Shrivastava, G. (2016). Network forensics: Methodical literature review. In *3rd International Conference on Computing for Sustainable Global Development (INDIACom)* (pp. 2203-2208). IEEE.

Sonamjain, T. (2014). A Review of Cloud Forensics Issues & Challenges. *International Journal of Advanced Research in Computer Science & Technology*, 55-57.

Srinivasan, C. R. (2019). *Cyber-security trends to look out for in 2019*. Retrieved from https://telecom.economictimes.indiatimes.com/news/cyber-security-trends-to-look- out-for-in-2019/67471232

Walters, A. (2007). *Integrating volatile memory forensics into the digital investigation process*. Black Hat, DC.

EncryptionW. I. (n.d.). Retrieved from http://web.deu.edu.tr/doc/oreily/networking/puis/ch06_02.htm

KEY TERMS AND DEFINITIONS

Android/Mobile Forensics: Mobile device forensics is a branch of digital forensics relating to recovery of digital evidence.

Anti-Forensic Techniques: Anti-forensics methods to ensure the privacy of one's personal data.

Cloud Forensics: Cloud Forensics is cross-discipline between cloud computing and digital forensics.

Data Forensics: Data forensics, also known as computer forensics, refers to the study or investigation of digital data and how it is created and used.

Memory Forensics: Memory forensics is the art of analyzing computer memory (RAM) to solve digital crimes.

Network Forensics: Network forensics is a sub-branch of digital forensics relating to the monitoring and analysis of computer network traffic.

Chapter 4
Trends in Malware Attacks:
Identification and Mitigation Strategies

Abhishek Kumar Pandey
*Babasaheb Bhimrao Ambedkar
University, India*

Ashutosh Kumar Tripathi
https://orcid.org/0000-0003-4021-9819
*Babasaheb Bhimrao Ambedkar
University, India*

Gayatri Kapil
*Babasaheb Bhimrao Ambedkar
University, India*

Virendra Singh
*Babasaheb Bhimrao Ambedkar
University, India*

Mohd. Waris Khan
*Babasaheb Bhimrao Ambedkar
University, India*

Alka Agrawal
*Babasaheb Bhimrao Ambedkar
University, India*

Rajeev Kumar
https://orcid.org/0000-0002-1813-1362
*Babasaheb Bhimrao Ambedkar
University, India*

Raees Ahmad Khan
*Babasaheb Bhimrao Ambedkar
University, India*

ABSTRACT

Security issues are ever-evolving in today's scenario due to the heterogeneous nature of software applications, multimedia features, multilingual interactive and responsible features, and rapid rise in third-party software products. The main objective of this chapter is to focus on the difficulties and components that the users have to contend with on the internet. This chapter investigates and manages ongoing malware attacks. It also explains the significance of the research, malware investigation, social engineering, and user awareness in the field of malware attacks. Cyber-attacks are the most common problem in recent years, and the increasing number of malware is becoming a challenging task for security experts. This chapter underlines key issues along with various aspects for experts to discuss and focus on reducing the threats posed by malware and planning the strategy for prevention in the future. The chapter provides an effective future direction for researchers to produce impactful outcomes.

DOI: 10.4018/978-1-7998-1558-7.ch004

INTRODUCTION

The recent decades have witnessed a spate of cyber-attacks that have led to disastrous results for both business organizations and the individual users of the cyber world. Every business is computerized now and every organization has its existence on the internet, but the main problem is that most of the online organizations don't understand security factors or issues (threats) of the cyber world. This lacuna creates a massive platform for hackers to attack commercial enterprises and to make money through a digital platform. In today's era, attackers are easily able to infiltrate systems because of malware. Attackers find it very easy to employ malware as it infects the system directly and that is the reason for malware emerging as a major threat for cyber-security. Software companies have to constantly work to write newer versions and security patches, and release them so that the existing and in-use software system can be upgraded to confront new forms of threats. Furthermore, it has been observed from the recent studies that software security breaches have dramatically increased around online financial activities such as- online banking, debit and credit card transactions, ATM transactions and other such activities.

According to a survey, "*In December 2018 to January 2019, the malware activity has increased by 61%* (Outpost24, 2018). This is indeed a cause for alarm as it creates a major issue for today's cyber-security experts. According to the India Times survey 2019, "*58% of data breach victims are the organizations who have a small business and do not have a proper cyber setup* (Srinivasan C.R., 2019). Surveys also cite that 10 years ago malware attacks were relatively less as compared to the frequency with which they are implemented by attackers today. This type of growth shows the weakness of human awareness and system security as well as the lack of quality research in gauging and finding effective solutions to contain malware attacks. Awareness is the key factor in every organization's security policy because if the employees are not aware of the possible threats they can be easily exploited by an intruder. Malware attacks can lead to huge losses for an organization not only in revenue but also in a brand niche, clients' trust, business secrets, and other such vital statistics.

Malware Analysis is the process that has gained considerable focus as an effective tool to eliminate malware attacks. Malware analysis is the methodology for finding the functionality and objective of any malware. This article, in particular, shows that malware analysis methods are an effective deterrent against malware attacks. The second section of this article deals with the related incidents in malware attacks. The third section highlights the types of malware which have been detected recently and are major threats to the cyber security of several organizations. Furthermore, the author attracts the focus on the factors and challenges that need significance to weaken the malware attacks.

Relevant Study Initiatives

The web has been expanding at such a progressive pace that its access is now exceptionally simple for everybody. However, simple accessibility leads to a high risk for any administration. The heavy measure of cyber-attacks is a consequence of simple and quality less availability of the web. Digital attacks are affecting people adversely. Recent studies show that most companies have unprotected and poor cyber security practices in place. Many companies are suffering from attacks daily just because of poor and quality fewer security mechanisms for web uses. Response strategy against any attack makes that attack less-harmful but according to the "2018 Hiscox Cyber Readiness Report", "*7 out of 10 enterprises are not prepared to respond against cyber-attacks. And this type of lack produces huge risk rate for industries and businesses* (thebestvpn, 2019). Some massive cyber-attacks that happened in the last 10 years have been enlisted below:

Arizona Beverages Ransomware Attack (2019)

England's multinational company Arizona Beverages was targeted by hackers. According to news reports **Dvidex malware class** ransomware was used in this attack (Malwarebytes Lab, 2019) & (Kacy Zurkus, 2019). The company was rebuilding its network for two weeks. A lot of the back-end servers were running obsolete Windows working frameworks that had never been bolstered again. Most hadn't got security fixes in years. The attack shows the urgent need for updating security practices for organizations.

Hack in US Universities

In March 2018, the Department of Justice, USA published a statement that more than 100 US universities got hacked by Iranian hackers and their data got leaked over the internet (Lily Hay Newman, 2018). The attacker sent colleges to stick phishing messages doctored to show up as though they originated from accomplice colleges, yet they released a malicious payload when opened. This type of attack shows the importance of social engineering awareness in society.

Equifax Data Leak

Multinational credit reporting company Equifax got hacked in early 2017 and more than 800 million consumer financial data was leaked online. This caused a big loss of respect and revenue to the company (calyptix, 2017). Hackers attack the website vulnerability for accessing data. This attack shows the importance of awareness for businesses' online security.

Yahoo Data Breach

In 2016, the world faced one of the biggest data breaches in the world's oldest internet company- Yahoo. The same year two major data theft took place in Yahoo. The first data theft occurred in September 2016 affecting over 500 million user accounts, the other data theft occurred in December 2016 which affected a total of 1 billion user accounts. This data theft compromised the security of the user account and information such as email addresses, passwords, date of birth, security question and even contact information was leaked (cisecurity, 2019).

Some other important and noticeable events caused by software security failure in 2016 are- The Bangladesh Banks Heist, the Legion Crew Hacks (India), Cyber-attacks on servers of Dyn, Philippines Voter Data leak, Russian Interference in US elections, Mark Zuckerberg hack, and Oracle MICROS hack.

Types Of Malware Attacks

Malware has a variety of classes. Malware classes are called types of malware. Many types of malware are in use. Different malware has different functionalities and use. Threat actors use these malware types to perform a specific type of harmful action.

Backdoors

Backdoors are a common and dangerous type of malware that formed nearly 34% of attack ratio last year (Malwarebytes Lab, 2019). Backdoors are any type of methods, authorized or unauthorized, that gives full (root) access to the attacker in the system or network. Backdoors are not only for the attacker, but they also help the software or hardware makers to connect with their technology after the implementation. In 2018 backdoor attacks increased by 34-173% (malwarebytes, 2019).

Ransomeware

Ransomeware is a specific type of malware that performs a specific harmful activity on your system and demands some type of ransom to stop the attack. In general, the patterns demonstrate a drop in the volume of ransomware attacks for the year. Statistics show that in 2017 the count of a ransomware attack was 8,016,936 and in 2018 the number decreased by 26% and the total count was 5,948,417 (Malwarebytes Lab, 2019).

Trojan

The Trojan is a sort of malware that is frequently masked as genuine programming. Trojans can be utilized by hackers and bad programmers endeavoring to access clients' frameworks. Trojans can compromise your data or spy on your activity. There are different types of Trojans. Every Trojan has its special functionality. According to a survey of Kaspersky Labs, the growth ratio of Trojan malware is 12% in the comparison of last year.

Phishing

Phishing keeps on being a noteworthy concern, not just because the rate of the incident is expanding but also because the attack strategies are becoming progressively modern. Phishing is the best practice for data breach attacks for attackers. Phishing is a method for taking on the appearance of a disclosed in substance hoodwinks an injured individual into opening an email, text, or instant message. The beneficiary is then fooled into clicking a noxious connection which can prompt the establishment of malware, the solidifying of the framework as a major aspect of a ransomware attack or the noteworthy of delicate data. According to a study of Retruster *"estimated cost loss by data breach with phishing attacks are $3.86 million and Phishing attacks have grown by 65% in the past year* (retruster, 2019).

DDOS Attacks

DDOS attacks are old but effective and that is the reason behind the growth ratio of 430% in the first quarter of 2019 (serverius, 2019). In 2019 DDOS attacks have been more professional and modern as compared to those in 2018. A conveyed forswearing of-administration (DDoS) attack is a malevolent endeavor to upset typical traffic that is focused on server, administration or system by overpowering the objective or its encompassing framework with a surge of Internet traffic.

Worms

A PC worm is a type of malware, much the same as its progressively famous cousin, the virus. Unlike an infection, a worm ordinarily doesn't taint or control documents without anyone else. Rather, it just clones itself again and again and spreads utilizing a system (state, the Internet, a neighborhood at home, or an organization's intranet) to different frameworks where it keeps on repeating itself. Worms formed 7% of the attack ratio in 2018. In the last one year, the cybercrime economy increased to $1.5 trillion (thesslstore, 2019). Security breaches also increased by 67% and the issue of

Figure 1. Graphical Representation of attacks in recent years

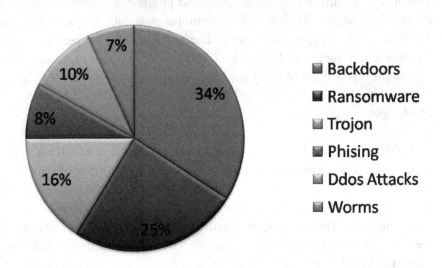

cyber security has become even more complicated because of modern cyber-attacks like updated ransomware and modern DDOS attacks, etc.

The above figure demonstrates different kinds of cyber-attacks and their attack rate. As indicated by Malware byte labs in the last two years backdoor attacks have increased to 34% (Malwarebytes Lab, 2019). Ransomware assaults have become more prevalent lately. The overview of Malware bytes Labs demonstrates that 740 million digital attacks were implemented in 2018 (Malwarebytes Lab, 2019). An investigation of Digital Guardian demonstrates that 184 million of them were ransomware assaults (digitalguardian, 2019). So, the assault rate of ransomware in 2018-19 was 25%. Beta news study demonstrates that 16% of the digital attacks in the last two years have been that of Trojan (betanews, 2018). Scurelist.com and forbs. com cite that DDoS assaults and phishing assaults make for 10% (securelist, 2018) and 8% (Forbes, 2019) assault rates, respectively. Worms are a regular infection and very useful as well. Investigation of mindsight demonstrates that worms' assault rate is at 7% (gomindsight, 2018). This examination demonstrates that the malware assault proportion is developing enormously and there is an imminent need to stop the developing rate of malware assaults.

DIFFERENT TYPES OF METHODS FOR MALWARE ANALYSIS

Malware is the biggest issue after 2017 ransomware attacks. Malware Analysis is a method of uncovering the dark and hidden functionality of malware and helps the security experts in prevention. There are three basic methods available for Malware analysis and these are:-

Static Analysis

In the static examination, the analyst removes data from malware documents while it isn't in the running stage. The data that is gathered amid static malware examination can extend from the easiest to the most perplexing.

Dynamic Analysis

The dynamic examination is a procedure of removing the data while malware is running. For any sort of powerful investigation, an inspector needs to set up (I) Analysis Test Environment and (ii) Dynamic examination instruments. The dynamic instruments break down inbound and outbound system correspondence and any working framework assets utilized by the malware.

Reverse Engineering

Figuring out malware is the way towards taking a caught executable and doing what might be compared to an MRI. Reverse Engineering gives a key to examiners for analyzing encrypted or protected malware files. In reverse engineering, the examiner works on a binary machine level that helps the examiner a lot.

Challenges For Malware Analyst

In tune with recent trends, malware attacks are creating various challenges in cyberspace and also gaining attention from industrics, experts and research communities. As a solution to the problems related to malware attacks, developers should try to explore more avenues to constantly upgrade the security parameters of the software. Since software security is the prime concern of developers, newer and faster ways of making the security policies more efficient and result-oriented should be adopted by the developers. Some popular and conceivable challenges that affect the organization and individuals directly are written below:-

Figure 2. Graphical Representation of Infection Ratio of Malware

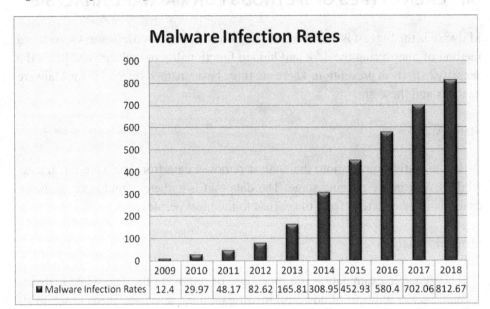

Malware Infection Rates

	2009	2010	2011	2012	2013	2014	2015	2016	2017	2018
■ Malware Infection Rates	12.4	29.97	48.17	82.62	165.81	308.95	452.93	580.4	702.06	812.67

Growing Number of Data Breach

No major attack was implemented in 2018 like ransomware in 2017, but it was a year of a data leak. Popular global organizations like Facebook, Marriott, Exactis, Quora and many more were infected with the data breach attacks. A study reveals that in 2018 the number of records that were compromised saw an increase of 133% in the comparison of those that occurred in 2017 (Malwarebytes Lab, 2019) Infection Ratio is the term that is used by technical experts to define the attack statics of malware. In the last 10 years, the growth of malware attacks infection rates has increased rapidly.

The above graph (figure 2) represents the growing infection ratio of malware attacks. As shown in the graph, in 2009 the internet was not popular among the common people so the ratio of attack was 12.4, but from 2013 the attack ratio has shown a steep increase because of the revolution of the internet and the increasing use of internet services by people. According to a survey, the attack ratio in early 2019 increased by 67% which is the highest when compared to the last 5 years (thesslstore, 2019). The above graph is a quantitative representation of malware attack statics that demonstrates the seriousness of malware attacks and tells the importance of developing a mitigation strategy for cyber-attacks.

An Updated Version of Ransomware

2018 was the year of revolution for computer-related persons in both positive and negative ways. On the positive side, Sir Tim Burners-Lee introduced his new solid project to the world that can make revolutionary changes on the internet in the future and on the negative side many malware coders update their code and changed the old attack strategy. Ransomware is one of the most widely used and dangerous malware and the world saw an updated code of ransomware in 2018, coder of ransomware updated the shotgun mechanism and replaced it with Brute-force in the updated version.

Malspam Takes First Place in Favorite Infection Vector

In 2019 every cyber expert is aware and has a prevention mechanism to prevent attacks with exploits and other new infection vectors, that's why attackers are now using an old technique like the infection vector named malspam. Malspam is an old infection vector in which the attacker creates an attractive spam mail with an infected attachment or URL and due to lack of awareness, most of the time victim click or download the attachment or URL.

Big Amount of Fake or Malicious Apps Present on Web Stores

The knowledge of computer and coding language is very normal and easy to learn nowadays and this is the reason for so many fake, malicious and harmful apps or software that are present on web stores that adversely affect the net users. The reason behind this type of breach is permitting the apps to use the phone's entire services without specifically verifying them and not reading the terms & policies of any app carefully. In early 2019, the internet giant Google removed 28 fake apps from its app store.

Google released a statement that said that all these apps do not have their legitimate functionality related to their name (indiatoday, 2019).

FUTURE DIRECTIONS

These are just some of the cases extracted from the long list of cyber-attack episodes. Studies point out that in every 40 second a cyber-malware attack is executed, but only 60-70% of them can be traced or identified. Others remain anonymous due to the lack of knowledge and awareness. So some important and determining factors

Figure 3. Factors that need Importance

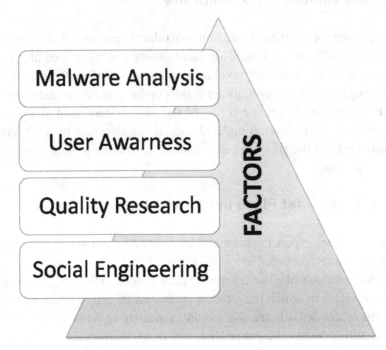

that can make an immense change in cyber security must include malware analysis, user awareness, quality research, and social engineering.

Malware Analysis

Malware is the biggest weapon for hackers. Malware is like an atom bomb in the cyber world as it is small software that can do what the owner wants. Malware analysis is a process to identify malware by their class, behavior, purpose and many other characteristics and after the analysis, the expert finds the solutions to mitigate them. In today's era malware analysis field is not so popular and this is the main reason why malware is growing and affecting systems worldwide without any fear.

User Awareness

The user is the easiest exploiting point for an attacker. The system, software, applications are built for the users, but if the users are not aware of the threats that are related to the system they can be easily exploited. In the current situation, many organizations and individuals don't understand the risk factors, threats related to their work or system, weak points in their IT infrastructure and the vulnerabilities related to digital environments. Hence, it becomes an important factor that needs focus and importance for mitigating attacks.

Quality Research

Research is a field that helps every topic or issue to be solved because research can help everyone to find vulnerabilities and scope of solutions and give a path for future researchers. Malware attacks are not so popular with researchers who are more inclined towards coding. This dearth in substantiative research has led to many issues in cyber-security.

Social Engineering

Social engineering is a term that is used in hacking, but after seeing the current scenario, it is important to teach and tell about the social engineering to the users and organizations for their security as social engineering is the key of success for hackers. Kevin Mitnick a famous hacker and security expert of the USA tells the importance and effect of social engineering in hacking. Mitnick tells that, *"Social Engineering is the art of influencing people to do something that can make a system compromised or accessing the information with which a hacker can exploit the victim"* (Mitnick, 2019). Kaspersky Lab announced a survey that tells that 45% of enterprise employees hide the cyber-security incidents because of the fear of losing a job or facing punishment. The survey also shows that most of the times employees are the reason for causing an incident on the internet like malware attacks (Kaspersky Lab, 2019). This type of study shows the importance of mitigation strategies. If the world is not aware of the impact of social engineering, it can result in the most dangerous attacks on enterprises.

CONCLUSION

After analyzing the challenges and attacks, there is an immediate need to concentrate on the aspects that would help in decreasing the number of malware attacks. Software systems are ubiquitously used in both personal and professional life and have become an important source of vital information; hence their security is of utmost concern. The study also shows that users are one of the weakest points of any security mechanism and social engineering is the technique which helps the intruders to exploit them. This article discusses the concerns about social engineering and raises a question for the abatement strategy from social engineering. Malware analysis has also been discussed in this article because only prevention is not sufficient for any security mechanism. It is imperative to find the objective of malware attacks to give advice for future experts and plan relief tactics related to the same patterns of malware attacks. Researchers must dedicate their efforts to the in-depth identification and mitigation of security issues emanating due to malware.

ACKNOWLEDGMENT

This work has been sponsored by the Council of Science and Technology, Uttar Pradesh, India.

REFERENCES

betanews. (2018). *Banking Trojan Attacks Up By 16 Percent In 2018*. Retrieved from https://betanews.com/2019/03/07/banking-trojan-attacks-2018/

calyptix. (2017). *Biggest Cyber Attacks 2017: How They Happened*. Retrieved from https://www.calyptix.com/top-threats/biggest-cyber-attacks-2017-happened/

cisecurity. (2019). *Top 10 Malware January 2019*. Retrieved from https://www.cisecurity.org/blog/top-10-malware-january-2019/

digitalguardian. (2019). *A History of Ransomware Attacks: The Biggest and Worst Ransomware Attacks of All Time*. Retrieved from https://digitalguardian.com/blog/history-ransomware-attacks-biggest-and-worst-ransomware-attacks-all-time

Forbes. (2019). *Four Phishing Attack Trends To Look Out For In 2019*. Retrieved from https://www.forbes.com/sites/forbestechcouncil/2019/01/10/four-phishing-attack-trends-to-look-out-for-in-2019/#17dddc404ec2

gomindsight. (2018). *History of Cyber Attacks From The Morris Worm To Exactis*. Retrieved from https://www.gomindsight.com/blog/history-of-cyber-attacks-2018/

indiatoday. (2019). *Google removes 28 fake apps from Play Store, Delete Now If You Have Any Of These Apps On Your Phone*. Retrieved from https://www.indiatoday.in/technology/news/story/google-removes-28-fakes-app-from-play-store-delete-now-if-you-have

Kacy Zurkus. (2019). *A Spot of Ransomware Hits AriZona's Tea*. Retrieved from https://www.infosecurity-magazine.com/news/a-spot-of-ransomware-hits-arizonas/

Kaspersky Lab. (2019). *Kaspersky Lab Survey: One-in-Four Hide Cybersecurity Incidents From Their Employers*. Retrieved from https://usa.kaspersky.com/about/press-releases/2017_kaseprsky-lab-survey-one-in-four-hide-cybersecurity-incidents-from-their-employers

Lily Hay Newman. (2018). *The Worst Cybersecurity Breaches of 2018 So Far.* Retrieved from https://www.wired.com/story/2018-worst-hacks-so-far/

malwarebytes. (2019). *What is a backdoor?* Retrieved from https://www.malwarebytes.com/backdoor/

Malwarebytes Lab. (2019). *2019 State of Malware.* Retrieved from https://resources.malwarebytes.com/resource/2019-state-malware-malwarebytes-labs-report/

Mitnick, K. (2019). *Exclusive Interview with Kevin Mitnick Ask Me Anything.* Retrieved from https://blog.knowbe4.com/exclusive-interview-with-kevin-mitnick-ask-me-anything-video

Outpost24. (2018). *TOP 10 of the World's Largest Cyberattacks.* Retrieved from https://outpost24.com/blog/top-10-of-the-world-biggest-cyberattacks

retruster. (2019). *2019 Phishing Statistics and Email Fraud Statistics.* Retrieved from https://retruster.com/blog/2019-phishing-and-email-fraud-statistics.html

securelist. (2018). *DDoS attacks in Q3 2018.* Retrieved from https://securelist.com/ddos-report-in-q3-2018/88617/

serverius. (2019). *Increase of DDoS attacks Q1 2019.* Retrieved from https://serverius.net/increase-of-ddos-attack-q1-2019/

Srinivasan, C. R. (2019). *Cyber-security trends to look out for in 2019.* Retrieved from https://telecom.economictimes.indiatimes.com/news/cyber-security-trends-to-look-out-for-in-2019/67471232

thebestvpn. (2019). *14 Most Alarming Cyber Security Statistics in 2019.* Retrieved from https://thebestvpn.com/cyber-security-statistics-2019/

thesslstore. (2019). *80 Eye-Opening Cyber Security Statistics for 2019.* Retrieved from https://www.thesslstore.com/blog/80-eye-opening-cyber-security-statistics-for-2019/

KEY TERMS AND DEFINITIONS

Malspam: Malspam, malicious spam, is a method for delivering emails that contain infected documents or links that redirect users to websites that contain exploit kits.

Malware Analysis: Malware analysis is done to provide the necessary information to deal with malware attacks.

Malware Attacks: Malware analysis by using reverse engineering method become one solution that can be used to extract data in a malware.

Malware Infection Ratio: Using extensive experiments spanning multiple malware and countries, we show that ESM can effectively predict malware infection ratios over time.

Reverse Engineering: Reverse engineering is taking apart an object to see how it works in order to duplicate or enhance the object.

Social Engineering: Social engineering, in the context of information security, is the psychological manipulation of people into performing actions or divulging confidential information.

User Awareness: User awareness of IS security policies is positively associated with perceived severity of sanctions.

Chapter 5
Digital Terrorism Attack:
Types, Effects, and Prevention

Parkavi R.
Thiagarajar College of Engineering, India

Nithya R.
Thiagarajar College of Engineering, India

Priyadharshini G.
Thiagarajar College of Engineering, India

Abstract

In this rapidly growing era of technology, terrorist organizations do not ultimately depend on weapons, army, bombs, and lethal weapons to inflict terror. As the entire earth is developing at a rapid pace, so do the terrorists. The strategies adopted by them have become cannier and more sinister. In addition to that, they no longer involve in training, making tedious plans, undergoing physical training, and subjecting their allies to physical attacks. Rather, they impose serious threats by attacking their victims by vandalizing the online infrastructure. This can be done conveniently from any part of the globe, thus enabling them to use the dark side of the internet. This chapter focuses on digital terrorism attacks, its impact, and it furnishes certain methods for prevention.

INTRODUCTION

Digital terrorism can be defined as a threat or harm that is done for personal motives that use the internet and networks. These intentions are most likely to be political, religious or ideological. It is one in which well experienced cyber terrorists having

DOI: 10.4018/978-1-7998-1558-7.ch005

great skill in the hacking handle. They cause severe damage to government systems, records and national level security which affects that particular country or a particular society thus making it more vulnerable. This pushes government agencies like the Federal Bureau of Investigations (FBI) and Central Intelligence Agency (CIA) to undertake efficient efforts to put a stop to digital terrorism.Significant steps must also be taken to create a sense of general awareness among the public.

BACKGROUND

In our day-to-day life, we come across many cyberattacks happening all around the world. These attacks inflict major damage to the person and the entire network upon which that particular system is connected to. These attacks are increasingly at an alarming speed which becomes inevitable to miss our notice. Some major incidents have happened that have shaken the entire world which left us at a state where people started wondering what the hell was happening. Before they could even realize the attacker would have vandalized them and would have stolen the valuable and private data that is extremely important to them. Let's look at some particular cases where the security was heavily damaged and the attackers gained access to illegal data.

In the middle of 2009, the famous dominator search engine Google also had to go through a similar crisis where the security was breached and data was got. The Chinese Google which was launched back in 2006 suffered from continuous attacks of digital terrorism. This particular event was known as Operation Aurora aimed at stealing intellectual property from Google. It did not just put a stop after attacking the security of Google. The operation went a step further and attacked also 30 major companies as they also, unfortunately, became the target of this operation of digital terrorism. On the overview, we can see this attack as a means to gain access to a Chinese public activist's account. Although a blog released by Google thereafter stated that the attack did not succeed in achieving its objective it should be considered as a major threat or danger because in this case, we are talking about a multinational company that has its roots and branches etched everywhere in the part of the world. When such a highly secured spot can be breached it automatically puts a serious and impending threat on all others and thus making them more cautious and alert. It was also analyzed that all the breaches happened only due to using Internet Explorer and this also resulted in German, Australian, and French governments asking their people to switch to alternative browsers. But pen-ultimately they were able to track down to two Chinese schools that have a partnership Baidu which happened to be the main rival search engine of Google in China. But the ultimate thing that we have to consider is that any amount of security can be breached via the modern aspects of technology thus always leading us to a state of probable vulnerabilities. And we must also take the prevention steps rather than trying to recover ourselves from the attacks after our systems have been attacked.

When we look at the case of Heart bleed, it wasn't a virus but it was a bug that was mistakenly written into OpenSSL. This paved way for hackers thus making their work effortless and easy and thus enabled the hackers to create a gateway that will enable them to access the databases. Some arguments are put forth stating that it is the biggest attack in the history of cyber-attacks. It is reported that it has nearly affected 17% of all the websites thus making it potentially threatful. The most horrible thing was that the infested bug was found only two years after the bug was almost gone. The late discovery was detected by Google security in 2014.

Another case emerged when yahoo asked all its users to change their passwords if they haven't done so since 2014. It was followed by a release of a statement saying that about 500 million users had seen their data being stolen by hackers. The stolen data included numbers, personal information, passwords. The level of infestation is much higher than the other recent attacks like MySpace and Adobe.

Sony play station also was aware that it lost some functionality during mid-April. Although the attack lasted only for 2 days the effect prolonged for a whole month. The most horrendous discovery was the stolen credit and debit card details. It resulted in an answering session by the US House of Representatives and it ended up with Sony paying a huge fine for allowing a loophole in their security that enabled the hackers to gain access to sensitive and private information of users. Sony further revealed that the 23-period attack resulted in a sum of around 140 million US dollars.

Now lets' look into another attack that shook the world-SONY pictures attack. In the year 2014 during November the early signs of the attack surfaced as images of skulls started appearing on the employees' screens exposing a message to issue a threat to Sony that secrets from data will be released in public. This was supposed to happen through a sophisticated and well-planned attack plan on hacking the infrastructure of Sony Limited. This initially led to the company asking the employees to estrange their systems and work with pen and paper. Sony at the beginning covered the news by releasing a press statement that stated that they were dealing with an "Information Technology matter". But later they came out with the truth that it was a digital terrorist attack that was launched on the company and they also named it a "brazen attack". So initially everything revolved around one question. Who was responsible for this attack? Because only if the answer is found for the before mentioned question they can find a permanent solution to prevent such attacks further. At that time an unknown group calling itself Guardians of Peace claimed that it was responsible for the attack. This led to an investigation by the FBI. But the initial doubts were laid on North Korea. The reason behind this is the controversial statement by a North Korean foreign ministry spokesman in which he mentioned the movie as an "act of terrorism". Naturally, North Korea defended them but went onto calling the hack a righteous deed and showered praises on it. This led to the cancellation of the movie premiere and cancellations of screenings across the US. People including actor Rob Lowe and comedian Jimmy Kimmel heavily criticized Sony for their decision that showed their defeat to the hackers and their cowardice. So actually what did the hackers then got hold of..? Certain scripts of movies including James Bond was leaked which resulted in a major halt in production works. In addition to this many films were illegally available on websites for the public to download and view them at a free cost. Also, all the important private information was revealed. This included the salaries paid to the employees and the bosses and social security information of the employees. In the end, the hackers achieved what they wanted to do so successfully and thus brought a bring corporation such as Sony under their regime even if it was for short notice of time.

Thus all these attacks pinpoint only one important thing: ATTACKS ARE UNAVOIDABLE WITHOUT PROPER AWARENESS AND HIGH-SECURITY MECHANISMS. Thus to provide better prevention it is necessary to know about the different mechanisms the attacks could be launched. We should also have a clear idea about the effects of its causes. Becausethen only we will realize the seriousness of it which will push us more towards a much-secured path. Hence finally after analyzing all the associated risks and undergoing a detailed study about it, we can draw certain methods of prevention against such attacks. Even though we can't completely prevent them i.e. be a hundred percentage we can employ various methods that include encryption and decryption and various other security mechanisms to make the situation secure and safe from various and all kinds of attacks. Thus the types, effects and prevention mechanisms will be indulged in a detailed analysis in the upcoming paragraphs.

LITERATURE REVIEW

As a general thumb-rule, cyber-warfare conjures up pictures of information warriors that unleash harmful attacks that cause severe havoc and thus affecting nations very potentially. Cyber attacks, information, and network security cause and inflicts serious havoc problems and disasters that reach into undiscovered areas for public policy and national security.Cyber-terrorism is the process of shutting down critical national infrastructures by the usage of various computer network tools.Almost nearly all of the literature on digital terrorism or cyber terrorism takes an assumption that the vulnerability of critical and major infrastructures and the vulnerability on the computer networks are the same.This in turns put forth the national security at a significant risk that can cause harmful effects and prolonged side-effects.(James A. Lewis,2002)

The mass and print media can be seen publishing a variety of reports and documents every day. These reports and documents are primarily based on attack especially deeply discussing the riots of terrorist attacks around the entire world. Recently there was also an attack launched on the Indian soldiers by the Pakistanis which was widely criticized as the critical attack. The attacks that are carried out majorly employ the same method-a group or individual causes an explosion at a target.The sad part in this is that the attackers are majorly representing only a tiny petite portion of the society to which they belong whereas on the contradictory side the victims are an innocent person who unluckily happens to be nearer to the place of attack by the attackers.This bringsforth a solid conclusion that a lack of symptoms of a particular case or phenomena does not mean that that particular phenomena or case does not exist.Another valid conclusion is that all the scientific technology that has been created and developed in due course time could majorly benefit us but at the same time can also be used against us that can cause destruction to us and can b against us at a particular period.Information security,the wonderful marvel of $20^{th}/21^{st}$ centuries dramatically changes all the aspects of the basic behavior of humans.At present terrorism has become the most vandalized and widespread form of creating violence and causing damage to individuals that at times are hardly aware of the attacks and the vulnerabilities.(Lech J. Janczewski,2007)

Hackers, in general, are represented by wide and well-known threats and are significantly responsible for the serious degree of disruption and eternal damage to the computer systems and machines. But however, they are not the sole reasons that have to be taken into consideration when we regard in aspects of criminal view. Scientific evidence suggests that the potential tool for terrorists nowadays is the rapidly growing technology. This in turns leads to the emergence of a novel threat in the way of digital terrorists. These digital or cyber terrorists attack all the technological infrastructures that include the internet to help them to launch their attacks synonymously without arousal of any doubt. (Furnell. S. M, Warren. M. J,1999)

In today's rapidly growing world we are becoming and tend to be more connected via information technologies and communications to an extent that has never occurred before. They enable us to access information on a global level that could transmit millions of data within a few seconds literally. This increasing global infrastructure is the basic foundation for the present integration of society's cultures and economies. It, in turn, allows a free flow of data, thoughts, ideas, and events that can be used to impact a greater sense of freedom across the entire community of people. But the major thing to be noted is that these capabilities have failed to harness the benefits of the economic side as a very competitive advantage. (Andrew M. Colarik,2006)

Recent days have seen a lot of speculations on cyber or digital terrorism regarding fictional characters such as Clear and Present Danger, Patriot games and many more. The gap between known cyber terror behavior and presumed threat suggests that an attack could be imminent at any time. It also furnishes that the reason for digital or cyber terrorism is the failure to distinguish between the use of digital means for organizational purposes and what Denning referred to cyber terrorism (Michael Stohl,2015)

Recent digital attacks such as Stuxnet and Anonymous' have kind of rekindled the fears that hint at cyber terrorism is an imminent threat. But the fact and truth are that the concept lies poorly perceived and understood. Although every day we see victims of cyber attacks in the newspapers and journals the truth s that none have one to a degree of causing cyber terrorism. What we are experiencing is only in terms of little effects that can be classified as cyber-attacks and ni as cyber terrorism. The major thing to be understood is that cyber-attacks are completely different from cyber terrorism. The former causes little or no effect whereas the latter causes a destructible effect on a large scale affecting nations and their economy and people. (Michael Kenney,2003)

Elliot and Lockhart had demonstrated in their personal and own studies that despite wonderfully and remarkably matching social and economic backgrounds juvenile scheduled offenders were found to be more intelligent and also found to possess high educational attainments. These kinds of people showed less and very little evidence of early developmental problems and fewer appearances at court. This is in comparison to normal people or other juvenile offenders who end up as cyber terrorists.(Andrew Silke,2009)

Cyber espionage can be defined as the usage of information technology systems and computer networks to gather information about a particular organization or a person or a society that is often to be in the realms of secret and confidential. This is generally done without the permission of the person who is responsible for holding the information. Cyber espionage is caused by a wide array of actors that includes groups, companies or even individuals and sometimes even nation-states. The FB I has also pinpointed that Chinese espionage activities are being a major threat to United States national security. (Irving Lachow,2008)

Not only has the world seen a change of geopolitics and social changes but it has dramatically changed with the advent of Information technology. The potential that these developments offer has created or put forth differing forms of warfare in cyberspace.These war fares seem unlimited as cyber terrorism can only be seen as a logical outcome of it.(Andrew Rathmell,2013)

The major question that arises is that can organizations achieve a strategic advantage in the current cyber terrorism game. A general game-theoretical model is proposed to conduct a detailed study of the optimal Information System. These studies are then used to apply and compare the losses that have been caused by common hackers and cyber terrorists. Simulations with varying levels of attacker's preference and deterrence level are carried out extensively to determine the sensitivity to the optimal Information System security investment. (Jian Hua &Sanjay Bapna,2004)

The United States experienced the worst largest terrorist attack in its history on 11th September 2001. Security practices and procedures were reviewed carefully by government agencies after this event. Awareness of other avenues was also spread where the terrorists might choose to achieve their goals, inclusive of cyber terrorism. Politically induced attacks in cyberspace can be defined as Cyber Terrorism. These attacks are mainly intended to make severe destruction such as loss of life or high economic damage. Mostly the term "weapons of mass disruption" is used in defining those potential computer-based threats. The threat of these attacks wanted us to have more knowledge of computers and the need for more computer professionals for computer security experts. It also became necessary for students to have knowledge of computer-related fields to be exposed to topics in computer security, especially the threat caused by cyber terrorism. A random sample of sixteen textbooks in the field of computer security was taken for examination to determine the coverage provided for cyber terrorism. These Textbooks more often provide resources for faculty to teach students about various topics in a subject – as here, students gain an understanding of techniques, potential threats, and targets of cyber terrorists. The results came out that the computer security textbooks provided do not give cyber terrorism the depth of coverage warranted by its importance/use for the IT industry. Therefore, faculties are forced to find their references and resources to address cyber-terrorism adequately in their class to cover most of the important topics. It is concluded by providing several web sites and trade books that can be used to help the faculty provide detailed information to their students on digital terrorism. (Janet J. Prichard &Laurie E. MacDonald,2018)

The ultimate goal of terrorism is to undermine civilians' resilience by indulging in them a sense of fear or panic and vulnerability that erases confidence in the ability of the law enforcement agencies and the government to protect their citizens against future attacks. How about Cyber Terrorism? Do Conventional terrorism and Cyber terrorism result in the same psychological effects? It is said that the psychological effects of digital terrorism have a high impact than conventional terrorism and in some cases, it is less effective. Do they affect the confidence in government agencies? Sadly, it does. (Michael L. Gross.et.al,2007)

The conceptual framework of knowledge management to analyze various aspects of knowledge as a resource for terrorist communities, and for confronting them, in the post-modern era is applied here. Terrorism is a societal phenomenon that is closely involved with changes in our knowledge of society. Nowadays, Terrorist organizations have become knowledge-centric, networked organizations, with a modern approach to organizational paradigms. Cyberspace is considered to be the habitat for knowledge and information and the terrorists involved are known as knowledge workers' expertise in it. Cyber terrorism is a combination of cyberspace and terrorism, filled with "nonvirtual" terrorist activities and global terrorism. A similar societal power-shift is provided by Information Technology from large organizations to small groups and individuals. (Gil Ariley,2017)

The arrival of new weaponry often comes with great fear over its potential for damage and destruction. Cyber weapons are not spared. They also certainly come in the same case. This is because so many damaging effects have occurred before on a large number of systems due to internet attacks. This caused the conclusion that cyber weapons are necessarily indiscriminate. But the facts do not bear this out. Cyber weapons are targetable. Many of them have already been so. Since cyber weapons are software, they are replicable and they can be designed in a way to reduce proliferation risks. (Steven M. Bellovin.et.al,2016)

Disintermediation of government has been one of the major challenges in cyber space. Historically, governments always had a reputation provided to their value as intermediaries both within states and between them. Their service as intermediaries in disputes between people—civil, criminal, and international is quite known. They also served as intermediaries in the physical world, investigating and prosecuting crimes, protecting borders and creating much of the infrastructure upon which real-world interactions take place. At the very core of the definition of government, lies the intermediary function. (David Aucsmith,2005)

Tomorrow's terrorist may be able to cause much damage with a keyboard than with a bomb. Psychological, political, and economic forces altogether promote the fear of cyber terrorism. If we notice from a psychological view, two greatest fears of the modern era are combined in the term "cyber terrorism." The fear of random, indiscriminate, violent victimization segues well with the distrust and fear of computer technology. No single case of cyber terrorism has been recorded yet, hackers are always taken for terrorists, and cyber defenses are more robust than is commonly supposed to be. Even so, the potential threat cannot be denied and it seems to get increased, making it all the more important to address the effects without inflating or manipulating it. (Gabriel Weimann,2002)

The term cyber terrorism is becoming more common in modern popular culture, yet a solid definition of the word is hard to define. While it is loosely defined, a large amount of subjectivity is present in defining what cyber terrorism is, and what it constitutes. To define cyber terrorism more logically, a study has been made of definitions and attributes of terrorism and terrorist activities. These attributes further developed a list of attributes for traditional terrorism. This list is then exposed to examine in detail with the addition of the computer and the Internet considered for each attribute. With this methodology, the online space and terrorism are synthesized to produce a broader but more useful assessment of the potential impact of computer terrorists. The concept of 'traditional' cyber terrorism, which defines the computer as the target or the tool is intended to be only a limited part of the true risk faced. More importantly, the breadth of the issue poses significant queries for those who argue for vertical solutions to what is a horizontal problem. (Sarah Gordon &Richard Ford,2012)

To deter cyber terrorism, first, it is important to identify the terrorists, since punishment or sentence may not deter them. The identification probability heavily based on tracking cyber terrorists. However, there are technical and legal challenges for tracking terrorists. Suggestions and insights on overcoming these challenges are provided. To deter cyber terrorism, the presence of three types of infrastructure is a must. They are technical, policy, and legal. (Sanjay Bapna & Jian hua, 2013)

The New YorkTimes reported that in March in the year 2107, the Obama administration initiated, and the Trump administration inherited, a covert action program to manipulate data inside North Korea's missile systems. Cyber and electronic warfare methods to sabotage missile components impair command and control systems, or jam communication signals to pre-empt enemy weapons shortly after they are launched. Because of the beginning of the U.S. program, popularly called Nimble Fire, North Korea has suffered numerous unsuccessful tests, including some catastrophic failures. (Erik Gartzke, Jon R. Lindsay,2015)

There is considerable debate about whether cyber terrorism poses a serious threat to society. Although so much has been dramatized in the most popular and well-known media, there is a legitimate danger. Because the term cyber terrorism has been improperly used and overused, a clear understanding of the danger of cyber terrorism must begin with a clear definition. At present, computer networks are attacked much and are subjected to compromise daily because of the security's inability to keep pace with the growth of connectivity and because of readily available hacking tools and techniques. Because most of the critical infrastructure is networked, it is at potentially high risk. Although much of the regular invasions are hackers trying to get in just to see if they can, acts of vandalism, or denial-of-service attacks, individuals are gaining access to sensitive information. The real danger of cyber terrorism, however, lies in the computer's use as both a terrorist tactic and a force multiplier. (Ayn Embar-Seddon,2002)

THE THREAT OF DIGITAL TERRORISM-A BRIEF INTRODUCTION

In general, cyberterrorism is the coming together of terrorism and cyberspace. People generally tend to get confused with the terms of cyber terrorism and cybercrime. Any happenings that create terror in cyberspace are defined as cyber terrorism whereas cybercrime is defined as using the required skills and knowledge to perform cyber attacks (Even a simple non-threatening one). It is said to be a cyber crime when the attack is more economically motivated rather than ideologically. Cyber terrorism is done by individuals or persons who are impacted by violent terrorist groups. It also leads to large scale destruction in terms of physical and psychological ways and results in inflicting damage beyond the target, i.e., affecting a plethora of people like a society or a country in general.

The rapid growth of the internet has led to marvelous development in human beings in terms of pursuing their endeavors. However as the age of the internet is booming, and as people are more into social media, the threats are also increasing at an alarmingly higher rate to its pros. As computers and networks expand globally, terrorists find it easier to launch cyber-terrorist attacks on them. The foremost and main reason is the ability to be anonymous. Being anonymous, aids the terrorists to be secretive in nature and at the same time do their work effectively without getting caught. Other reasons include the prospect of accessibility. Digital terrorism can be launched anywhere and on anyone on the earth. There is no need for closer proximity and hours of planning an attack as in physical attack. They are also done at a cost much cheaper and they do not require plenty of weapons or manpower. Many cyber-terrorist attack groups use denial of service attacks to attack their enemies. A Denial of service attack is one in which a machine or network is made inaccessible to its legitimate users. This is generally done by crashing the system by sending data that will result in the crash. It can also be achieved by flooding the target with unwanted traffic.

Personal data is something that is not to be compromised. Though we lose, imagine it on a large scale when it happens to some of the main databases such as a bank database or a country's army database or something that is extremely of utter importance. We end up concurring heavy losses both in terms of finance and data. Nowadays countries fret cyber terrorism more rather than everything. Although there are various forms of terrorism, cyberterrorism proves to be more and more dangerous as it easily falls into the category of unpredictability. So we must do everything in our power to be aware of it and thus prevent it from happening.

Physical Vs. Digital Terrorism

Although physical attacks for instances like war create major havoc and destroy property, it also takes away many and many lives of innocent people who are fighting for their nation or their leader, the digital attacks seem to pose a dangerous threat. This is because although digital terrorism attacks do not cause any damage to lives it invariably affects people's physiological and mental health. This is because private data is got by breaching even the high levels of security. When data like credit card and debit card numbers are received along with their passwords then these attacks cause serious economic loss to the person or nation or whosoever concerned. When we look at natural disasters like tsunami and earthquakes their effects are also devastatingly painful. For instance, hurricanes Katrina cost approximately 125 billion dollars. But when we look on the other side i.e. digital attacks, they too cause a mammoth economic loss. For example, the digital attack launched on MyDoom coast about 38.7 billion dollars which is also quite huge and devastating. We can say that digital attacks inflict more damage to a nation rather than a physical attack because physical attacks damage only a part of the geographical location whereas the digital attacks can vandalize the entire nation by gaining access to the important data of the nation and thereby making some major modifications or altering or even simply gaining access to the data can cause severe damage to the economy of the nation. The accessed data can be morphed modified and the risks are dynamic. The attacker can even sell the data to the enemy nations and this may, in turn, reflect in exposed warfare between nations. Thus digital terrorist attacks pose a serious threat and cause major damage when compared to physical attacks. So it's the digital attacks to which we must build our fortress strong and higher to prevent any hackers invading our fortress.

History of Digital Terrorism

The word "terrorism" is derived from the French word "terrorism" based on the Latin verb 'terror' which means 'to cause tremble'. In 1795, when it was used to describe the actions of the Jacobin club during their rule of post-revolutionary France, the so-called "The reign of terror". The rumor states that they coined the term Terrorism to refer to themselves. Terrorism is defined as the strategy of using coordinated attacks, violence, social threats to create fear and cause disruption and finally brings about compliance with specified ideological, political or religious demands.

The term terrorism civil war insurgency revolution, guerilla war, intimidation, and extremism are most commonly interchanged and used very loosely. It all refers to a common point, violence. An organized system of intimidation is called terrorism.

It is also defined as "A method were an organized society or party which seeks to achieve its common aim and tends to gain it through the use of violence".

The main characteristics of terrorism are:

- Terrorism is against a particular state or community and even over an individual incase of cyber terrorism.
- Politics plays a main purpose.
- It is considered to be illegal and unlawful.
- It aims at creating an impact of fear and panic not only for the victim but also for the people atlarge, causes to coerce a subduing.
- It stops rational thinking.
- It is accompanied by a feeling of impotence and helplessness on the part of the masses.
- It leads to a reaction of fight or dies.
- It contains arbitrariness in violence as their method to select victims is just random and there is no discrimination.

Computers and the Internet have become an essential part of our lives daily. Nowadays, maximum societies and individuals use these technologies to make their life easier. The technologies are mainly used for information storage, data processing, sharing messages, communications, typing, editing, designing and every other aspect of needs. This evolution of technology led us to the most deadly and destructive consequence that emerged in the name of "Cyber Terrorism". The term Cyber Terrorism indicates the negative intentional usage of advanced information technology for destructive purposes. Earlier, the traditional methods of terrorism were less harmful whereas now it has taken a whole new dimension that tends to be deadly in nature. For example, manipulating valuable data through hacking the victim's computer system is just a part of Cyber Terrorism.

Anyhow cyberspace always paves a way for new methodologies and the invention of technologies. The two elements cyberspace and terrorism combine as a common term of Cyber Terrorism. Virtual World, an alternate word for cyberspace, is a world where computer programs and data move. There is also a thought that defines there is no such existence of cyber terrorism and it is a matter of hacking or information warfare. It is most likely a creation of fear or panic using electronic means and technologies.

A computer system and internet facility used by terrorist communities to develop their websites and networks to send and receive messages from each other worldwide is an effective mode of cyber terrorism. They also use encrypted programs and digital signature for email service which cannot be read by anyone. Access to global electronic networks and information is a way to facilitate cyber terrorism. Viruses and worms are flown to cause collateral damage in government departments such as Academic, Health, Intelligence, Defense and Commerce.

Information and communication technologies are sometimes misused as targets and sometimes as weapons. Terrorists, for their existence, always try to establish their command and control to earn money. Terrorist uses the information processing devices for breaking, cracking, hacking, flowing of virus and altering valuable data or deletion of data.

Some Notable Incidents of Cyber Terrorism:

- In 1998, Sri Lankan embassies were swamped with 800 emails a day over two weeks by ethnic Tamil guerrillas. The messages read that claiming them to be Internet black tigers and the cause of this act is to disrupt the communications. It was characterized as the first known attack against a nation's computer systems by the Intelligence authorities.
- In 1999, during the Kosovo conflict hacktivists made a protest against the NATO bombings with denial-of-service attacks and NATO computers were blasted with email bombs. Adding to it, highly politicized virus-laden e-mails were received by many businesses, public organizations, and academic institutes from a range of Eastern European countries.

In Romania, crackers gained illegal access to the computers that controlled the life support systems at an Antarctic research station, leaving behind the 58 scientists endangered. This is one of the worst cyber terrorist attacks. Recently, in May 2007 Estonia played victim to a mass cyber-attack by hackers inside the Russian Federation and some evidence suggests that the attack was coordinated by the Russian government. Though the Russian parties deny this attack, it seems to be in response to the removal of the Russian world war II memorial from downtown Estonia.

Hierarchy of Cyber Capability

- *Enabling*
  - Includes online activities that support the operations performed by the terrorist organizations
  - For example, publicity and propaganda, fund-raising, disseminating manuals, reconnaissance, and clandestine communications between members and know-how to incite and facilitate the attacks by others.
- *Disruptive*
  - These include the online activities that generally disrupt the information technology of opponents.

- ○ For example, the cyber breaches of network security using hacking, dissemination of malware, financial theft and fraud, denial of service attacks, ex-filtration of digital information, phishing and other Information Technology activities that induce harm.
- *Destructive*
  - ○ These include cyberattacks that trigger injury or physical damage utilizing spoofing operation technology(OT) and digital control systems.
  - ○ For example, it includes attacks on Supervisory and Data Acquisition(SCADA) systems and also disabling control and safety systems.

Candidate List of Scenarios For Possible Attacks On These Places

- Airports-The air traffic is spoofed i.e. it is a duplicate scenario is brought into play and it is made by others to believe that it is true.This can be done to create an airplane crash,airport emergency crash, and even fuel store fire
- Construction Projects-In construction sites the damage can be done by hijacking the controls of the crane
- Transport-In transport the crashes can be made to occur between two trains when data about the trains is hacked and altered and thus resulting in a crash. Similar crashes can also occur to tankers resulting in two tankers crashing against each other.Similarly, an explosive chemical cargo explosion can also be made to occur.Eurostar fire is also quite possible.
- Real Estate-In this case the attacks may include boiler explosion,manipulation of building sway control, smart meter hijack, door locking, electrical fires that are caused by system overloads,spoofing backup generators,sabotage or manipulation of vital alarm, targeting of sprinkler systems,targeting Halo fire suppressors and shutting of cooling systems on server farms or data center battery power UDS.
- Retail-Here the major target is towards the food security and also includes panic/stampede creation with spoof announcement or alarm
- Pharmaceutical-Here the attacks could be mass poisoning that could effectively affect loads and loads of people in the view of the attacker and thus succeeding in their attempts of attacks and vision.
- Chemicals-This can be induced by causing a chemical reactor to explode. Sometimes it can also be done by chlorine explosion or poisoning and even causing an explosion of a fertilizer plant and grain silo. It also includes targeting a lumber mill or particulate removal with HVAC.

- Healthcare-Critical targets on medical equipment can induce severe damage. Automation attack on prescriptions can also be used. Pathogens can be released just so to increase the sales of medicine or to create false demand. Uninterrupted power system attacks and targeting HVAC systems also can be done to affect this particular industry.
- Power/Energy-Causing fires to the oil refinery and chemical spills are major attacks in this particular type. Aurora and Erebos-style UK outage are some of the other techniques of attacks being employed to inflict damage.

MAJOR FORMS OF CYBER TERRORISM

To bring forth some solutions to digital terrorism, it is essential to first and foremost understand the two major forms of cyber terrorism-hybrid cyber terrorism and pure cyber terrorism.

Hybrid Cyber Terrorism

It involves the extensive use of the internet for activities such as propaganda, communication, and training, fundraising and planning for actual terrorist attacks. The terrorist groups use the internet to spread their motives and ideology to other parts of the globe. It also uses the internet to bring in more people to their terrorist organization by employing them. It is also found out that terrorist organizations have been more lately using telegram applications. This is due to the aftermath of closing down all the terrorists' social media accounts. Terrorist groups also actively use messaging apps and social media for discussing their plans. Fundraising is nowadays done with the usage of even bitcoins.The money raised by funding is used generally to purchase lethal and dangerous weapons.

Pure Cyber Terrorism

Pure cyber terrorism is defined as the attacks that are inflicted directly on cyber infrastructure by attacking the cyberspace. This is done to achieve the desired objectives in the field of politics, religion and other ideologies. Further, this can be broadly categorized into Destructive cyber terrorism and Disruptive cyber terrorism. Destructive cyber terrorism is defined as the usage of computer viruses and Trojans to cause damage or to ruin and tear down the physical and virtual assets. Disruptive cyber terrorism is defined as hacking that primarily was designed to bring the websites down and thereby create havoc in the normal lifestyle. The latter primarily depends on important infrastructures such as financial systems, transportation, and medical utility.

The major way is to take down the path of the legislative framework by issuing an internet regulation that will foresee and monitor all the social platforms for malicious activity and thereby detect, react and prevent further spreading of any unwanted propaganda else it will result in serious damage. At the same time, adequate and correct measures must be taken to allow people to express their natural thoughts without any struggle. Primarily, privacy must be preserved. The monitoring should be rigorous in nature and should be consistent with the ultimate aim of targeting the terrorist groups.

To create a strong bond between the stakeholders of the public and private sectors is also another efficient method.i.e., bringing together government forces that include network operators, Internet service providers, civil experts, and cybersecurity experts. It has become extremely crucial to scrutinize the digital terrorism attacks more precisely. This involves the process of investigating the objectives and the resources that are needed. It also includes examining and evaluating the risks that could lead to destructible damage. So it is of paramount importance for nations to adopt national strategies thus resulting in more sense-awareness among the public. There should also be a cordial relationship between the countries by signing agreements related to digital terrorism so that the countries together can fight against the invisible forces of terrorism.

Phishing Scams

An attempt where the scammers contact you out of the blue and trick you into giving out your personal information like credit card numbers, bank account numbers, and passwords. They normally contact via email, text messages, and a phone call or even through social media pretending to be a legitimate business such as your bank telephone or even internet provider.

These scammers ask you to update them on your details so that they can get access to you. They might even ask you to fill any survey or poll as you can win a prize at the end. But here is where they gain accessto your email accounts, phone, and other information.

Another way they use to get hold of your access is by sending you that unauthorized or suspicious activity is happening in your system' and ask you for your details so that they can sort it out. Infact they tend to steal from you. Phishing scams are same as fraudulent phonecalls. People are now being educated to be aware of phishing scams.

Online scams

Online scams are generally scams that take place online. It is more like a phishing scam that happens online. Tricking you into giving your personal information by popping up an ad that tells you have won something and asking for your card details to pay for shipping. Sadly, you'll never receive anything but start noticing weird transactions happening from your bank account.

Malware

Malware is malicious software onto your system. It's a piece of software that can cause harm to data and devices. It is an overarching name for different types of viruses namely 'Trojan' and 'spyware'. Malware is done through a range of viruses that will penetrate your computer, phone or other devices to cause damage so that the culprits can steal your personal information.

Email Bombing

An email bomb is more like a way of internet abuse. It is done by overloading one's email address by sending numerous emails at a time. This will cause the person who receives the emails server to become sluggish or even crash. This is not particularly done for stealing but to show the pain of the sluggish server and making it hard to fix.

Virus Dissemination

This is a form of cyber crime. It not only gets the malware (as we have seen above) onto one part of the system but also spreads to other pieces of software. Lacking a safe environment to test in, when you tend to open a piece of infected software the process begins all over again.

Logic Bombs

Logic bombs are small programs or sections that act like a virus. They are triggered by an event. This event can be a certain date or time, a percentage of disk space filled or the removal of the file and so on.Critical sections of code could be deleted in a program making your software useless. The people who generally implement logic bombs happen to be most commonly installed by insiders who already had access to the system.

Theft

Internet theft is the approximate term for any theft that happens over the internet. The ultimate goal of internet theft is to steal your personal information which paves the way to steal money from your bank accounts or make use of your details for their purpose. This can be done in many ways such as fake ads fake emails, viruses and snooping.

Social Media Hack and Spamming

Social media hacking is an invasion of privacy often done as a joke. Usually, it happens to celebrities or a brand to defame or make fun of them. Celebrities end up with following people they usually wouldn't or putting up random statuses in their account. Even though it is funny it is still invading someone's privacy.

The hacker can also spread unauthorized content that can cause stress to people who view them or can end up with the account getting reported. Social media spamming is when a person creates a fake account to be friends with a normal person, therefore to spam their inboxes with bulk messaging. This is done to spread malware.

Spamming can also spread malicious links that are intended to harm or damage the user or a device. By clicking on the link, we think we are directed to some random advertising sites but the truth is that we unknowingly download the malware which leads to theft of personal information.

Another dark side of social media is creating malicious accounts to spam your activities by constantly giving negative comments. This is said to be a form of trolling. While you can report such behavior to the social media platform to delete these accounts or block them, they continue their attack with other accounts in no time.

Electronic Money Laundering

When money is generated in a large amount, it is illegally laundered before spent or invested. The technique called wire transfer is used to launder money electronically through messages between banks. Previously it had been tough to track wire transfers as a large number of money transactions occurred daily. But anyhow banks nowadays seem to overcome the issue and began filing any suspicious activity.

Sales and Investment Fraud

By knowing the contact details and available account information for savings and investment account holders the fraudsters easily adopt the persona of an investment broker. Then they make contact with the customers obviously to cheat them. They seem to be quite trustworthy as they talk about the accounts you already own and real results.

Eavesdropping and Surveillance

It is a crime to eavesdrop over the phone or online without the consent of the parties. Wiretap is the common way to eavesdrop, a practice where the criminal connects a listening device probably to a telephone line to monitor the conversation secretly. Since the evolution of new technologies, computers can be hacked for eavesdropping and surveillance.

Software Piracy

Software piracy is defined as unauthorized use or distribution of computer software. Nowadays we can easily find any software or almost every movie and song for free online. Even though pirated materials seem good since they are free, it contains its risks. These risks include Trojan, viruses, worms and other forms of malware. But it's also considered as stealing as no proceeds reach the producers of the content. Film producers are the most affected in the piracy world.

Data Diddling

Data Diddling is the action of skewing data entries into the user's system. The name might seemingly be humorous and less complicated action compared to other cybercrimes, it has huge results, however.

They include altering financial figures up or down marginally or it could be more complex, making the entire system useless.

Salami Slicing Attack

Salami slicing attack is a technique used by cybercriminals to steal money or resources a tiny bit at a time so that there is no noticeable difference found initially in the bank accounts. The criminal does this continually to different resources until a considerable amount is stolen over time. Salami slicing attackers generally use this method to steal money.

Hacking

Hacking is when some intruder gets access to your system without your permission. Hackers usually do this for many reasons, let it be greed, fame or power as it reflects their capabilities and cleverness and they enjoy it. However, some do this to steal personal information, banking details and financial data. Hackers are one's who have advanced knowledge of computers and generally tend to be computer programmers.

Cyber Stalking

Cyber Stalking is especially known among teenagers and youngsters. There are so many numerous cases of cyberstalking across the entire globe and the world unknown to us. The twist is that the victim and the stalker know each other. The victim is often subjected to online harassment in forms of a barrage of online messages and emails. The ultimate aim of online stalking is to make the victim miserable by taking control of them. It is just like normal stalking.

Cyber Bullying

Cyberbullying is similar to cyberstalking; however, the messages can be harmful toxic and quite offensive. The bully intends to create fake profiles and post an image, video or send abusive messages that will offend the victim. Either way, it is still a crime. It sounds like normal bullying but it is usually done online through social media channels.

Identity Theft

One of the most common types of cyber crime is identity theft. The criminals usually steal information like credit card information, addresses and email addresses and more. The identity theft usually occurs to create fraud for financial gains. Stealing and cheating on identity is a big issue than it looks like. It is more like hijacking a person itself with these information they pretend to be someone else and create new bank accounts.

Child Soliciting and Abuse

It is a type of cyber crime where the criminals solicit children for pornography. It is done via chat rooms online. Here, a child is considered to be under the age of 16. It also describes the form of sexual abuse towards children. This type of cyber crime is strictly monitored by police.

Figure 1. Cyber-attack classification

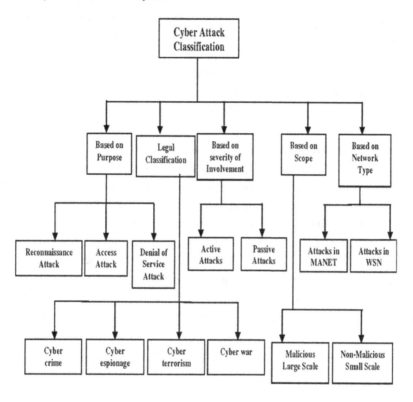

Ransom ware

Ransomware is a threat to many companies and has affected NHS and other big corporations all over the world. Ransomware enters your system, encrypts your files which means you don't have any access to them. The criminals will then threaten you to give a large sum of money to get your data back. Once the data is encrypted, it is virtually impossible to get it back.

(Source: Cyber-Security Incidents: A Review Cases in Cyber-Physical Systems)

DIGITAL TERRORISM AND ITS EFFECTS

The ultimate goal of terrorism is to undermine civilians' resilience by indulging a sense of fear that erodes confidence in the ability of the government and law enforcement agencies to protect citizens against further attacks. Findings suggest that cyberterrorism aggravates stress, anxiety and intensifiesfeelings of vulnerability and radicalizes political attitudes. In these ways, cyber terrorism causes similar effects as conventional terrorism. As the threat of cyber terrorism grows, strengthening emotional restrictions and confidence will prove as critical as bolstering deterrent and offensive cyber capabilities. Conventional terrorist attacks can be weathered by emotional resilience whereas in the face of cyber-terrorism will need the usage of authorities to implement policies to reduce the fears and insecurity of cyber terrorism, educate and create awareness the public about better cybersecurity practices and convey accurate information about the scope and the probability of cyber-attacks. Conventional terrorism employs kinetic means such as suicide bombers or advanced explosive devices and attacks in many ways. Terrorism causes death, injury and property destruction and also generates fear and anxiety in the target population. Terrorists may use terrorism to demoralize a civilian population to pressure their government to refrain from a specific policy. Sometimes terrorists are effective.

Unlike conventional terrorism, cyber terrorism employs malicious computer technology rather than kinetic force. But similar to conventional terrorism, cyber terrorism aims to political, religious, or ideological goals by harming people physically or psychologically. Cyber-terrorists tend to terrify their victims by crippling digital and financial resources, social networks and threatening physical harm. First, cyber terrorism causes stress, anxiety and personal insecurity along with heightened perceptions of threat. Second, many people are willing to exchange security with civil liberties and privacy.

PREVENTION AND SOLUTION

To deal with terrorist activities in cyberspace, consider these three stages of defense:

Prevention: How can we manage an attack from happening? How can we make it a failure before reaching the target?

Incident management, damage limitation: When an attack has reached the target, how do we prepare for and make defense during an attack? How to defeat the attack without loss? How to identify and limit the damage?

Consequence management: What to do after an attack?

These must be the first priorities when an attack actually happens. Recovery and Response are very important to face consequences.

Figure 2. General steps required for investigation

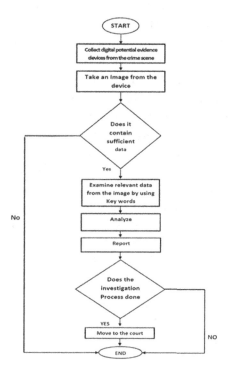

Tasks that would fall under recovery might include

- The removal of hostile or defective entities
- A survey of damage assessment, what is broken or altered, and what is not
- An automated process for assessing quickly and effectively rationing and reallocating what is left
- Functions to be reconstituted must be prioritized
- Restoration to pre-attack status without destroying evidence.

Tasks that comes under response include

- Capturing the right culprit: strong forms of accurate trace-back and forensic tools may be similar to "fingerprinting"
- Asymmetries: How to react about attackers with few IT assets or vulnerabilities?

We can also deploy anti-social behavior to detect cyber terrorism in the text contents. To do this, the text documents are to be converted to numerical vectors that consist of numerical weights of the terms that are present in the text documents. Vectors can be calculated by using different weighting methods. Some methods include the binary weighting, term frequency-based weighting, term frequency, and inverse document frequency-based weighting, and fuzzy set-based weighting methods. Naive Bayes Multinomial (NBM) and Support Vector Machines (SVM) can be used as classifiers to compare the performances of the weighting methods. The certain analysis shows that a fuzzy set based weighting method with SVM classifier gives the best and correct classification accuracy which reaches up to 99% escalation. (Vahide Nida Uzel ; Esra Sarac Essiz ; Selma Ayse Ozel,2018)

For too officially police a crime there must be an act that will consider a digital crime and that should make it punishable under the law. There also must particularly exist the capability to investigate for all the potential and possible suspects and obtain circumstantial or physical evidence of the crime to be used in future and upcoming criminal proceedings. The act of gaining unauthorized access to a particular network system is a criminal act under federal law. The attack planning cycle for traditional terrorist and then cyber terrorists planning used to penetrate a network system can be compared. (P. R. Neely, Jr. and M. T. Allen,2018)

(Source: Fuzzy Crime Investigation Framework for Tracking Data Theft based on USB Storage)

FUTURE RESEARCH DIRECTIONS

As the battlefields are turning their attention towards the technology side, we can expect fewer more advancements in the field of digital terrorism. As Nicole Eagan, CEO of Darktrace cites that the digital battlefield is quickly shifting to a war of Artificial Intelligence algorithms. When Artificial Intelligence is combined with digital terrorism the autonomous cyber-attacks sustain their presence. This will enable them to spread their roots stronger and hence the attacks become harder to interpret the attacked and impossible to put a stop to them. Hence we will be left in a status of extreme vulnerability where attacks can be easily executed and the attackers find it easy to identify their targets. These targets are the brutally attacked with no means of any remedial measure.

As these attacks by time grows are becoming more refined, we will face a situation where the cyber-attacks will mimic our online traits and thereby impersonating people. These weaponized AI may become more and more refined that they will pose a threat of convincingly impersonate a person we trust whole-heartedly. The next potential step towards this would be to target the defenses that have been deployed against them itself. Thus this will break into the security of the system and will enable the attacker access to the entire private data which we don't want to fall in the hands of the attackers especially. These security mechanisms that Artificial Intelligence would break would include the firewalls and how the system handles the threats. These processes will be learned by Artificial Intelligence and thus they will pose a major threat to us and the data.

Thus the potential future research should be in the field of study that combines both digital terrorism and Artificial Intelligence that cause damage that is beyond our wildest dreams. Thus our energy must be unleashed by examining more about such cases and how they can be prevented effectively. Or we can direct our research on how to stop combining Artificial Intelligence and digital terrorism.Thus this is what future research should be based upon.

CONCLUSION

Thus a crucial method of preventing cyber-terrorism before they happen is to make security mandatory in all the software and devices that are being developed. The ways of finding the terrorist must also be viewed from the perspective of the attacker. This will enable fast procuring of ideas to re-counter the attack. Intrusion detection is one of the major research areas in the field of prevention of cyber terrorism. The earlier methods include encryption techniques using passwords. But as more and more vulnerabilities are coming into the scene it is also necessary to constantly develop new methods of intrusion detection which will enable the detection of digital terrorism attacks. By intrusion detection, we can lessen the probability of an attack on our systems. Also, the responses to cyber terrorism attacks can be primarily centered on preserving data during the course of the attack.

REFERENCES

Aucsmith, D. (2016). Disintermediation. Counterinsurgency and Cyber Defense. Academic Press.

Colarik. (2006). *Cyber Terrorism: Political and Economic Implications*. Academic Press.

Embar-Seddan. (2002). *Cyber terrorism: Are We Under Siege?* Academic Press.

Rathmell. (2008). Cyber-terrorism: The shape of future conflict? *Defense & International Security*, 40-45.

Silke. (2003). *Terrorists, Victims and Society: Psychological Perspectives on Terrorism and its consequences.* Academic Press.

Gartzke, E., & Lindsay, J. R. (2015). *The Cyber Commitment Problem and the Destabilization of Nuclear Deterrence.* Academic Press.

Weimann. (2005). Cyber Terrorism: The Sum of all Fears? Studies in Conflict and Terrorism, 28(2).

Ariely, G. (2007). Knowledge Management, Terrorism and Cyber Terrorism. *Terrorism,* 10.

Janczewski & Colarik. (2007). *Warfare and Cyber Terrorism.* Academic Press.

Kenney, M. (2015). Cyber-Terrorism in a Post-Stuxnet World. *Orbis, 59*(1), 111–128. doi:10.1016/j.orbis.2014.11.009

Lachow. (2009). Cyber Terrorism: Menace or Myth? *Cyber Power and National Security.*

Lewis, J. A. (2002). *Assessing the Risks of Cyber Terrorism, Cyber War and Other Cyber Threats.* In Center for Strategic and International Studies.

Prichard, J. J., & MacDonald, L. E. (2004). Cyber Terrorism: A Study of the Extent of Coverage in Computer Science Text Books. *JITE-Research, 3*(1).

Gross, M. L., Canetti, D., & Vashdi, D. R. (2018). Cyber Terrorism: Its Effects on Psychological well being, Public Confidence and Political Attitudes. In *Bytes, Bombs and Spies: The Strategic Dimensions of Offensive Cyber Operations.* Brookings Institution Press.

Stohl. (2006). Cyber terrorism: a clear and present danger, the sum of all fears, breaking point or patriot games? Crime, Law, and Social Change, 46(4–5), 223–238.

Bapna & Hua. (2012). How can we deter Cyber Terrorism? *Information Security Journal: A Global Perspective, 21*(2).

Bapna, S. (2013). The economic impact of cyber terrorism Jian Hua. *The, 22*(2), 175–186.

Bellovin, S. M., Landau, S., & Lin, H. (2017). Limiting the Undesired Impact of Cyber Weapons: Technical Requirements and Policy Implications. *Journal of Cybersecurity, 3*(1), 59–68.

Furnell, S. M., & Warren, M. J. (1999). Computer hacking and cyber terrorism: The real threats in the new millennium. *Computers & Security*, *18*(1), 28–34. doi:10.1016/S0167-4048(99)80006-6

Gordon, S. (2002, November). Cyber Terrorism: An Overview. *Computers & Security*, *21*(7), 636–647. doi:10.1016/S0167-4048(02)01116-1

Neely, P. R. Jr, & Allen, M. T. (2018). Policing Cyber Terrorism. *Journal of Cybersecurity Research*, *3*(1), 13–18. doi:10.19030/jcr.v3i1.10227

Uzel, V. N., Saraç Eşsiz, E., & Ayşe Özel, S. (2018). Using Fuzzy Sets for Detecting Cyber Terrorism and Extremism in the Text. *2018 Innovations in Intelligent Systems and Applications Conference (ASYU)*, 1-4. 10.1109/ASYU.2018.8554017

KEY TERMS AND DEFINITIONS

Anonymity: Restraining oneself from revealing their true identity.

Attack: Something that causes potential harm and destroys a thing or affects a thing.

Cyberattack: An attack that is launched onto the network so as to gain illegal access to the system.

Cyberspace: It denotes an environment where internet and systems communicate actively.

Decryption: It is the process of converting cipher text back to plain text generally using a key and thus finding the actual content.

Digital Attack: A violent case where the attacker attacks the offender by means of attacking the network infrastructure.

Encryption: It is the process of converting plain text to cipher text that makes it harder for the hacker to figure out.

Hashing: Method of converting a string of characters into a shorter fixed length value for easy storage and retrieval.

Phishing: The process of sending emails or messages pretending to be another person who results in getting personal data from others such as credit card number or phone number.

Spam: Unrelated things sent over the internet that is completely irrelevant.

Threat: Anything that can cause damage or harm the system or the network. It is only a warning and it does not mean the happening of the event. It only hints at the happening of the impending danger.

Chapter 6
Development and Various Critical Testing Operational Frameworks in Data Acquisition for Cyber Forensics

Abhineet Anand

(iD) https://orcid.org/0000-0003-3505-8563
Chitkara University Institute of Engineering and Technology, Punjab, India

M. Arvindhan
Galgotias University, India

ABSTRACT

Digital forensics is the science of preserving and analyzing digital data; this data can then be used in court cases as well as for crime detection and prevention. Digital forensics began in the 1970s and was initially used as a tool for fighting financial crime. Today, with computers and digital devices being an integral part of our professional and private lives, digital forensics are used/needed in a wide variety of disputes. Data Acquisitions is described and discuss different techniques or methodology obtain the data, facts, and figures from different resource and at a different level of the system.

DOI: 10.4018/978-1-7998-1558-7.ch006

INTRODUCTION

The field of digital forensics is continually changing as new technology is developed both as the focus of a digital forensic practitioner's activities and concerning the tools available to undertake those activities. This has led to the difficulties being faced by the U.S. National Institute of Standards and Technology (NIST) who have been unable to keep pace with new digital forensic software being released or even updates to existing software (Allemang D., 2011). For instance, the NIST handbook revised on 1 February 2012 refers to the testing results of EnCase version 6.5, but by 23 February 2012, the production version of EnCase was v7.03. This problem comes about because the tools themselves are victims of the fast-moving environment of digital forensics and the need for those "tools designed solely for forensic purposes to keep abreast of the broad range of technology" (Alzaabi M., 2013). Digital forensics is the science of preserving and analyzing digital data; this data can then be used in court cases as well as for crime detection and prevention. Digital forensics began in the 1970s and was initially used as a tool for fighting financial crime. Today, with computers and digital devices being an integral part of our professional and private lives, digital forensics are used/needed in a wide variety of disputes (ALfahdi M, 2016).

Common Data Acquisitions Considerations

Broadly classification of data acquisition can be done into two categories

1. Static Acquisition: In this environment, data is copied from a hard drive from a powered-off system. The normal procedure is taking out the evidence form the suspected computer, by using any of the write blockers is attached to the investigating system, which makes copies/images of the original files. With the help of different tools various type of analysis is done on this evidence and try to find out the proof for any type of unethical breach (Ayers D., 2009).
2. Live Acquisition: In this type of environment, the tools are directly included in the system, which runs various background processes on the suspected system. From the live stream, images are created and different analysis is applied on online mode and the targeted system are being protected from any type of threat. This type of Acquisition is used most nowadays because shutting down the servers or websites is nowadays being not possible. For Live Acquisition, write blockers are in use at the various level of data acquisition. Mainly these devices are used to monitor the commands given to hard disk. They never allow data to be written or copied to any other device. Even they don't allow the disk packs to be mounted on the system with write access on them, only

read-only permission is given. Write protectors works in both of the hardware as well as software type of protection (Benredjem D., 2007). Host Protected Area and Device Configuration Overlay are used to enable the write Blockers. Hardware writes blocker's example are Tableau T3458is Forensic SATA/SCSI/IDE/USB Combo Bridge, Tableau T35es-R2 Forensics eSATA/IDE Bridge, UltraBlock Firewire - The First Portable Firewire Hardware Write Blocker, etc.

Data Acquisitions is described and discuss different techniques or methodology obtain the data, facts, and figures from different resource and at a different level of the system. It describes some contingency planning for data acquisition and explains how to use some basic acquisition tools. Figure 1 is discussing the different data acquisition consideration which may be the basis of classification of these techniques also. Here it will be discussed how it can be used for remote networks and how the different tools will work and used in the remote networks. It will also be required to see how different RAID levels will be the different methodologies to use the acquisition techniques. So, when we are looking at the different types of storage formats. explained the best type of technique for acquiring that data (Beebe N. L., 2014). So, before starting the acquisition techniques it is required to know various storage format which may come across while discussing and acquiring data from places. Data in forensic acquisition tools are stored as an image file; which can be of three different formats that can be used as digital.

Raw Format

It makes possible to write bit stream data to files. A bit stream is a contiguous sequence of bits, representing a stream of data, transmitted continuously over a communications path, serially (some at a time). The term bit stream is frequently used to describe the configuration data to be loaded into a Field Programmable Gate Array(FPGA) (Buchholz F., 2004). The advantage of the raw format is fast data transfer. It ignores minor data read errors on source drive and most computer forensic tools can read raw format. The biggest among these is it ignores the minor data errors and clones them. The disadvantage of this type of data storage is that it requires lots of storage and tools may not collect marginal or bad sectors. It ignores read errors but bad sectors create problems.

Property Formats

Most forensic tools have their formats. They are only open to their software features offered which could be the company based on their algorithm. But, sometimes it depends on the software with the format and property kind of the thing which cannot be understood by other parties, which creates a problem for other companies. Now, talking about the images of data whether those are compressed or not compressed. Some software uses the compression step some do not. And that too, even though the software uses the compression what level of compression is used by them is also matters. These compressions will be again used to splitting those files into smaller parts. The other aspect is with the feature of the integration of metadata into the image file. The main disadvantage is the inability to share an image between different tools/companies/recovery agencies. It will be limited to use that specific tool. In these category file size limitation for each segmented volume. The expert witness format in unofficial standard, so communicating or transferring images or data from one software to another is always a big task in these types of formats. Different expert proprietary formats are used by tools like EnCase, FTK, x-Ways Forensics or SMART. The file extension may be used by these are .E01, .E02 or so. These tools can produce compressed or uncompressed files according to the requirement of the situation and need (Case A., 2008).

Advanced Forensic Format(AFF)

To overcome the drawback of unofficial standard in the property format Dr. Simon L Garfinbel of Basis Technology Corporation has designed an open-source acquisition format. The basic design goal of this structure provides in both of the compressed or decompressed files with no file size restriction. It provisioned the concept of extra space in the image file or segmented file for metadata. It was having a simple file structure and open source can be used with different tools or software. Different file extension which comes across this format are .aff (Advanced Forensics Format) data. The next file format which stores metadata in a single file is .afd. If it is for multiple files, then .afm is used. If the raw format and metadata stored in a separate file then .afm extension is used (Casey E., 2011). Based on research, digital forensics can be divided into various group which further can also be categories into different subgroups. In figure 3 the detail of these categories has been addressed.

Figure 1. Common Data Acquisition Considerations

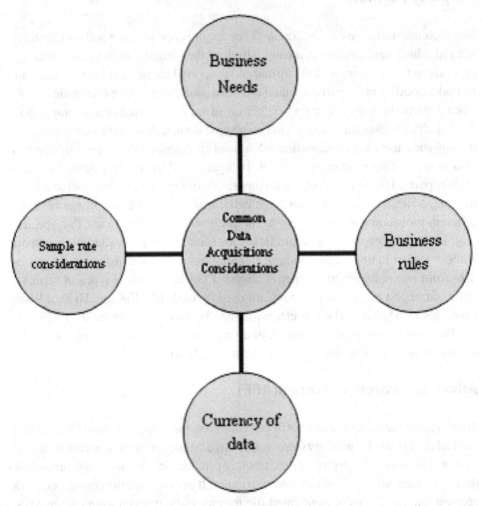

Figure 2. A different part of the signal during transition

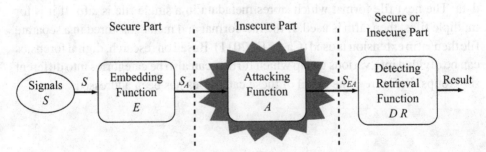

As per the direction and requirement for the minimum qualification and requirement of different trending and collaboration of education and legal categories are merging, the above discussed hierarchical chart can further be modified. It is starting with Data Volume as the volume of data that is generated is increasing day by day it is very important to secure and check different devices which may be the area of cyber forensics (Abhineet Anand, 2017).

The dedicated storage devices which are dedicatedly used by a particular organization tend to decrease because of Cloud storage; private cloud or high secure or confidential data will still be part of our system in that case Storage Area Network(SAN). It will be required to make these data more secure. And with that taking the same example of Cloud, the use of data exchange which tends to increase in the Network Storage Area(NAS) which is required to be scan and protect from the unethical uses. The different categories driving this category are Tools that Image and look for evidence at the same time, User History Timelines, Carving in Parallel, Imaging in Parallel, Traffic generation (Gholap P., 2013). A Live Acquisition is a method of checking or gathering data from one running system, just like we switch on the system and start getting the list of the applications running in the system. It mainly stores or analyzes the logs, temporary files created by the applications, supporting files for the main process, threats and other links. The other information which it may trap may be networked connection links or requests, various encryption keys, and the data generated after encryption, a different list which is produced by the application, different codes which are being modified by application presently running in primary memory. Different topics that can be identified in this category are RAM Analysis, Interrupt execution for Live Acquisition, Legal Ramification. Process Control System (SCADA system) is being used in almost every case of manufacturing or operation environment which tends to and forced to also to make these systems more secure and record the data to make it safe. Many industries which lakes to cope with the system results in more accident and loss. A lot of research and innovation is also being generated because of the same reason. Different subcategories that are identified in Control System are Evidence Collection in the Absence of Persistent Memory, Hardware-Based Capture Devices for Control System Network Audit Tools, Honeypots for Control System (as Part of Investigation), Radio Frequency Forensic(900Mhz), IDS for Control System (Kataria M., 2014).

The Computer Forensics has been changed to Digital Forensics, which indicates a broad verity of devices that can be considered in this category. Various devices like mobile phones, media players, various types of control devices in virtualized as well as real machines and many more digitally supported equipment are considered in the field of digital forensics. These are the various Media Types which has broaden the study. Evidence Modeling- Different type of investigation process has been kept under this category of digital forensics. This category is mainly dealing with the

Figure 3. Category of Digital Forensic

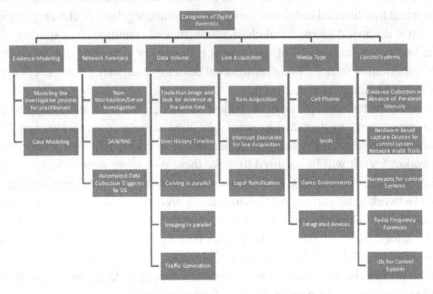

process of capturing the evidence associated with a particular crime. For the various category of crime different model is already suggested. If any of the crime occurs, it may be suggested to follow the particular set of steps to record the various evidence, which has been found very much successful for large organizational structures. These types of models are used to guide and train newly appointed officers to retrieve data at a different level, as well. The legal issues associated with digital forensics were also considered an overarching theme that would be difficult to incorporate into a single hierarchy. Identified legal categories include Cybercrime, Constitutional Law, Property Law, Cyber War, Contract Law, Tort Law, Criminal Procedure, Evidence Law, as well as special issues (Abhineet Anand, 2017). Beyond the categories listed, there are additional complications associated when the arena is extended to an international playing field. Thus International Law is a secondary overarching legal issue that merits further research. This work is also being undertaken by a subset of the participants.

There are some of the data acquisitions being listed below:

3. **Business Needs:** In this kind of consideration, we mainly focus on business needs like:
   (a) Source of data
   (b) Problem definition
   (c) Why data are being used
   (d) Techniques/strategies needed
   (e) Implementation
4. **Business rules** are the rules which have constraints under which business organization operates and those rules are also being used in managing the company (Alzaabi M., 2013).
5. **Sample rate considerations:** Like the isolation part where we can break or make the statement. This kind of considerations may either express sampling interval in unit time or we may express them by sampling interval in hertz.
6. **The currency of data:** The currency of the data may deal with many types of work which may require the data being made available to them currently. Meaning that there may be cases where we need data over a specific period while some may need data for reasons.

Authoritative data source:

1. ADS is defined as a single officially designated source having any type of information and providing information to fields where business depends.
2. Here, information is trusted meaning information provider uses management practices to produce/generate information for making sure to integrity, security, and quality.
3. The main aim of ADS to provide information which is visible, understandable in information consumers.
4. Analysis and recommendations which are documented can only help in the assessment and designation of ADS (ALfahdi M, 2016).

Data collections considerations:
The person who will do the data collection should have the following:

1. **Skills:** if a person having certification of data collection and if any company does not have any authorization they will be contracting
2. **Frequency:** how many times the data sets being collected will need a justification
3. **Timely:** period in which data will be needed

Data collection is an area where the cost-saving mechanism is needed.

Before we collect data we must apply some of the practices like analysis, definition, and standards. Data be reviewed and updated in real-time to get high quality and along with them, metadata will be updated.

Converted data consideration:

1. **Legacy quality:** data being available to complete needs are sufficient or not.
2. **Technical issues:** are there technical issues with storage conversion of data in regular format.

Cyber Forensics:

1. Cyber forensics is being defined as the kind of science where there is investigation is being done and has some analysis techniques which help in gathering the data and preserving to present in the court of law.
2. In cyber forensics, investigation happens systematically to find out about the crime and find the responsible.
3. A digital way is being made after being made from original and store it in a location with no one's access (Ayers D., 2009).
4. Various methods are being used by investigators and also paid software applications to check digital copy for deleted, damaged and encrypted files.

Impact Of Cyber Forensics:

- Computer
    1. With the introduction to the forensics and with the computers, it has been a facet of the forensic investigation
    2. Also, the report writing helped in reducing the paperwork. (Benredjem D., 2007) & (Beebe N. L., 2014)
    3. Spell check removed the errors in the spelling mistakes in an automated way.
- AFIS
    1. The automated fingerprinting scanning replaced the earlier the fingerprinting method (being involved the ink work and many of the criminals used to escape from jail as a hell).
    2. This fingerprinting scanning is being digitally scanned and is being stored in databases.
    3. But still, now the latent prints are being recorded and being put into the search engine to match at the time of the crime scene.

Figure 4. Impact of Cyber Forensic

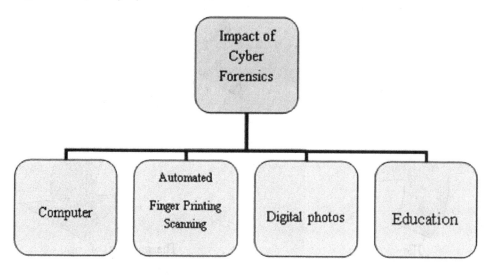

- Digital photos
  1. These days the digital photos are dominating the world rather than the old way of taking photos.
  2. With the help of digital photos, we can save time.
  3. With these photos available, they are being shared in the world through the internet.
  4. Besides, many kind of stationery cameras are also helping in the cyber forensics as they are taking the photos and are coming to know before and after the crime.
- Education
  1. Teaching forensic investigators to look at the newest technology used in cyber forensics (Buchholz F., 2004).
  2. Proper training is being given to the investigators to deal with techniques and they become enough educated to investigate the crime (Case A., 2008).

FUTURE OF CYBER FORENSICS

The future of cyber forensics is very interesting as it will be a part of every sector including governments, institutions, companies where we will have some of the automated systems identifying the crime and also each of the investigator will help

Figure 5. Elements of Data Forensic Computing

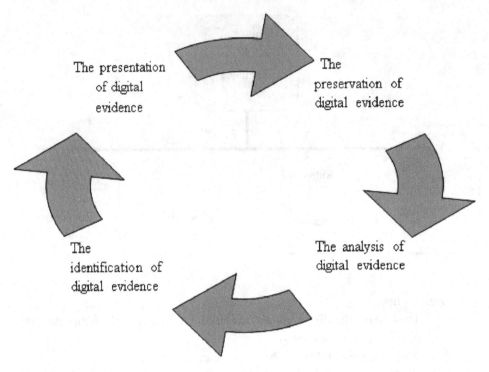

us to find the guilty which will be found by the evidence being founded or collected at the time the crime happen (Casey E., 2011) & (Abhineet Anand, 2017).

The future of cyber forensics will help us to reduce the crimes by what it is now.

Four Key Elements in processing Data Forensic Computing identifying, preserving, analyzing and presenting digital evidence.

Computerized measurable examinations have confronted numerous troubles to defeat the issues of dissecting proof is huge and enormous datasets. Different arrangements and systems have been proposed for managing enormous information examination, for example, triage, man-made brainpower, information mining, information bunching, and information decrease procedures. In this manner, this area displays a writing audit of the current research in enormous information criminology and talks about a portion of the open issues in the space (Gholap P., 2013) & (Kataria M., 2014).

Big Data Acquisition and Analytics

The standard engine was utilized to keep up enormous information gathering, decide issues and find the purpose behind breakdowns; while the limited state machine

Table 1. Some of Input Metadata Parameters for Forensics Tools

S. No.	Input Source	Input Parameter	Data Type
1	Log File Entries (Security Logs)	Event ID	Integer
2		User Name	String
3		Data Generated	Date
4		Time Generated	Time
5		Machine(Computer Name	String
1	File System Metadata Structure(NTFS)	Modification Time	Date & Time
2		Access Time	Date & Time
3		Creation Time	Date & Time
4		File Size	Integer
1	Application Logs	Name	String
1	Network Packet	Packet Length	Integer
2		Class	String

was used to depict the condition of enormous information procurement. All together for obtaining to be fruitful, a few stages are required. At first, the standard engine should be made, including rules set up and refinement. In endeavoring to manage huge information analysis, (Noel G. E., 2014) recognized the significant difficulties engaged with finding significant data for computerized legal examinations, because of an expanding volume of information. They proposed the utilization of Latent Dirichlet Allocation (LDA) to limit professionals' overhead by two stages. In the first place, LDA removes concealed subjects from records, what's more, furnishes rundown subtleties of substance with at least human intercession. Furthermore, it offers the likelihood of separating pertinent data and archives utilizing a watchword look. The assessment of the LDA was conveyed out by utilizing the Real Data Corpus (RDC); the execution of the LDA was likewise tried in examination with current customary articulation look procedures in three zones: recovering data from imperative reports, (Kataria M., 2014) organizing and subdividing the recovered data, and examining covering themes. Their outcomes demonstrate that the LDA procedure can be utilized to help channel clamor, separate pertinent records, and produce results with a higher pertinence.

Metadata and Digital Forensics

Metadata describes the attributes of any files or applications in most digital resources It provides accuracy, logical consistency, and coherence of files or applications that they describe. It provides accuracy, logical consistency, and coherence of files or applications that they describe. Semantic search by metadata is one of the important functions to reduce the noise during information searching. Several metadata types exist and provide some attributes which are important in processes as shown in table 1 (Khan M. N. A., 2008) & (Li H., 2014). Some of the Input Metadata Parameters for Forensics Tools are discussed in Table1.

(Neil Rowe, 2012) built up an apparatus (for example Dirim) to naturally decide abnormal or suspicious documents in a huge corpus by examining the catalog metadata of records (e.g., the filename, expansions, ways, and size) through a correlation of predefined semantic gatherings and examination between document groups. Their investigation was led on a corpus comprising of 1,467 drive pictures with 8,673,012 documents. The Dirim approach found 6,983 suspicious documents dependent on their augmentations and 3,962 suspicious records as per their paths. However, the principal challenge with this methodology is its capacity to discover shrouded information. Additionally, it isn't successful at identifying the utilization of hostile to criminology (Liu Y., 2010) & (Mezghani E., 2015).

The yield from the past layer is numerous ancient rarities identified with the occurrence structure heterogeneous assets. Amid this layer, counterfeit shrewd strategies will be utilized in request to discover the relationship between these ancient rarities and remake the occasion dependent on that. Likewise, so as to decide the evidential ancient rarities, all the yield relics from the last layer ought to be examined that were made, gotten to or adjusted nearer to the season of a detailed episode that is being examined; nonetheless, to produce a course of events over numerous assets, it presents different challenges (for example timestamp translation) (Najafabadi M. M., 2015) & (Noel G. E., 2014).

As an outcome, it is important to create a brought together course of events between heterogeneous assets; in this manner, a few instruments will be utilized to adapt to these issues. The appropriate responses will be given to the inquiries that will be raised amid the crime scene investigation examination. Fundamental research embraced by Fahdi (ALfahdi M, 2016) has appeared robotized ancient rarity recognizable proof is an incredibly encouraging methodology amid the legal sciences investigation stage (Palmer G., 2001).

To accomplish and approve the methodology requires future research. This exertion will be focused upon the advancement of tests to assess the plausibility of using metadata also, semantic online ontologies to comprehend the issues of enormous information and heterogeneous information sources separately. The utilization of the cosmology based legal sciences gives a semantic-rich condition to encourage proof examination. Further trials will likewise be directed to Further assess the utilization of AI in the capacity to recognize and correspond to pertinent proof. Various situation based assessments including various partners will happen to assess the viability of the proposed methodology (A Hashmi, 2018).

REFERENCES

Abhineet Anand, A. G. (2017). Ethical Hacking and Hacking Attacks. *International Journal of Engineering and Computer Science*.

AlFahdi, M. (2016). *Automated Digital Forensics & Computer Crime Profiling* (Ph.D. thesis). Plymouth University.

Allemang, D. H. J. (2011). *Semantic web for the working ontologist: effective modeling in RDFS and OWL*. Elsevier.

Alzaabi, M. J. A. (2013). An ontology-based forensic analysis tool. *Proceedings of the Conference on Digital Forensics, Security and Law*.

Ayers, D. (2009). A second generation computer forensic analysis system. *Digital Investigation*, *6*, S34–S42. doi:10.1016/j.diin.2009.06.013

Beebe, N. L., & Liu, L. (2014). Clusteringdigital forensic string search output. *Digital Investigation*, *11*(4), 314–322. doi:10.1016/j.diin.2014.10.002

Benredjem, D. (2007). *Contributions to cyber-forensics: processes and e-mail analysis* (Doctoral dissertation). Concordia University.

Buchholz, F. S. E., & Spafford, E. (2004). On the role of file system metadata in digital-forensics. *Digital Investigation*, *1*(4), 298–309. doi:10.1016/j.diin.2004.10.002

Case, A. C. A., Cristina, A., Marziale, L., Richard, G. G., & Roussev, V. (2008). FACE: Automated digital evidence discovery and correlation. *Digital Investigation*, *5*, S65–S75. doi:10.1016/j.diin.2008.05.008

Casey, E. (2011). *Digital evidence and computer crime: Forensic science, computers, and the internet*. Academic press.

Gholap, P. M. (2013). Information Retrieval of K-Means Clustering For Forensic Analysis. *International Journal of Science and Research*.

Hashmi, A. R. (2018). Security and Compliance Management in Cloud Computing. *International Journal of Advanced Studies in Computers, Science and Engineering*.

Kataria,, M. (2014). BIG DATA: A Review. *International Journal of Computer Science and Mobile Computing*, *3*(7), 106–110.

Khan, M. N. A. (2008). *Digital Forensics using Machine Learning Methods* (Ph.D. thesis). University of Sussex.

Li, H. (2014). Challenges and Trends of Big Data Analytics. In *Ninth International Conference on P2P, Parallel, Grid, Cloud and Internet Computing (3PGCIC)* (pp. 566-567). IEEE.

Liu, Y. L. X. (2010). Analysis and design of heterogeneous bioinformatics database integration system based on middleware. In *International Conference on Information Management and Engineering (ICIME)*. IEEE. 10.1109/ICIME.2010.5477628

Mezghani, E. E. E. (2015). A Semantic Big Data Platform for Integrating Heterogeneous Wearable Data in Health- care. *Journal of Medical Systems*, 1–8. PMID:26490143

Najafabadi, M. M. (2015). Deep learning applications and challenges in big data analytics. *Journal of Big Data*, 1-21.

Neil Rowe, S. L. (2012). Finding Anomalous and Suspicious Files from Directory Metadata on a Large Corpus. *International Conference on Digital Forensics and Cyber Crime*. 10.1007/978-3-642-35515-8_10

Noel, G. E., & Peterson, G. L. (2014). Applicability of Latent Dirichlet Allocation to multi-disk search. *Digital Investigation*, *11*(1), 43–56. doi:10.1016/j.diin.2014.02.001

Palmer, G. (2001). A road map for digital forensic research. *First Digital Forensic Research Workshop*, Utica, NY.

Patrascu, A. (2013). Beyond digital forensics. A cloud computing perspective over incident response and reporting. In *8th International Symposium on Applied Computational Intelligence and Informatics (SACI)*. IEEE. 10.1109/SACI.2013.6609018

Chapter 7
Cyber Forensic Lab Setup and Its Requirement

Mohammad Z. Khan
Integral University, India

Mohd. Shoaib
Aligarh Muslim University, India

Faiyaz Ahmad
Integral University, India

ABSTRACT

The year 1978 was the year when the first computer-related crime took place; it was alteration or deletion of data. The day-by-day level and intensity of cybercrime has strengthened and is getting stronger in nature in the current era. So, to achieve accuracy during the investigation, an intensive investigation environment or lab is needed. This will help the investigation team in various ways. More advanced techniques and tools are used in a current age lab setup, and solutions to forensically examine a variety of digital devices apart from computers are made.

INTRODUCTION

Lab setup will be the strong motivating behind the elaboration of the investigation of evidence related to digital forensics. To set up a cybercrime investigation related lab, studying the case study of new generation cybercrime plays a key role (Guo, H., Jin, B., & Huang, D. 2010). Many levels of analysis are required in the advanced level of cyber-attack. With your own Cyber Lab setup, precisely investigating an entire range of digital forensic cases is possible under one roof. Starting from Computer

DOI: 10.4018/978-1-7998-1558-7.ch007

Best rated software and set of related hardware are required for setting up a cyber-forensic lab; additionally, we need related services, data transmission facilities and accessories, and devices that are forensically equipped for specialized digital forensics. These essential set of components will enhance your analytical skills towards the forensic investigation of digital data evidence available at different places like hard disks drives, different categories of flash drives, Random Access Memory, circuits, or even cloud-based storage. While most of the equipment is designed to help in a different type of analysis such as evidence-based analysis, etc. and also provide support to preserve and prevent evidence tampering (Baryamureeba, V 2004).

forensics, Mobile forensics, Network forensics, to even the latest; Cloud forensics; all cases can be undertaken and investigated with the help of a fully equipped Cyber Lab.

CYBER FORENSIC LAB SETUP

This figure 1 shows the general lab setup view in a modelled approach where commuters are well equipped with different basic components as discussed above (Hardware, Software, other forensics-related components)

Equipment Required

These are the most essential list for the setup of; these are very basic in nature:

- Hardware Devices
- Software Applications
- Specialized Accessories

Figure 1. Example of Cyber Forensics equipment

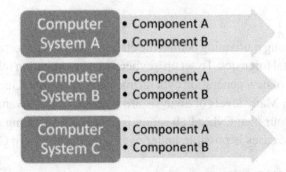

- ○ Evidence Collections
- Specialized Devices
  - ○ Evidence Preservation
- Specialized kit
  - ○ Digital Data Investigation Kits
- Other hardware Assemblage Tools
- Transmission Cables
- Data Connectors

Hardware Devices

Hardware devices can be categorized as follows:

Input- The number of basic input devices likes Keyboard, Mouse, Scanner, Light pen.

Output- The number of basic Output devices likes CRT & Flat Panel Monitors, Headphones, Printer, Projectors, Sound Card, Graphic Card, LCD Projection Panels, and Surround Sound Speakers

Processing Devices- Number of Processors is required for lab setup to achieve high-end results like Multiple Core Processor, Multiple Processor Motherboard, and Chips

Storage- High storage capacity is essential for lab setup; it can be further classified into two categories

Internal and external storage RAM – DDR1 & DDR4, 5 TB & 6 TB - Hard disk drives

Others - Internal/External/PC card modem, Network Card, Laptop Computers, Palmtops, Breadboards

Transmission Cables / Data Connectors

Cables / Connectors- different connectors are required like Ethernet Cables, Modular Adapters, Ribbon Cables, Din splits Cables, VGA Split Cable, USB Cables, Audio Cables, Cable Extenders, HDMI 1, 2, 3 Cables, DVI Cables, S Video Cables, DVI to DVI Cable, Serial Cables, Custom Serial Cable, SATA Cables, Optical Fibre Cable, Serial Attached SCSI

Additional Evidence Storage Devices

TB size external hard drives, 16 GB or higher capacity pen drives, all disk formats supporting live or bootable CDROMS, Mobile device/camera/camcorder memory cards

Software Services

Software programs required for digital forensic evidence investigation that will be installed on lab workstations will include:

- Forensic Disk Imaging Tool
- Mobile Field Kit
- Registry Rebuilding Application
- Different Operating Systems
- Tools for Password Recovery and Data Decryption
- Tools Media Content Indexing Tool
- Toolset for Digital Media Procurement and Backup
- Toolset for Packet Capturing and Analysis
- Antivirus Program
- Data Recovery And Restoration Tool
- Programming languages
- Viewers for Open Source File

OTHER ASSORTED REQUISITES

Specialized Forensic Workstation

These are set of high capacity hardware devices and configured and Pre-installed with forensic related software-based solutions, Evidence protection and preservation of evidence are integrated into single devices

Evidence Collection Accessories

Specialized Mobile Data related Investigation Kit such as Momentum L2 Digital Forensics Laptop Workstation.

Evidence Preservation Devices

RF Shield Bags are available in three sizes Large, Medium, Small.

Rest of Hardware Assemblage Tools

Wiring connector, Wall mounts, Cable ties, Wall plugs, Stainless steel Hose clamps, Fibreglass sleeves, and tubes for wires, Round cable clips, Crystal plug connectors, Power cords, Hand-tools, Anti-static pads.

LABORATORY PRACTICE

It is essential for every forensic laboratory working every discipline, around the world should make every effort to maintain and achieve good practice and should also meet their Client's expectations by providing quality of service and related quality products.

To achieve this, several organizations have produced good guidance documentation (guidance, standards, or procedures) for advising a forensic laboratory on how to achieve this. A number of these are general in their nature and some are sector-specific. Generally, these apply to all types of forensic laboratories, and these include (Peisert, S 2008).

- Quality Management Systems series are covered in ISO9000
- Competency of testing and calibration for laboratories general requirements are covered under ISO17025.

Other quality standards and related auditing are defined for digital forensics laboratories are as follows:

- FRS stands for Forensics Regulator; it is a UK based regulatory authority that works for Codes and conducts related to forensic science providers and practitioners in the Judiciary System, V-1, launched on 2011 December. Ziese, K.J 1996)
- SWGDE know as Scientific Working Group on Digital Evidence it provides Quality Assurance and also provides Standard Operating Procedures with Manual, V-3, 2o12;
- ENFST named as European Network of Forensic Science Institutes provides the Guidelines for the Best Practice during the Forensic Examination of Digital Technology, V-6, 2o09;
- National Voluntary Laboratory Accreditation Program, Procedures, and General Requirements are provided in NIST Handbook 150, published in 2o06;

ACCREDITATION OF THE DIGITAL FORENSICS DISCIPLINE

After discussing the basic lab setup requirements, technical accreditation is also mandatory for the cyber forensics lab. Underestimating the importance of measuring and examining the accurate, technically competent and valid results cannot be tolerated. Accreditation of Laboratory accreditation can help to provide a benchmark that can certify the result and provide subsequent confidence to the examination of digital evidence. Education and training programs for digital forensics has expanded with a high velocity in both the private and public sectors. As a result, several public & few private laboratories are now examining digital media on a routine basis. An all-encompassing definition of the discipline is: "the application of specialized scientific techniques to the preservation, recovery, and examination of digital or electronic data which may be used in legal matters." This includes the examination of computers and their hard drives, cellular telephones, PDAs, digital cameras, smart media cards, CDs, DVDs, USB thumb drives, digital audio and videotapes, and so forth. The commonality is that they all contain digital or electronic data ("0s" and "1s" or representations thereof) stored in particular sequences (Hailey, S 2003).

DISCIPLINE IN PERSPECTIVE

Digital data recouped during forensic assessments frequently winds up probative and may demonstrate that a crime, (for example, wholesale fraud or ownership of child pornography) has been perpetrated. Since any digital data recouped is evidence, it must be treated all things considered. Anyway dissimilar to a bleeding shirt or a dormant lift found at a crime scene, there is no genuine physical evidence to outwardly evaluate for pertinence. This is because the evidence is digital and can't be seen by the simple eye. Be that as it may, the "portrayal" of what the "0s" and "1s" convert into is noticeable and might be applicable (for instance, an SSN or an image). When managing digital evidence, applicable logical standards identifying with the accumulation, preparing, and assessment of evidence must be followed (Abdullah, M.T 2008).

Digital evidence found on digital media can be dynamic, erased, encrypted, scrambled, or as is once in a while the case, in part overwritten. Analysts have numerous forensic instruments and techniques accessible to look at digital media for its essence or nonattendance. Since any or the majority of the digital evidence might be essential for the suit, the legal framework must be guaranteed accurate, dependable, certain, and repeatable outcomes. This goes a long way past simply finding and extricating the data, looking at and translating its pertinence, and producing a report (Ziese, K.J 1996).

An analyst might be called to testify in court and their testimony can wind up basic for the effective indictment of the case. That testimony can be exceptionally specialized and complex and it is impossible that legal hearers will have the information to survey its precision, validity, and trustworthiness. Notwithstanding, from forensic science, numerous inquiries, issues, and concerns can emerge:

- Was the digital evidence corrupted or bargained in regards to how it was gathered and where it was put away?
- Is the chain-of-custody complete and accurate?
- Is a hand-on-training alone adequate to qualify the analyst as a specialist?
- Are archived, checked/approved methods accessible for the survey?
- Is the case record documentation complete and point by point to such an extent that another inspector can reproduce the consequences of the examination(s)?
- Were the assessment results companion looked into?
- Is the analyst skilled to play out the examination(s)?
- Was the analyst proficiency tried?
- How are the forensic PCs and forensic software kept up and refreshed?
- Are the software tools utilized authentic, licensed, approved variants?
- Were the software tools execution tried before their utilization?
- Did the software or hardware equipment modify or change the first digital evidence?
- Were logical and scientific standards pursued during the assessment(s)?

Examiners must give satisfactory, accurate, and complete responses to address these inquiries and concerns.

Contingent on the jurisdiction, their testimony may likewise need to meet the necessities of (Frye, 1923) or (Daubert, 1993) regarding the tolerability of expert testimony into legal procedures. This at that point brings up the issue, What 'guidelines' or 'best practices' are set up in the digital forensics community that can address these inquiries and concerns? At the point when other forensic orders confronted comparable to concerns, they were effectively moderated or eased by the reception of a Quality Management System which included practices, for example,

- Documented preparing programs
- Competency testing examiners before enabling them to perform independent assessments
- Participation in yearly proficiency testing projects to assess singular analyst fitness and the quality execution of the lab
- Documented arrangements, policies, and techniques for the distinguishing proof, accumulation, conservation, and security of evidence from misfortune, tainting, or malicious change
- Documented, execution tried specialized strategies
- The utilization of suitable benchmarks and controls during assessments
- Using discipline suggested best practices and methodology
- Attaining research facility accreditation

ACCREDITATION PROCEDURE FOR LAB

The importance of correct, technically competent, and valid examination results can't be unpretentious. If the associate degree examination result's incorrect, an individual is also sentenced to jail for a protracted time. Laboratory certification will give a regular which might guarantee confidence within the results obtained from the examination of digital proof. Though many states already need laboratories playacting forensic examinations at intervals their state becomes licensed, the bulk doesn't need certification. (Guo, H., Jin, B., & Huang, D. 2010) but, that will shortly modification. The 2009 National Academy of Sciences report titled "Strengthening rhetorical Science within the United States: A Path Forward" enclosed the subsequent recommendation:

Recommendation: Laboratory accreditation and individual certification of forensic science professionals ought to be necessary, and every one forensic science professionals ought to have access to a certification method. In crucial acceptable standards for certification and certification, the National Institute of Forensic Science (NIFS) ought to take under consideration established and recognized international standards, like those published by the international organization for Standardization (ISO) (Wagner, E.J 2006). No person (public or private) ought to be allowed to apply in an exceedingly forensic science discipline or testify as a forensic science skilled while not certification. Certification needs ought to embrace, at a minimum, written examinations, supervised apply, proficiency testing, continued education, recertification procedures, adherence to a code of ethics, and effective disciplinary procedures. All laboratories and facilities (public or private) ought to be accredited, and every one forensic science professionals ought to be certified, once eligible, inside a fundamental quantity established by NIFS (Ziese, K.J, 1996).

Beginning in 1982, the American Society of Crime Laboratory Directors/ Laboratory Accreditation Board (ASCLD/LAB, www.ascld-lab.org) began providing voluntary accreditation to public crime laboratories. (Daubert v. 1993) in 2003, they accessorial the Digital evidence discipline (which is comprised of 4 sub-disciplines: Audio Analysis, laptop Forensics, Image Analysis, and Video Analysis) to their legacy accreditation program. Afterward, the discipline name was modified to Digital proof in 2005. Today, accreditation may be obtained by public and personal crime laboratories in one or a lot of the sub-disciplines below ASCLD/LAB's International Program. The program uses the ISO/IEC 17025:2005 International normal and therefore the ASCLD/LAB – International Supplemental needs (2011 Edition) for its accreditation needs (Guo, H., Jin, B., & Huang, D. 2010).

ISO/IEC 17025:2005 is a world quality normal utilized by accreditation bodies worldwide for the accreditation of each Testing and activity laboratories. Rhetorical laboratories comprise the testing part of the quality. The 2 primary sections within the standard area unit "Section 4: Management needs," and "Section 5: Technical needs." Management needs concern operational parameters and therefore the implementation and effectiveness of the standard Management System. The unit area requirements are the same as those per the ISO 9001:2000 standard. There are 131 doubtless applicable clauses below Section four. Technical needs concern workers' competency, testing methodology, equipment, quality assurance measures, sampling, and therefore the news or take a look at results. Most of those needs derive from the ISO Guide twenty-five. There are one hundred seventy doubtless applicable clauses below Section five (Casey, E, 2004).

Many of the ASCLD/LAB – International Supplemental demand clauses was derived from the "ESSENTIAL" standards that were a part of the ASCLD/LAB heritage Program (currently being phased-out). There square measure 121 doubtless applicable clauses that integrate with Section four and Section five ISO/IEC 17025:2005 clauses. Currently, ASCLD/LAB has accredited fifty-eight laboratories within the Digital evidence discipline, nineteen below their international program and another thirty-nine below their heritage Program.4 By attaining ASCLD/LAB enfranchisement, a laboratory demonstrates that its management, operations, personnel, procedures, equipment, physical plant, security, and health and safety procedures all meet "established and recognized international standards." Accreditation will offer a way to enhance quality, assess performance, offer an independent review, meet established standards, and serve to confirm the promotion, encouragement, and maintenance of the best standards of forensic apply. Testimony from associate degree examiner operating in an accredited laboratory will assist in meeting the challenges of Frye or Daubert and assure the court that examination results square measure correct, technically competent, and valid primarily based upon needed quality assurance practices. An associate degree external independent review will demonstrate management's commitment to making sure that it's Quality Management System and its physical plant meet or exceed documented standards of practice.

CHALLENGES IN DIGITAL FORENSICS

To attain ASCLD/LAB – International accreditation, a laboratory should reach 100 percent compliance with each applicable clause within the accreditation needs. The requirements don't offer guidance on that of the 422 clauses square measure applicable or what objective proof is important to demonstrate agreement. Usually unmarked is that the indisputable fact that around each sentence or lists of things within the accreditation needs are taxable clauses to that the laboratory should demonstrate agreement or indicate that the clause is "not applicable." Some non-applicable clauses are obvious, like those concerning different forensic disciplines. (Tilstone,

W.J 2006) several others aren't therefore obvious. Frequently, a word or phrase in a very clause results in a misunderstanding, an interpretation, or associate degree oversight. As an example, ISO/IEC 17025:2005 Clause five.5.2 states the following:

Equipment and its software system used for testing, activity, and sampling shall be capable of achieving the accuracy needed and shall fit specifications relevant to the tests and/or calibrations involved. Activity programs shall be established for key quantities or values of the instruments wherever these properties have a big impact on the results. Before being placed into service, instrumentality (including that used for sampling) shall be marked or checked to determine that it meets the laboratory's specification needs and complies with the relevant standard specifications. It shall be checked and/or calibrated before use.

The clause is usually taken as follows: "Equipment used for testing should be capable of achieving accuracy. No calibrations are conducted within the laptop Forensics sub-discipline, thus no activity programs ought to be established. Instrumentality ought not to be marked before being placed into service. Instrumentality ought not to be marked before use."

Software that operates instrumentality and software system used throughout examinations (acquisition software system, knowledge analysis software system, etc.) is roofed by the primary clause. {This is usually this can be} often unnoticed, leading to a non-conformance. (Abdullah, M.T 2008) The second clause isn't applicable. Since clauses 3 and 4 create relevance activity, several can interpret that they are not applicable. Though, the instrumentality and its software system (i.e. rhetorical computers, write blockers, acquisition software system, etc.) aren't mark, each those clauses square measure applicable. Instrumentality and its software system may be checked before being placed into service and before getting used for examinations mistreatment acceptable standards and controls. Failure to try to, therefore, would be a misunderstanding of the wants and result in further non-conformances.

Once all the applicable clauses are known, any/all existing laboratory practices and documentation and therefore the physical plant itself should be reviewed and evaluated for connectedness, compliance, and agreement. Laboratories can oft acquire Quality Management System documentation from different commissioned laboratories and habitually implement that documentation with the least changes. This application may be harmful. The documentation ought to be viewed as a model and not as a finished product. For instance, a top-quality Manual developed by associate degree commissioned laboratory can address specific circumstances and practices distinctive thereto laboratory (Baryamureeba, V 2004). The style during which they address a clause might or might not address the problems associated with that clause in another laboratory. A higher approach is for the laboratory seeking enfranchisement to raise the question, "What benefit science and/or apply demand we tend to do to evolve to the clauses?"

Examiners should be concerned with the enfranchisement method. A lot of usually than not, initially they're going to be reluctant and proof against participate. From their viewpoint, enfranchisement pertains to the laboratory; to not them since it will not help in getting individual certification(s). Once they understand that enfranchisement needs objective proof within the style of formal documentation, they complain that they're going to pay longer on work and fewer time performing arts examinations. Examiners believe they follow smart analytical practices and knowledge to conduct digital rhetorical examinations. However, they're going to understand that associate degree enfranchisement demand, like necessary proficiency testing, queries their competence. Examiners even have to be convinced that the standard Management System can cut back the probability of issues occurring which mechanisms square measure in situ to reduce the impact of issues if/when they are doing arise(Guo, H., Jin, B., & Huang, D. 2010).

When confronted with these and lots of different challenges, laboratories can usually look for the services of associate degree ISO/IEC 17025:2005 accreditation authority to supply steering and sensible solutions to help them in achieving accreditation in Digital Forensics.

CONCLUSION

The Forensics laboratory plays a vital role in our justice system. Well conferred rhetorical proof may be persuasive to a jury. Many, several cases activate the forensic proof itself or the dearth thence. The forensic laboratory thus plays a crucial role in the way of seeking justice.

Quality should be a priority in each rhetorical laboratory and to each forensic skilled. Digital forensics is no different. Quality is achieved through strict adherence to established quality standards as a part of associate degree overall quality assurance program. Accreditation of a digital forensics laboratory is a way to confirm agreement to those standards. The recognized world leader in the enfranchisement of rhetorical labs is ASCLD/LAB. Standards for digital forensics are written by the ASTM.

Accreditation and certification aren't substitutable. The first distinction is that accreditation pertains to the physical work wherever certification applies to the personnel conducting the examinations. Not solely ought to examiners be tested to demonstrate that they're "functioning properly," therefore to ought to their tools. Solely tools that are tested and evidenced reliable ought to be used once process a case. This testing procedure is thought of as validation.

Digital rhetorical practitioners use each software system and hardware tools in their work. Nobody single tool will everything or will it well. Almost all labs have different sorts of tools at their disposal, it offers them the broader capability as needed they have given the big selection of technology they see returning within the door for analysis.

REFERENCES

Abdullah, M. T., Mahmod, R., Ghani, A. A. A., Abdullah, M. Z., & Sultan, A. B. M. (2008). Advances in computer forensics. *International Journal of Computer Science and Network Security*, 8(2), 215–219.

Baryamureeba, V., & Tushabe, F. (2004). The Enhanced Digital Investigation Process Model. *Digital Forensics Research Workshop*.

Casey, E. (2004). *Digital Evidence and Computer Crime* (2nd ed.). Amsterdam: Elsevier Academic Press.

Daubert v. Merrell Dow Pharmaceuticals, Inc., 509 U.S. 579 1993

Frye v. United States, 293 F. 1013 D.C. Cir. 1923.

Guo, H., Jin, B., & Huang, D. (2010, November 11). *Research and Review on Computer Forensics*. Retrieved from https://link.springer.com/chapter/10.1007/978-3-642-23602-0_21

Hailey, S. (2003). *What is Computer Forensics*. Retrieved from http://www.cybersecurityinstitute.biz/forensics.htm

Hui, L. C. K., Chow, K. P., & Yiu, S. M. (2007.). Tools and Technology for Computer Forensics: Research and Development in Hong Kong. Information Security Practice and Experience Lecture Notes in Computer Science, 11–19. doi:10.1007/978-3-540-72163-5_2

Peisert, S., Bishop, M., & Marzullo, K. (2008). Computer forensics in forensic. *Operating Systems Review*, 42(3), 112. doi:10.1145/1368506.1368521

Tilstone, W. J. (2006). *Forensic science: An encyclopaedia of history, methods, and techniques*. Academic Press.

Wagner, E. J. (2006). *The Science of Sherlock Holmes*. Chichester, UK: Wiley.

Ziese, K. J. (1996). Computer based forensics-a case study-U.S. support to the U.N. *Proceedings of CMAD IV: Computer Misuse and Anomaly Detection*.

KEY TERMS AND DEFINITIONS

Certification Related to Cyber Forensics: These are provided by IACIS, The International Association of Computer Investigative Specialists, and ISFCE, The International Society of Forensic Computer Examiners.

Cyber Forensics: Computer forensics (also known as computer forensic science) is a branch of digital forensic science pertaining to evidence found in computers and digital storage media.

Forensics Lab: The DFS's Forensic Science Laboratory Division (FSL) collects, examines, analyzes, and reports on physical evidence submitted in criminal cases.

Hardware and Software for Lab: The Cyber Center lab will establish a baseline (golden) hardware and software configuration that is ready to execute lab exercises.

ISO Quality: The ISO 9000 family addresses various aspects of quality management and contains some of ISO's best known standards.

Laboratory Accreditation Process: Laboratory accreditation can provide a standard which can ensure confidence in the results obtained from the examination of digital evidence.

Chapter 8
Digital Crime Evidence

Parkavi R.
Thiagarajar College of Engineering, India

Divya K.
Thiagarajar College of Engineering, India

Sherry Ruth V.
Thiagarajar College of Engineering, India

ABSTRACT

With the advent of computers, there came computer-related crimes; hence, there comes the need for cybercrime judicial proceedings. And for any trial, evidence plays an instrumental role in bringing the victim to justice. So, there is a need for digital evidence. Digital crime evidence forms a core for the field of computer forensics. Breaking down the term digital crime evidence to be understood in simple words, it is the collection of data and information that plays a crucial role in digital crime investigation and that is usually stored and transmitted in electronic formats. Digital evidence is defined as any data stored or transmitted using a computer that supports or refute a theory of how an offense occurred or that address critical elements of the offense such as intent or alibi. This data is commonly a combination of text, audio, images, and videos. This evidence is generally invisible, fragile, time-sensitive, and integrity will be lost if they are mishandled.

INTRODUCTION

Crimes in the bygone era were committed to gaining property or for personal vendetta. These crimes were done in the actual presence of both the attacker and the victim. However vicious these events may be, they were advantageous in two aspects. One,

DOI: 10.4018/978-1-7998-1558-7.ch008

the perpetrators could be caught easily and justice can be brought to the victim. Secondly, it checked the number of crimes as the hooligans were aware that their rate of survival once found guilty was low. But with the advent of digitization, there was a huge sprout of electronic devices computers, storage devices...etc. They acted as a comfortable zone for a new range of crimes popularly labeled as cybercrime or digital crime. They provided the much-needed anonymity for the attackers and offered more scope than the previous model. Though computers have been aiding criminals in their ventures, they also have acted as a valuable resource for investigating officials to establish digital evidence (Casey. 2011). Thus, the evolution of the digital world is a two-sided coin. Digital evidence has offered more promising results than ordinary results, in that this evidence can be transported afar without much ado. Also, this evidence can be duplicated and stored in multiple backs up areas to safeguard the evidence from being destroyed or being tampered with.Digital evidence plays a vital role in the proceedings of the judicial body. There are variedroles that digital evidences play in our daily life.Digital evidence, it's everywhere. Consider the ubiquitous nature of electronics: in our society, interaction with electronic devices is inevitable. Most of us interact with them hundreds, if not thousands, of times a day. And most of those devices are "smart" enough to retain information about who you are, and where you were when you interacted (Vacca, 2005).

SOURCES OF DIGITAL EVIDENCE

Starting from the very basics, a computer system is the primary source of digital evidence. A computer system can be a PC or a laptop. Breaking down the broad spectrum of computer systems, the following list can be arrived at:

- Monitor or video display device
- Keyboard
- Mouse
- Peripheral or externally connected drives, devices, and components.
- The case contains circuit boards, microprocessors, hard drives, memory, and interface connections.

Storage devices like hard drives and other removable media like floppy disks, zip disks, CDs, thumb drives (commonly called flash drives) and memory cards. Joining the list with the advent of mobile phones is a whole range of handheld devices. (Ozel Bulbul Yavuzcan, 2013).

The sources of digital evidence are many. They can be sourced from many of the electronic devices like PC, mobile phones and from the network layers like the Physical layer, Data link layer...etc. Collection of digital evidence involves a whole lot of supporting equipment like camera, cardboard boxes, notepads, gloves, evidence inventory logs, evidence tape, paper evidence bags, evidence stickers, labels, or tags, crime scene tape, antistatic bags, permanent markers, and non-magnetic tools. Electronic devices act as primary sources of solid evidence like computer documents, text and emails. Other images, Internet history, and the transaction also act as vital evidence. For instance, mobile devices are proving as a single prominent destination for access to text messages and images. They are backed up on cloud storage, which facilitates easy retrieval of data by forensic investigators. (Singh Gupta, 2011)

Certified Digital Media Examiners are investigators who have the education, training, and experience to properly exploit this sensitive evidence. That said, there is no single certifying body, and certification programs can contain different courses of study. Generally speaking, these professionals have demonstrated core competencies in pre-examination procedures and legal issues, media assessment and analysis, data recovery, specific analysis of recovered data, documentation and reporting, and presentation of findings. While certification of examiners is not required in most agencies, it is becoming a widely valued asset and the numbers of certified examiners will increase. Vendor-neutral (not software-based, but theory- and process-based) certification is offered through the Digital Forensics Certification Board (DFCB), an independent certifying organization for digital evidence examiners, the National Computer Forensics Academy at the High-Tech Crime Institute and some colleges. (Seaskate, 1998)

Computer documents, emails, text and instant messages, transactions, images and Internet histories are examples of information that can be gathered from electronic devices and used very effectively as evidence. For example, mobile devices use online-based based backup systems, also known as the "cloud", that provide forensic investigators with access to text messages and pictures taken from a particular phone. These systems keep an average of 1,000–1,500 or more of the last text messages sent to and received from that phone.

Also, many mobile devices store information about the locations where the device traveled and when it was there. To gain this knowledge, investigators can access an average of the last 200 cell locations accessed by a mobile device. Satellite navigation systems and satellite radios in cars can provide similar information. Even photos posted to social media such as Facebook may contain location information. Photos taken with a Global Positioning System (GPS)-enabled device contain file data that shows when and exactly where a photo was taken. By gaining a subpoena for a particular mobile device account, investigators can collect a great deal of history related to a device and the person using it. Given the care that digital evidence is given before collection, it is given even more safe passage while examination in the laboratory. A qualified analyst is a person who should be left in charge of the lab examinations.

Files on a computer or other devices are not the only evidence that can be gathered. The analyst may have to work beyond the hardware to find evidence that resides on the Internet including chat rooms, instant messaging, websites and other networks of participants or information. By using the system of Internet addresses, email header information, timestamps on messaging and other encrypted data, the analyst can piece together strings of interactions that provide a picture of activity. Computers are used for committing a crime, and, thanks to the burgeoning science of digital evidence forensics, law enforcement now uses computers to fight crime. (Rosen, 1982)

Digital evidence is information stored or transmitted in binary form that may be relied on in court. It can be found on a computer hard drive, a mobile phone, a personal digital assistant (PDA), a CD, and a flashcard in a digital camera, among other places. Digital evidence is commonly associated with electronic crime, or e-crime, such as child pornography or credit card fraud. However, digital evidence is now used to prosecute all types of crimes, not just e-crime. For example, suspects' e-mail or mobile phone files might contain critical evidence regarding their intent, their whereabouts at the time of a crime and their relationship with other suspects. In 2005, for example, a floppy disk led investigators to the BTK serial killer who had eluded police capture since 1974 and claimed the lives of at least 10 victims.

To fight e-crime and to collect relevant digital evidence for all crimes, law enforcement agencies are incorporating the collection and analysis of digital evidence, also known as computer forensics, into their infrastructure. Law enforcement agencies are challenged by the need to train officers to collect digital evidence and keep up with rapidly evolving technologies such as computer operating systems.Add to this the massive amounts of digital information office workers deal with every day: emails, the web, calendars, word processors, spreadsheets, and security systems. It's a vast amount of information. And, all of these systems collect "digital fingerprints" when they are used. This leads to large amounts of "indirect" information available to anyone who knows to look for it.

Digital evidence is overlooked very much like fingerprints were overlooked way back in time. Mostly, the professionals who are adept at studying digital evidence are scarce. And the worst thing that can ever happen is botching up the investigation by being clumsy around the actual crime scene. Digital evidence is ubiquitous. Digital evidence is fragile and utmost care has to be taken while dealing with it. Even an activity assumed to be so simple can put potential evidence is the risk of being destroyable.

Digital crime and physical crime have much in common since the former emerged from the latter. The late arrival of the police into the crime scene could cause a serious loss of potential evidence. Similarly getting the victim computer into the hands of the digital forensics' expert is vital, so that no evidence is compromised. (Richards, 1999) (NFSTC, 2009)

Whenever physical crimes occurred, the investigators make it a point to arrive at the scene well in advance and they make sure to leave everything untouched till a forensic expert is in the scene. Digital crimes also follow in the same path and every possible care is taken to preserve it. Only someone who knows technology and the law can adequately protect that valuable digital forensic evidence. Companies are usually deterrent to the idea of investing in forensic experts, as they consider it as an extra burden. What is to be known is that some legal proceedings must just end way sooner if the companies have a robust framework of forensic experts.

The checklist for System Discovery includesthe layout of the computer system, including the number and types of computers and the types of operating systems and application software packages used. The structure of any electronic mail system, including the software, used the number of users, the location of mail files, and password usage. (NFSTC,2009)

ELECTRONIC MEDIA COLLECTION CHECKLIST

Data Files

- office desktop computer/workstation
- notebook computer
- home computer
- computer of personal assistants/secretary/staff
- palmtop devices
- network file servers/mainframes/mini-computers

Backup Tapes

- system-wide backups (monthly/weekly/incremental)
- disaster recovery backups (stored off-site)
- personal or "ad hoc" backups (look for diskettes and other portable media)

Other Media Sources

- Tape Archives
- Replaced/Removed Drives
- Floppy Diskettes & Other Portable Media (e.g., CDs, Zip cartridges)

CHECKLIST FOR ELECTRONIC MEDIA EXAMINATION

- Assign a unique number to each piece of media. (The number series used for numbering electronic media should be distinct from that used for paper documents.)
- Write-protect all media.
- Virus checks all media. Record any viruses discovered and immediately notify the producing party.
- Print directory listings for each piece of media. Make sure the listing has the media number printed on it.
- Virus check the drive that you are restoring the data to and make sure the drive is free from any other data. (Restoration should be to a distinct drive, dedicated to a single case.)
- Restore each piece of media to a file with a name that corresponds to the number assigned to the media being restored (e.g., a diskette numbered 123 should be restored to a file named "Disk 123").
- Verify that all files on the directory listing appear in the copy restored.
- Run an undelete or salvage utility and restore any residual data to a separate sub-file for the media (e.g., Disk 123residual).
- Secure the source media.
- When printing a particular document, insert a distinct header or footer that gives the full directory listing for a document printed (e.g., Disk 123corrsmokinggun.txt). (Grimm, 2016)

The collection of digital devices can be done on the scene. First responders need to take special care with digital devices in addition to normal evidence collection procedures to prevent exposure to things like extreme temperatures, static electricity, and moisture.

While collecting evidence, computer forensic investigators make it a point to follow the below steps:

1. Send preservation of evidence letter. Because the information stored on computers changes every time a user saves a file, loads a new program or

does almost anything else on a computer, it is critical that you put all parties on notice that you will be seeking electronic evidence through discovery. The sooner the notice is sent the better. The notice should identify as specifically as possible the types of information to be preserved and explain the possible places that information may exist. If necessary, obtain a protective order requiring all parties to preserve electronic evidence and setting out specific protocols for doing so.

2. Include definitions, instructions and specific questions about electronic evidence in your written discovery. This is a continuing process, with three objectives to accomplish:

    i)   First, use a series of interrogatories to get an overview of the target computer system. These interrogatories will be followed up by the deposition of the Information Systems department.

    ii) Second, all requests for production should make clear that you are requesting electronic documents as well as paper. You can do this by defining documents to include items such as data compilations, e-mail, and electronically stored data. You should also draft requests that specifically ask for different types of computer-based evidence such as diskettes, e-mail, and backup tapes.

    iii) Finally, if necessary, include a request for inspection so you can examine the computer system first hand and retrieve any relevant data.

3. Take a deposition of the Information Systems department. This is the single best tool for finding out the types of electronic information that exists in your opponent's computer systems. The checklist for System Discovery can be cross-checked with the list with the investigators. The layout of the computer system, including the number and types of computers and the types of operating systems and application software packages used. When asking about any types of software make sure to ask for the software maker, program name and version of each program. The structure of any electronic mail system, including the software, used the number of users, the location of mail files, and password usage. Specific software used. This includes software applications for things such as calendars, project management, accounting, word processing, and database management.

4. Collect backup tapes. One of the most viable sources of evidence is the routine backup created to protect data in case of disaster. This information is normally stored on high capacity tapes but may exist on any type of media. When collecting backup tapes in discovery, make sure to also gather information on how the tapes were made.

5. Collect diskettes. Data selectively saved by users to diskettes or other portable media is another fertile, but often overlooked, source of evidence. Users save data to diskettes for any number of reasons. Users create "ad hoc backups" of key documents or files to use in case an important document or file is lost. Users may also copy e-mail files to a diskette to prevent them from being deleted in automatic purging routines. Finally, users will use diskettes to save data they do not want to keep on company computers.

6. Ask every witness about computer usage. In addition to the discovery directed at the computer system, every witness must be questioned about his or her computer use. The most overlooked source of electronic evidence is the home computer. Data usually end up on home computers in one of two ways. First, data can be transferred to and from the workplace on diskettes or other portable media. Second, an employee may be able to log on to the company network from home. In this situation, the home computer acts just like the employee's office workstation. Regardless of how data is transferred, the critical point is to find out whether the witness works from home and how data is transferred to and from that home computer. Palmtop devices and notebook computers are other good sources of evidence.

7. Make image copies. It is no secret that deleted files and other "residual" data may be recovered from hard drives and floppy disks. How do you make sure that you capture this data? Answering this question first requires a brief explanation of why "residual" data exists. When working with computers, the term "deleted" does not mean destroyed. Residual data includes "deleted" files, fragments of deleted files and other data that is still extant on the disk surface. To assure that this residual data is captured, you must make an image copy of the target drive. (Glasser Legal Works).

With the ever-growing use of computers as business and communication tools, data generated and stored electronically are becoming an increasingly important target for discovery. As with all other discovery, the goal in the discovery of electronic information is finding useful information and collecting that information in a manner that assures it can be admitted into evidence. There is no magic in accomplishing this goal. What is required is a proven, methodical approach. While technology will undoubtedly continue to change, the basic techniques for collecting electronic evidence should continue to prove effective. Improve investigations and reduce your potential for litigation and fines with the strict chain-of-custody protocol our experts follow at every stage of the data collection process. (NFSTC, 2009)

A defensible incident response starts with reliable evidence. When sensitive information is compromised, it's critical to ensure electronic evidence is handled with precision and cares to prevent it from being overwritten, destroyed, or otherwise corrupted. With Kroll, you can feel confident knowing our data collection and data preservation experts follow a strict chain-of-custody protocol at every stage of the process to improve the outcomes of on-site investigation and reduce your potential for litigation and fines.Preserving critical electronic evidence during the on-site investigation and threat containment/eradication paves the way for successful incident analysis. At Kroll, the trained and certified forensic experts adhere to strict data preservation standards to ensure all potentially relevant data is captured and remains intact during an on-site investigation. They can quickly and efficiently capture electronic data from email servers, network shares, desktop or laptop computers, handheld, and portable devices and backup media. (Guo Jin Huang, 2011)

Whether gathering digital evidence from a single source or multiple sources organization-wide, they apply forensically sound methods to preserve key digital evidence so you can establish a clear picture of the incident and launch an effective response. And because they've worked on hundreds of cases involving multiple data collection sites around the globe, the clients can trust them to perform an optimal on-site investigation, giving the clients the flexibility to pursue any available legal remedies. Computer forensics experts ensure that no digital evidence is overlooked and assist at any stage of an investigation or litigation, regardless of the number or location of data sources. Claims of fraud, financial tampering, computer crime, employee misconduct, and other wrongdoing require corporations, law firms, and government agencies to follow digital trails to piece together facts that lead to the truth.

Various types of digital devices can be used as a source of digital evidence. The most familiar devices are computers and cell phones. Any piece of technology that processes information can be a valuable source of digital evidence. For example, flash drives, PDAs, wearable devices, digital recorders, smart home appliances printers, and network devices are all valuable sources of digital evidence. Digital evidence can be classified into two categories:

- Computer-generated evidence: which is an output of computer instructions without manual intervention? This will include the output of programs, log files, receipts, and reports.
- Computer-stored evidence: This is based on human-generated content. This will include Emails, word documents, spreadsheets, and text messages. Regardless of the source and category of digital evidence, on-site forensic investigators must be able to recognize and properly seize potential digital evidence from the various potential sources. (Kent Chevalier Grance Dang, 2006)

Wearable devices, also known as "Wearables" are the next generation of portable technology that has become an integral part of everyday life for so many people. The International Data Corporation has reported that the total volume of smart "Wearables" will reach 25.7 million units in 2015. Wearables are "devices worn, applied, or ingested that are designed to measure or capture health-related data in digital format without intervention by the subject and their associated apps". (Schoenwaelder President, 2017) Examples include Biometric watches, ingestible sensors, and smart contact lenses. The data stored on these devices can be an important source of intelligence. One of the most popular wearables on the market is the Fitbit fitness trackers "Fitbit". A Fitbit is designed to measure the wearer's activity levels by collecting data using sensors that monitor the user's location, vital signs, sleep patterns, and physical activity. A Fitbit is capable of creating detailed descriptions of the user's everyday activities and habits. The data gathered by the Fitbit is synced to the user's account on the Cloud to monitor their exercise progress, sleep quality, and medical statistics. This data can also be synced to a mobile application for easy access by the user to their activity history. There are several technologies behind the Fitbit tracker that enable it to achieve its purpose, these are GPS, WIFI, NFC, Bluetooth, Gyros and Accelerometers and heart rate monitors.

These sophisticated technologies enable the Fitbit to track steps, distance, calories burned, active minutes, stairs climbed, sleep habits, stationary time, continuous heart rate, breathing patterns, location, pace, elevation, and routes, among other calculable figures. The admissibility of wearable as digital evidence is a topic of debate. The value of digital evidence retrieved from Wearable devices has been recognized in several courts. Under the US Federal Rules of Evidence, admitting data collected from portable devices and computers as the evidence does not require much more than the admission of standard evidence. There are legal requirements in most jurisdictions for the admissibility of digital evidence in legal proceedings. These requirements apply to all sources of digital evidence including evidence extracted from Wearable devices.

Wearable devices store endless amounts of data about the user's location, activity levels, sleep patterns, and moving habits; thereby creating a detailed narrative of the user's everyday life. Evidence extracted from Wearable devices has not yet been used on a wide scale due to arguments regarding the reliability and accuracy of these devices. However, these wearable devices are being improved continuously, their accuracy and reliability and thereby admissibility are improving specially when they are synced to other devices like mobile phones and computers which are already used as admissible evidence in court. Provided that the evidence meets the requirements of admissibility, Wearable devices should be considered as one of the sources of digital evidence that can be helpful in many legal cases. (Vinez, 2017). The use of wearables has revolutionized the arena of formulating evidence, but it faces serious challenges. There will be arguments regarding the validity and credibility of evidence obtained from wearables. They are broadly classified into three areas namely: Legal, Operational and Misuse challenges. (Antwi-boasiako Venter, 2017) (Leroux, 2007). These requirements are Legal authorization, digital evidence relevance, digital evidence authenticity, digital evidence integrity, and digital evidence reliability.

Universal four step approach of digital forensics

There is a universal four-step approach in the collection and analysis of digital evidence(Casey, 2011). They are Identification, Preservation, Analysis, and Presentation.

PROCESSING AND MANAGING DIGITAL EVIDENCE

Processing and managing digital evidence comes under the category of analysis and presentation. The analysis includes proper processing of the collected evidence to separate redundant and obsolete information from useful chunks of data and mapping them together into a meaningful chain of events. All the victim devices seized must be analyzed carefully to obtain all forms of digital evidence. This involves keyword lookups, picture analysis, timeline analysis, registry analysis, mailbox analysis, database analysis, cookies, temporary and Internet history files analysis, recovery of deleted items and analysis, data carving and analysis, format recovery and analysis, partition recovery and analysis, etc. on the storage media depending on the severity of the case. Computer forensic experts with rich knowledge about the procedure must be called in for this process. The presentation involves the effective conveyance of the true events which took place. This plays a vital goal in the trial room in deciding the judgment of the case. The presentation must be valid and liable. It is an important attribute to be held by the presenter of the case. Now let us take a deep dive into the subject and have in-depth knowledge about this topic. The road map of computer evidence processing usually proceeds with the following mandatory steps (Casey, 2011):

Shutting Down the Computer

Normally instead of shutting down a system, it is pulled from the plug. It is a common practice rather than shutting down the system manually because even leaving it idle lets operation like perform reading and writing between the CPU, operating system, RAM hard drives, and the other resources. There is a high risk of potential evidence being overwritten. Hence the common practice of pulling the power cord is used where the overwriting of data on the hard drive will not happen and the system will be maintained in the same state as it was when the investigators first reached the place. This also eliminates the remote wiping of the suspicious data. There is even some software that removes certain data during a normal shutdown.

Document The Hardware Configuration of The System

Before dismantling the seized evidence for analysis photos of the entire hardware system must be taken from all possible angles. All the connecting wires and the components must be labeled so that it will be easy when assembling the components again.

Make Bit Stream Backups of Hard Disks And Floppy Disks

Bit by bit copies of all the hard drives and floppy drives have to be made. It is a thumb rule in forensics that usually two copies or backups are made. All processing and managing of evidence should be made on only the backup copy of the evidence. The original copy must be left untouched unless given legal permission to check it. Preservation of digital evidence is inevitable as they are too fragile and are easily exposed to alteration.

Mathematically Authenticate Data on All Storage Devices

To prove that the data has not been altered after the seizure of the evidence some kind of authentication has to be made. Hash algorithms are used and the source and copies are compared to make sure both the values are the same. This proves that the copy made is a replica of the source. Law enforcement and military agencies have been using 32-bit validation techniques. But today several advanced techniques exist.

Document The System Date And Time

Dates and times of the evidence play a crucial part in the collection of evidence. If the system clock is faulty all the file timestamps will also replicate the same faulty timing. To overcome these faults the date and time of the system when the device was seized must be taken into notice.

Make a List of Key Search Words

The data collected from the evidence are voluminous and cannot be examined by the individuals. Hence some automated tools are used for this purpose. To check the seized floppy drives and diskettes, a certain set of keywords are needed.Some keywords will be generated through the known information about the crime, the device user and the alleged associates. Using people who know the case is necessary and this list should be kept as small as possible.

Evaluate the Windows Swap File

Windows swap files are a space on a hard disk used as an extension to the virtual memory extension of a computers' RAM.The manual processing of such a file eats the time out. Now automated software has been introduced to analyze them in a short period. They are dynamically created and will be erased during the shutdown of the computer. However, everything will not be lost. They can be captured and evaluated.

Evaluate File Slack

Slack space is something which remains leftover on a hard disk drive when a computer file does not need that whole space allocated to it by the operating system. It serves as a base for security leakage and raw memory dumps. This space is not known to many computer users. Many forensic tools are used to investigate this space. The raw memory dump in this space provides vital data that provides relevant keywords and leads that had remained concealed till that point of time. This collection of relevant keywords should be added to the expert's word search list.

Evaluate Unallocated Space

Unallocated spaces are good resources of temporary files created by computer applications. On an average billion of bytes of storage space are found to contain data regarding formerly deleted files. These spaces can be analyzed using forensic tools to get a rich set of relevant keywords. This keyword is added to the previous set of collected list.

Search Files, File Slack and Unallocated Space for Keywords

The keywords obtained in the previous steps must be used for searching in the physical entities obtained.A lot of such text search utilities are available and most of them are validated by the intelligence authorities.The output must be carefully reviewed and documented.When some relevant data is identified they should be noted and the identified data should be completely reviewed for any new keywords. If any new keywords are identified they should be added to the former list and again a search should be made.

Document File names, Dates and Times

From the view of an evidence filename, their creation dates and their modification times and dates are more important. Hence all these data must be recorded for all the files including the erased files. The files need to be sorted based on file size, name, content, date and time of creation, last modified date and time. This can give a timeline of the evidence used.

Identify File, Program and Storage anomalies

Files that have been encrypted, compressed and graphic files are stored in binary format. Hence the content of these types of files can be read or analyzed with bare eyes, so suitable techniques should be used to decrypt the content. The partitioning in the seized hard disks is an important area for data collection. Even the data in the recycle bin must be analyzed because if they have been deleted then it must post some value of importance concerning the evidence standpoint. If any such suspicious contents are found they must be recorded immediately.

Evaluate Program Functionality

While scrutinizing an application used in the victims' computer, the entire working functionality of the application must be known to the forensic expert. The running of any programs which are intended to destroy the evidence must be examined. They'll be usually hidden and tied onto the click of hotkeys or the execution of regular OS commands.

Document Findings

Documenting the evidence is very important and it must be done at every step of discovery of data which could serve as evidence. Always beware to use licensed forensic software as the licensing of the software used in the trial will be always questioned by smart defense lawyers. The use of unlicensed software is also against the federal laws of the government. If possible, mention the license details of the forensic software you are using.

Retain The Copies of The Software Used

A copy of the software used during the process of investigation is recommended to be included in the forensic report being submitted. Sometimes it is necessary to duplicate the forensic reports before the trial. Duplication can become tough if the software has been upgraded or modified. There is a high possibility of experts encountering this problem because the software is upgraded routinely.

Some of the major reasons for inefficient evidence collection are the lack of proper policies, lack of proactive measures for incident response, and broken chain of custody. Chain of custody is a roadmap that shows the collection, analysis, and preservation of the evidence.

TOOLS TO COLLECT DIGITAL EVIDENCE

The forensic tools can be classified based on the task they perform as follows:

- Network forensic tools
- Operating system analysis tools
- Email analysis tools
- Registry analysis tools
- Database analysis tools
- Disk and data capture tools

Now let us look into each category with example tools under each category:

Network Forensic Tools

Network data is usually dynamic and volatile in nature. Network forensics deals with the monitoring and analysis of the network traffic for information gathering, legal evidence collection and for intrusion detection purposes. It will be a nice measure if network forensics being a proactive one rather than being a reactive one.

NIKSUN Net Detector

It is a complete package for security monitoring built on NikOS architecture. It is a unique software that integrates the signature-based IDS functionality with statistical anomaly detection, analytics and deep forensics with complete reconstruction and packet-level decoding. Experts can easily identify how a breach occurred, how and where the data was extracted, compromised data, and the victim people.

SAVVVIUS

SAVVIUS automates the collection of network traffic needed for security investigations. It integrates itself with leading IDS and IPS systems. It is an award-winning network forensics software.

Operating System Forensics Tools

OS Forensics allows us to identify the disreputable files and their activity with their hash value matching, drive signature comparisons, e-mail, memory and binary data.

OSForensics

It enables the discovery of relevant data through searching and indexing the data. It can be used to extract passwords, decrypt files and recover the deleted files in a blink of an eye. It mainly uses hash matching and drives signature analysis features to analyze suspicious activities.

Email Analysis Tools

E-mails are one of the keys to communication between people today and they tend to possess the voluminous amount of data needed for evidence processing. But the analysis of e-mail is becoming difficult with the advancement of new technologies.

MiTec Mail Viewer

It is useful for Outlook Express, Windows Mail /Live Mail, Mozilla, Thunderbird message databases. It has powerful searching and filtering capability and also extracting email addresses from all emails n opened folders to list by one click.

Registry Forensic Tools

In most windows systems, the registry acts as the dark cave entrance to the unfolding of many mysteries. It is considered to be an owner for a rich source of information. In most cases, the software used by the attackers will create a footprint with this unexplored part of the system. It contains information about the user activities and their accessing of the files.

Database Forensic Analysis Tools

These tools are used to perform forensic action related to databases and their actions.

Disk and Data Capture Tools

There are various tools to analyze and scrutinize the usage, partitioning of the disk structure and to make live capture of data.

Some Common Forensics Tools

Some other common and reputed forensic tools include:

SANS SIFT

SANS SIFT is a complete package of investigative Forensic toolkit which includes all the software for performing in-depth forensic or incident response investigation. It supports Expert witness, Advance Forensic format and Raw Evidence formats.

CrowdStrike CrowdResponse

It is a lightweight CLI based tool used to get lists of details like process lists, scheduled tasks and so on.

The Sleuth Kit (+Autopsy)

It is an open-source forensic tool that can be used to perform deep forensics. An autopsy is just a GUI version of The Sleuth Kit. The features of the sleuth kit include Timeline Analysis, Hash Filtering, File system Analysis and Keyword searching and it is flexible to the addition of new modules.

FTK Manager

It is a data preview and imaging tool that helps to examine files and folders on hard drives. Networking devices, CDs and DVDs. It also lets us review forensic image files, review and recover even the deleted files from the recycle bandit lets us examine the dump files which usually consists of a lot of evidence. It also lets us mount a forensic image to view its contents.

CAINE

Computer-Aided Investigative Environment is a live forensic tool that consists of a lot of forensic tools. The main features include user-friendly Graphic user interface, automated report generation for mobile forensics, network forensics, recovery of data. The other forensic tools can be launched from this interface.

ExifTool

It is a CLI tool used to read, write or edit metadata information. It is used to analyze the static properties of suspicious files caught.

Bulk Extractor

It is a computer forensic tool that scans disk images, files, directories and extracts information regarding credit card numbers, domains, e-mail addresses, URL s and zip files. The output information is sent as an output to a series of text files that can later be analyzed and use in the trial room as a source of evidence.

ENSURING THE VALIDITY OF THE DIGITAL EVIDENCE

Digital evidence is becoming vital in crime cases nowadays. So, when this evidence is presented at the trial room it must be substantial evidence such that the individual piece of evidence is so sufficient enough to convict a criminal of his crime. The digital evidence is processed in investigative and legal domains. The investigative domain includes the preservation of the evidence, locating the evidence, selecting the evidence, validating the evidence, it is preceded by the legal domain which involves the legal practitioners who construct and present the argument in the courtroom. Sometimes false evidence can surface up causing unreliable arguments (Boddington, Mann, Hobbs, 2008). This mistake is usually made by those practitioners who are unfamiliar with the realistic nature of the digital domain. However, there are errors in all kinds of cases. Some of the factors affecting the validity of the evidence include missing collection tools. failure to report exculpatory data, misinterpreted data taken out of context, falsely leading evidence, irrelevant evidence, minor system and application errors and so on. Owing to the complexity of the digital evidences these types of cases mostly tend to fail due to the poor reconstruction of the evidence.

The validation process of digital evidence includes the following steps:

Start
Validate the evidence
If (the evidence is valid):
Retain the evidence
Else If (the evidence is unclear):
Seek further explanation.
Else:
Reject the evidence.

The above pseudo-code gives a constructive idea of validating digital evidence. (Erbacher, 2010) On the first note if the evidence appears to be muddy further explanations are sought. If not, the evidence is retained. This requires a series of prompts where the prompts respond as "yes "or "no". Usually, if it is "no", then the prompt is unclear and further investigation has to be made. If it is a "yes" they can be retained and used as a valid piece of information in the trial. Each piece of proof which are to be included for the legal report must satisfy a weight of inference for some assertion used. This strategy of assertion will be applied hierarchically. If an assertion is confirmed then it will be taken to the next level of assertion for further interrogations. To assist legal practitioners in the process of validation interrogation, an interrogation checklist will be maintained. Giving such an interrogation list will help the practitioner to decide upon whether evidence has met the concerned categories of assertion or whether they require any further interrogations. The two-option provided for the user of the interrogation list to seek an assertion or else to seek negation. An interrogation list can be created on an individual's or the investigating party's point of view. The parameters could vary. for every interrogation list. Let us consider an instance in which an interrogation list consists of the fields: subject, assertion, different prompts, and known issues. It will be an effective one and can be used as a standard approach for any interrogation list.

On looking in this path one might question the privacy of the accused involved. It should be made clear that privacy and the path of digital crime evidence collection are not to be collapsed. Because, when undergoing the investigations, the protection of any private information is cent percent assured.

CASE STUDY

Cases Involving Smart Wearables

The most controversial criminal case where Fitbit data was used as digital evidence is a murder case in Connecticut on December 2015.

In this case, police found the victim - Connie Dabate -dead from two gunshot wounds in the basement of her house. Her husband – Richard Dabate - was found tied to a folding chair on the kitchen floor with several cuts on his body.

Richard told the police his version of the events leading to the murder of his wife; however, data from her Fitbit and other digital devices contradict his story. A year after the incident and with the help of several digital evidence, Richard was charged with the murder of his wife.

In his story, the defendant claims that while he was driving to work on the morning of Dec 23, he received an alert on his cell phone indicating that the home alarm at his house has been activated. He claims that he sent an email to his boss from his cell phone indicating that he will be late for work. He drove back home and claims to have arrived at approximately 9 am. The defendant claims that once he arrived at his house, he encountered a masked intruder. He claims that while he was struggling with the intruder, he heard his wife coming back home from the gym and arriving at the garage door. The defendant claims that the intruder was able to chain him to a chair in the kitchen and ran after his wife. The intruder followed Connie Dabate to the basement and shot her, and then escaped from the house. The defendant, although tied up to a chair, claims that he then managed to activate the panic button from the home's alarm system. After an initial investigation, the police found the husband's story a little suspicious. There was little sign of struggle in the house and no signs of forced entry. The dogs were not able to pick up the scent of an intruder, and there was no blood evidence to support the defendant's story. So, the police issued search warrants for the following electronic records

- Cell phone records for the defendant and his wife.
- Computer records from the defendant's laptop.
- Facebook records for the defendant and his wife.
- Text messages.
- Fitbit records for the wife.

After investigating the data from the aforementioned electronic records, the police found text messages showing that the defendant was involved with another woman and was discussing getting a divorce from his wife. Police were also able to construct a timeline of the events, which contradicted, with the defendant's version of the story. Following is an illustration of the timeline of events:

- At 8:30 am, the defendant claims to have left the house to go to work.
- At 8:46 am, the Wife's Fitbit records show idle time after activity, which is presumably the time she left the house.
- At 8:53 am, surveillance Cameras from the gym's parking lot shows the wife arriving at the gym.
- Between 8:30 and 9:00 am, the defendant claims to have received an alert on his cell phone from the home alarm system. The defendant claims that he sent an email to his boss from his cell phone and drove back to his house.
- At 9:00 am, the defendant claims to have arrived back at his house and was faced by the intruder. A little after, the wife arrived and was chased by the intruder to the basement, and then shot dead.
- At 9:04 am, records from the defendant's laptop show that an email was sent from the defendant's laptop, not the cell phone. Geo-location data shows that the email was sent from the defendant's home, not while being on the road as he claims.
- At 9:18 am, Google search records from the defendant's laptop showing that he searched his wife's exercise schedule at the gym.
- At 9:18 am, surveillance cameras show the wife leaving the gym. Cell phone records show that she made a call that lasted almost 4 minutes.
- At 9:23 am, wife's Fitbit data show activity after being idle between 9:18 and 9:23 which is the time she was presumably driving home.
- At 9:23 am, data from the home alarm system showing the garage door was opened.
- At 9:40 to 9:46 am Facebook data showing that the wife posted two videos on Facebook. The IP address for this transaction was traced to the house.
- At 10:05 am, the wife's Fitbit record shows the last movement. Between the time she came home and when it stopped, she moved a distance of 1,217 feet inside the house.
- At 10:11 am, the home alarm panic button was activated, which is approximately an hour after the defendant claims to have activated it.
- At 10.16 am, a call to the police was placed from the home alarm system company.
- At 10:20 am, the defendant called 911.

As seen from the above timeline, many sources of electronic devices and records provide digital evidence that tells another version of the story of how the events took place at the time of the incident. Correlation between the evidence gathered from several digital sources helped the police in knowing the facts of the incident. The most crucial evidence is the data retrieved from the victim's Fitbit, which shows that her last movement was at 10:05 am, which is an hour after the time her husband claimed that the intruder shot her. Also, Fitbit records show that the victim moved a distance of 1,217 feet inside the house, which is 10 times the distance from her car to their basement. (Khairallah, 2018)

Wearables as a source potential evidence have evolved recently. The following are some more proofs for that.

- In 2014, a Canadian law firm used the Fitbit data to show the effects an accident had on their client. The client's Fitbit data showed that her activity level had significantly decreased since the accident as a result of her injuries.
- In 2014, Police in Pennsylvania, US, proved that a woman was lying about being assaulted using data from her Fitbit. The woman claimed that she was asleep when an intruder broke into her home and attacked her. However, her Fitbit data showed that she was awake and walking around during the time of the alleged attack. She was later charged with filing a false report.

Andhra Pradesh Tax Case

A suspicious businessman from Andhra Pradesh was exposed to his fraudulent activities when forensic experts got hold of the computers used by the accused. He, a plastics firm owner was taken into custody and a huge bounty of Rs.22 Crores was recovered from him by the detectives of the Vigilance department. These officers sought an explanation regarding the unaccounted cash from the accused and gave a period of 10 days to show up the proofs. The accused person gave a proof of 6000 vouchers to prove the legitimacy of the unaccounted cash. But after scrutiny of the digital evidence like the computers he used, his mobile phones it threw light that they were all prepared after the raid took place. It was also later discovered that he had been running a whole of 5 different businesses under one company's name using fake and computerized vouchers to maintain the finances of the company. He did this to escape the amount of tax he had to pay (Cyber laws and Information Security Advisors).

Sony.Sambadh.Com Case

India's first cyber crime conviction was made for this case. A complaint was made by Sony India Private Ltd which runs a website named www.sony.sambadh.com for the Non-Residents of India who can gift or send products to their friends or relatives in India after they pay for the product. The company will then deliver the ordered goods to the intended recipients. During the wake of My 2002, a person under the identity of Barbara Campa ordered a Sony color Television and a cordless headphone to be sent to a person named Atif Azim residing in Noida. The payment was correctly transacted by the credit card company and the transaction proceeded. After proper checking, the product was delivered to Arif Azim and digital proof of the delivery of the items was taken as photographs. After a period of one and a half months, the credit card company informed Sony that this transaction was not legit and the real holder of the card had denied the transaction. The company then complained about the criterion of online cheating at the Central Bureau of Investigation where the case was registered under the sections of 418,419, and 420 of the Indian Penal Code. Digital crime investigations lead to the fact that Arif Azim who was an employee of a call center in Noida gained unauthorized access to the credit card of an American citizen. He misused this number on the company's website. The CBI seized the products and the CBI was able to prove the crime with the digital evidence caught. The accused was subjected to punishment based on the norms of the Indian Penal Code (Cyber laws and Information Security Advisors).

SMC Pneumatics (India) Pvt. Ltd. V. Jogesh Kwatra

It was one of the first cases of defamation of an organization in India. An employer of the company which had lodged the case in the court had been sending obscene, filthy, derogatory and defamatory emails to his employers as well as clients and beneficiary companies of the reputed company. His main aim was to defame the company and its managing director worldwide. After careful examination of his emails, it was proved that he had been sending mails there were truly offending and humiliating in nature which defamed the target organization (Cyber laws and Information Security Advisors).

The Murder Case of 22-Month-Old

This was a murder case that involved the death of a 22-month-old Georgian toddler named Cooper Harris who was left behind inside a car for near father Mr. Harris, forgot his child's presence inside the car and lacked it. But later interrogations with the father revealed that he had researched about child deaths inside vehicles and the temperature needed for it to occur. This caused a twist in the path the case was going. When the detectives seized Mr. Harris's work computer and on looking for the digital evidence he had searched about "child deaths inside vehicles and what temperature it needs to be for that to occur" (Michael Pearson, 2014). It was also stated he had some extramarital affairs with many women and he wanted to free himself from the current marriage. So, he had planned to kill the little toddler. The digital evidence obtained was crucial to prove the killer of the toddler. He was charged with malice murder, felony murder, and cruelty to children, criminal attempt to commit a felony and dissemination of harmful material to minors

The Death of Caylee Anthony

Caylee Anthony was the 3-year-old daughter of Casey Anthony. Caylee's grandmother Cindy was the first to report about the disappearance of Caylee. She had called 911 and reported that Caylee had been missing for 31 days and Casey's car smelled like there had been a dead body inside it. She also said that Casey had been giving continuously varied statements regarding the whereabouts of Caylee when questioned. She also lied Caylee had been kidnapped by her nanny named Zenaida "Zanny" Fernandez –Gonzalez. On investigation, a woman named by that name existed but she was in no way connected to Anthony's family. A meter reader Roy Kronk called the cops about some mysterious objects found in the forested areas near the Anthony residence. When the sheriffs underwent an investigation in that area a skull was found near a grey bag. A second search led to the discovery of what was found to be the remains of a small girl. A thorough investigation revealed duct tapes hanging from Caylee's hairs and some remaining tissues on her skull. In October 2009, crime scene investigators revealed documents related to the Anthony investigation which had proofs and records of Google searches of the terms "neck breaking "and "how to make chloroform" (Ashley Hayes,2011). A blanket found at the crime scene matched that of Caylee's bedding clothes in her grandparents' house. Among photos entered as evidence a photo from Casey Anthony's ex-boyfriend's computer was a poster depicted with the caption "Win her with chloroform". This digital evidence played a crucial part in proving the crime.

USE CASES

There have been cases where digital evidence has played an instrumental role in bringing the criminal to justice.

The intelligence agency of any country strives to work hard for preventing any untoward incident in the country. They work in close collaboration with the army and maintain peace in the country. They can achieve this mammoth task, utilizing smart monitoring systems. These systems detect unusual activities.

There is a case of a terrorist, in the guise of a normal citizen. He was nabbed after going through his web activities, thereby preventing any attacks or crimes he could have committed.

There are many cases of disgruntled employees making chaos in the office environment. One such case speaks of one such employee who used the CEO's IP address and sending offensive messages, making it appear as if it's the CEO who's sending them. On the proper study of the router and network traffic, the perpetrator was identified. (Narh Williams, 2016) (Kruse, 2015)

There was a case of a competitor stealing critical information about a target and information could not be obtained regarding IP addresses. But an IDS installed before saved the day by recording not only the IP address but all the associated network traffic. (Grimm, 2016)

There is an increased need for action by CFIs, as the reputation of key players is at stake here.

There are many leading forensic service providers. One of them is Kroll. Kroll assures of offering service of collection of digital evidence with no discrepancies. They also ensure that no digital evidence is overlooked. Also, they offer no limitations on the number of data sources that they will look into. Even the most sensitive and complex of the evidence are analyzed at Kroll. Any other litigation-based services like collecting electronic evidence and their preservation are all looked after securely. There is cybercrime investigation, data preservation, data collection, data recovery and forensic analysis, expert testimony and reporting services offered by Kroll. (Bock, 2018)

CONCLUSION

Long story short the importance of digital evidence in the perspective of being presented in a trial has been analyzed by the authors. This chapter gave a quick overview of how the digital evidence is collected, their different electronic origins, and why they are collected. It also aimed at the preservation and maintenance of such collected digital evidence. As a foundation block for forensics, the preservation step has the highest possible weight because this is where several mishaps are bound to happen. Next, several forensics tools and their usage were enlisted. They were categorized into different branches based on the type of service provided. A list of general-purpose tools that are offered as a whole and complete package for performing forensics were also discussed. As a next step, the part of authenticating and validating the digital evidence collected was briefed. This is also so vital because the jury will usually question the validity of the evidence during the trial. A potential amount of knowledge would have been gained by the user regarding the two domains namely the investigative domain and the legal domain. Finally, some interesting case studies were presented which would have surely enlightened the readers on how the cases involving e-crimes, homicides, murders are handled and how the accused is convicted with the help of digital evidence. The readers are requested to explore more in this field as it is not a topic to be held in the size of a hand. The more you investigate abiding the rules, the more you enrich your forensic skills.

REFERENCES

Ami-Narh, J. T., & Williams, P. A. H. (2008). Digital forensics and the legal system: A dilemma of our times. *6th Aust. Digit. Forensics Conf.*, 30–40.

Anthony trial. (2011). *Chloroform searched on computer*. Retrieved from http://edition.cnn.com/2011/CRIME/06/08/florida.casey.anthony.trial/

Antwi-boasiako, A., & Venter, H. (2017). A Model for Digital Evidence Admissibility Assessment. *Adv. Digit. Forensics XIII*, *511*, 23–38. doi:10.1007/978-3-319-67208-3_2

Boddington, Hobbs, & Mann. (2008). *Validating digital evidence for legal argument*. Australian Digital Forensics Conference, Edith Cowan University, Perth, Australia.

Casey, E. (2011). *Digital Evidence and Computer Crime: Forensic Science, Computers and the Internet*. London: Academic Press.

Computer Forensics Services. (2018). Retrieved from https://www.kroll.com/en/services/business-intelligence-and-investigations/forensic-accounting

Digital forensics: An Analytical Crime Scene Procedure Model (ACSPM) Forensic Science International. (2013). Retrieved from https://corporate.findlaw.com/litigation-disputes/top-ten-things-to-do-when-collecting-electronic-evidence.html

Erbacher, R. F. (2010). Validation for Digital forensics. *Conference Paper*, Army Research Laboratory.

Grimm, H. O. N. P. W. for Authenticating Digital Evidence. (2016). *Hot-car death highlights key role of digital evidence*. Retrieved from https://edition.cnn.com/2014/07/02/tech/web/digital-evidence/index.html

Guo, H., Jin, B., & Huang, D. (2011). Research and review on computer forensics. *Lect. Notes Inst. Comput. Sci. Soc. Telecommun. Eng.*, *56*, 224–233. doi:10.1007/978-3-642-25255-6_29

Gupta, Singh, Kaur Arora, & Mahajan. (2011). Digital Forensics- A Technological Revolution in Forensic Sciences. *J Indian Acad Forensic Med.*, *33*(2).

Important cyber laws case studies. (n.d.). Retrieved from http://www. cyberralegalservices.com/detail-casestudies.php

Kent, Chevalier, Grance, & Dang. (2006). *Guide to integrating forensic techniques into incident response.* Academic Press.

Khairallah, T. (2018). *Wearables as Digital Evidence Fitbit evidence case study.* Retrieved from https://www.preprints.org/manuscript/201812.0313/v1/download

Kruse, W. (2015). Your Employee May Be Wearing Their Alibi - Or Your Evidence Vice President for Digital Forensics. Academic Press.

Leroux, O. (2007). Legal Admissibility of Electronic Evidence. *International Review of Law Computers & Technology, 18*(2), 193–220. doi:10.1080/1360086042000223508

Loja, N., Morocho, R., & Novillo, J. (2016). Digital Forensics Tools. *International Journal of Applied Engineering Research., 11,* 9754–9762.

Manning, P. K. (1992). Information Technologies and the Police. In Modern Policing. Chicago: The University of Chicago. doi:10.1086/449197

N. C. J. U.S. Department of Justice. (2001). Electronic Crime Scene Investigation: A Guide for First Responders. *NIJ Res. Rep., no. NCJ, 187736,* 96.

National Forensic Science Technology Center. (2009). *A Simplified Guide to Digital Evidence.* Author.

Richards, J. (1999). *Transnational Criminal Organizations, Cybercrime, and Money Laundering: A Handbook for Law Enforcement Officers, Auditors, and Financial Investigators.* Boca Raton, FL: CRC Press.

Rosen, D. M. (1982, September). Police and the Computer: The Revolution That Never Happened. *Police Magazine, 5,* 5.

Saini, H., Rao, Y.S., & Panda, T.C. (2012). Cyber-Crimes and their Impacts: A Review. *International Journal of Engineering Research and Applications.*

Schoenwaelder & President. (2017). *Role of Wearable Devices for Real World Data Collection: Engagement or Today's.* Academic Press.

Seaskate. (1998). *A Technical Report prepared for The National Committee on Criminal Justice Technology.* National Institute of Justice, By Seaskate, Inc.

Vacca, R. (2005). Computer Forensics Computer Crime Scene Investigation (2nd ed.). Academic Press.

Vinez, K. E. (2017). The Admissibility of Data Collected from Wearable Devices. *Stetson J. Advocacy Law*, *1*, 1–23.

Yassir, A., & Nayak, S. (2012). Cybercrime: A threat to Network Security. *International Journal of Computer Science and Network Security*.

ADDITIONAL READING

Passi, H. (2018, May 23). *Top 20 Trending Computer Forensics Tools of 2018*. Retrieved from https://www.greycampus.com/blog/information-security/top-twenty-trending-computer-forensics-tools

Tripwire Guest Authors. (2014, April 15). *Free Computer Tools For Network And Email Forensics*. Retrieved from https://www.tripwire.com/state-of-security/incident-detection/free-computer-tools-network-email-forensics-4/

KEY TERMS AND DEFINITIONS

Database Analysis Tools: These tools are with features and comparison that connect with cloud databases, Amazon Redshift, and Google BigQuery.

Disk and Data Capture Tools: Encrypted disk detector can be helpful to check encrypted physical drives.

Email Analysis Tools: These tools will make email headers human readable by parsing them according to RFC 822. Email headers are present on every email you receive via the internet.

Network Forensic Tools: Network forensic analysis tools (NFATs) help administrators monitor their environment for anomalous traffic, perform forensic analysis and get a clear picture of their environment.

Operating System Analysis Tools: Tools for the analysis of operating systems from their source code were developed.

Registry Analysis Tools: Tools for registry forensics. Tool: MuiCache View. Whenever a new application is installed, the Windows operating system automatically extracts the application name from the version resource of the exe file and stores it for later use in a Registry key known as the "MuiCache."

Sources of Digital Evidence: There are many sources of digital evidence, but for the purposes of this publication, the topic is divided into three major forensic categories of devices where evidence can be found: Internet-based, stand-alone computers or devices, and mobile devices.

Chapter 9
Digital Steganography Security

Parkavi R.
Thiagarajar College of Engineering, India

Anitha S.
Thiagarajar College of Engineering, India

Gayathri R.
Thiagarajar College of Engineering, India

ABSTRACT

Steganography has been considered as a major instrument used for an unauthorized and destructive purpose such as crime and warfare, and forensics has been used for a constructive purpose such as crime detection and fraud detection. Hence, the combination of both steganography and forensics plays a major role in the present internet era for information exchange between two parties. It has been propelled to the forefront of the current security techniques. The main objective of the technique is to provide an imperceptible way of transferring secret messages to the recipient. Another issue to be noted is that the term steganography completely differs from cryptography. The above-stated analysis is used in digital forensics. There are many steganography software tools available for ordinary computer users.

INTRODUCTION

The word "DATA" is more valuable than money. Nowadays Data is flooding over the internet via social media like Facebook, Twitter, YouTube and the web browser itself. Even a search query and history data of a search engine can able to describe one's personal or societal status. Due to rapid increase in data mining, analytics as well as hacking technologies and tools, data can be easily processed to get valuable

DOI: 10.4018/978-1-7998-1558-7.ch009

information of a person or country like their favorites, daily routines, family and business, and even though unknown secrets which are not even known by the respective user. So the risky situation comes here to exchange data via the internet which is ineluctable in our fastest and modern world. There is a need for reliable techniques that helps to secure data roaming on the internet. Hence the security systems like Cryptography, Steganography comes to the digital world to secure the data, which is already used by our ancients to protect data that exist in physical matter.

HISTORY OF STEGANOGRAPHY

The word Steganography comes from the words "*Steganos*" means cover or secret and "*graphy*" means writing. The veiling of one form of data within another form of data is called Steganography. Many incidents are revealing that Steganography is not a new technique for this world. The first incident was, Ancient Greek Ruler Histaeus used to shave the head of his slave, tattooing in the scalp and wait for hair to grow. Then send the slave to recipients to convey the hidden message. The recipient would have shaved the slave's head to see the message. In the second incident, Demestrus wrote a message to his friend in the wooden carve of the wax tablet that seemed to be simple. In the third incident, During the American & British Revolutionary, they use invisible ink to exchange information. In the fourth incident, during World War 2, Germans used microdots. Later, Null ciphers were used i.e. unencrypted message send within the real readable format. For example, **P**olice **r**eport **e**mergencies **in d**owntown **e**nding **n**ear **T**uesday by taking the first letter on each word on the given sentence, it gives the result "PRESIDENT". This is called null cipher. As the years have grown, Steganographic techniques also grow and emerge as the strongest technique to secure the data. (Siper, Farley, R & Lombardo, 2005)

Cryptography vs. Steganography

Cryptography is the most frequent usable technique for data communication in the network where Steganography is not in that case but it is also used for secured data sharing.

Cryptography uses a key to encrypt or decrypt the data. For example, Mr. X wants to send the message "Hello Mr." to Mr. Y via the "ZZZ app". The "Z app's" security system encrypts the plain text of Mr. X i.e. altering the actual or original message to something like "HSJHDJHF SDKJSDJS" (just for example, not a real answer) as a ciphertext which is going to send in the network by using the public key of Mr. X. On another end, Mr. Y 's app receives the ciphertext sent by Mr. X and the security system decrypts the ciphertext into plain text by using the private key of Mr. Y and displays the real message. Here Mr. X and Mr. Y are not directly involved as a person to do cryptography and not even know their keys. All the above activities are done in a fraction of second in a system without human interaction. Here the cryptanalysis may be done but it will take much more time to crack the key used in encryption and decryption technique to know the actual data. Here the security sounds.

On the other hand, Steganography is a technique that veils the data within the data i.e. No alteration in actual data. For instance, Mr. X wants to send a secret message but not allow using cryptography techniques. Then He preferred another strongest technique called Steganography. Hiding of actual text data within the image, video, audio or vice versa, using various methods like least significant bit alterations of the image, not in the actual data to be sent. After doing stego functions, media with the embedded message sent in the network seems to be the same as before doing stego function.

It is tough for the hackers to find whether the media contains a secret message or not, by seeing it in the naked eyes but in the case of cryptography, it is known that the message was encrypted by seeing ciphertext but not known the actual message. To find the secret message, complete scanning of media sent in the network at the bit levels to find any modifications or addition of bits in comparison to unnecessary bits of original media. Steganography also sounds great in the area of security. Like the security techniques, the hacking techniques also reached its peak in development. Different and more specialized tools were developed to crack the security. So keeping the data secured until its expiry date is more than enough in this modern era. Instead of using security techniques as separate streams, combining both techniques to make the data much more secure, i.e. first do the cryptography function and then do the Steganography function. For example, Mr. X wants to send a text message like "Hello MR. y" which is embedded in the image of CAT. First the message "Hello MR. y" is encrypted using a key then stego function is implemented to hide the ciphertext within the image at the sender side. On the receiver side, first the stego functions are cracked and then the decryption has to be done using with the help of key. (Rathore, 2015)

CHARACTERISTICS OF STEGANOGRAPHY

Other than hiding messages in the media, the steganographic technique has several other characteristics to be noticed. They are as follows, (Codr, 2009).

Veiling Capacity

It is the capacity of the message going to hide in the media. Consider the image of pixel 200 X 200, i.e. Length X Height. Pixel is the smallest component in a digital image. Each pixel contains variable intensities and is represented by three or four color components in the color imaging system. Several distinct colors represented by a pixel depend on several bits per pixel. True color images contain 24 bits/pixel i.e. 2^{24} colors. So for each color component in RGB 8 bit is allocated with an extra 8-bit component for opacity. If we use one bit of all color components to hide data, then the hiding capacity is 120,000 bits or 15000 bytes. If we use 2 bit of all components, then the hiding capacity is 640,000 bits or 30000 bytes.

Robustness

It is another property, that message hidden in a media does not undergo any changes or alteration even if the media is manipulated by other techniques like cropping, blurring, adding additional colors in the image on the top, erasing the media file using specialized tools, etc. It should the same as at the bit level to retain the hidden data in it.

Tamper Resistance

It is a property in which hidden message's ability to continue to exist as the same without being affected even if the active measures were destroyed i.e. Message should be recovered itself or retain as same.

Undetectability

It is a property that defines how steganography techniques should be. The result of the steganography technique is as tough as possible to the core to find the difference between cover (media bits) and stego objects (hidden image) for a computer using statistical or other computational methods.

Invisibility

This property is also called perceptual transparency. Each medium like an image, video, audio has a certain capacity to hide data within it. If data to be hidden exceeds the threshold capacity of the media, results in distortion of original media i.e. visible differences are seen in the media from original media. This makes the steganographic technique weaker and useless. If the distortion in the stego media is noticed by the attacker, then the original data have loosed its security and it can be extracted or modified. So it is necessary to hide the data less than or equal to the threshold capacity of the media which is used as a cover media.

Signal to Noise Ratio

The signal to ratio is the property of the image. The contrast of the object in the image decides whether the object is visible or not. Signal to ratio is the ratio between the blackest black and whitest white. Higher the signal to ratio, the visibility of the object is higher. Lower the signal to ratio, and then the visibility of the object is lower or hidden. To hide the data within the image, the signal to ratio must be lower.

The good Steganographic technique should satisfy every property mentioned. If anyone of the property is not satisfied, the steganography method sounds low.

HOW STEGANOGRAPHY WORKS IN GENERAL?

Let's see how steganography is implemented, in general. The extensive components are the cover media that will hold the secret data, the secret message may be plain/cipher text/code, the stego function, and its inverse operation and an optional stego or password that helps in locking and unlocking of the secret message. The stego function conceals the secret message using the stego key into the cover media. On the receiver side, the inverse stego function unwrap the secret message. The core components used for modern steganography techniques are plaintext; still imagery; audio and video; and IP datagram. The cover media may be a document file, image file, video, audio, program or protocol. The steganography methods are Line-Shift Coding, Word-Shift Coding in Text steganography, Least Significant Bits and Transformations in Image Steganography, LSB Coding, Phase Coding and Echo Hiding in Audio Steganography. (Olguin, 2016) There are mainly 4 types or techniques for implementing steganography.

They are,

a) Text Steganography
b) Audio Steganography
c) Video Steganography
d) Image Steganography

Text Steganography

Text Steganography is the method of hiding the text data within the text files. It uses the text files as cover media. So this method is called as Text Steganography. This method is the trickiest one of all the other methods, due to the deficiency of redundant information in the text file. It is possible to change the structure of the text document by hiding data in it without making notable and observable changes. It requires less memory to store along with the stego object. There are various techniques used to implement text steganography for data transferring, (Agarwal, 2013).

Selective Hiding

In selective hiding is the process of hiding the characters at specific locations or beginning and end of the passage. This technique requires a huge amount of text. (Rani & Chaudhary, 2013)

Html Web Page

The secret text is hidden using HTML attributes. Using these characters, the original text can be retrieved. (Rani & Chaudhary, 2013).

Semantic Hiding

It is a type of text Steganography in which synonyms are used to the secret message. (Rani & Chaudhary, 2013).

Hiding of Text Using Whitespaces

In this type, the amount of whitespaces between words is used to determine the message. The smaller amount of whitespaces is indicated as 0 and a larger number of whitespaces is indicated at 1. (Rani, & Chaudhary, 2013)

Audio Steganography

It is a method in which the data to be sent is hidden among the modified audio signal in an indiscernible manner. The basic model of audio Steganography consists of three components such as carrier, message, and password. Carrier acts as a cover message, carries the secret message. The message is the information that the user needs to been sent. Password is the key used by the recipient to decrypt the cover file; it is also called as stego-key. The cover file with the message is called as stego-file.

The process of information hiding involves two steps; initially, the redundant bits are identified in the cover file. Then the redundant bits are replaced by the bits of secret information. The redundant bits should not damage or destroy the quality of the cover file. There are five methods involved in the audio steganography process. (Jayaram, Ranganatha, & Anupama, 2011)

1.   LSB coding
2.   Parity coding
3.   Phase coding
4.   Spread spectrum
5.   Echo hiding
     LSB Coding

Least Significant Bit (LSB) is a common algorithm used for audio Steganography, in which some of the least significant bits of a cover file are replaced by sequences of bytes of secret message. When the least significant bit is replaced by other bits of data it does not degrades the quality of the media. Hence some of the least significant bits have been replaced. The least significant bit in binary integer may be zero or one which determines whether the number is odd or even. In other words, consider a secret message **ready for war** is embedded into the normal audio file by replacing the least significant bits of data. The resultant data is obtained from the stego-file by converting the file into bitstreams.

The application decodes the cover file and obtains the possible hidden byte, by reading the eight-bit binary integers. The secret message is recreated by capturing the least significant bits of the binary integers. Nearly there is a fifty percent chance that the replacing bit is the same as that of the original bit, so it doesn't affect the quality. (Malviya, Saxena, & Khare, 2012)

Parity Coding

Parity coding is another type of audio steganographic technique, in this method, the single audio signal is divided into the number of separate samples, in these samples the bits of the secret message are embedded from the parity bit. If there is no match between the secret bit to be encoded and the bit in the selected region, the process may lead to an inversion of the least significant bit of one of the samples in the region. (Malviya et.al, 2012)

Phase Coding

Phase coding is one of the effective methods in audio Steganography. In the phase coding method, the initial part of the audio segment is replaced by a secret message. The remaining segments of the audio signal try to retain the relative phase between segments. In this case, the occurrence of noise may be possible. The phase component of sound which is not perceptible to the human ear is called noise. The noticeable phase dispersion may occur when there is a drastic change between the phase components.

1. Initially, the original sound is divided into small segments of sizes according to the size of the secret message.
2. Discrete Fourier Transform (DFT) is applied for building a matrix of those phases. The phase difference between the adjacent segments are been calculated.
3. 3. The phase shifts between these segments are easily detectable, that is we can easily change the segment of audio signal but at the same time, the phase difference between adjacent segments must be preserved.

$$Phase\_new = \frac{\pi}{2}, \text{ when message bit } = 0;$$

$$Phase\_new = -\frac{\pi}{2}, \text{ when message bit } = 1;$$

A phase matrix has been created using a new phase of the first segment and original phase differences

4. Inverse Discrete Fourier Transform is used for reconstructing the sound signal by combining the new segment along with the original sound segments.
5. At the same time, the receiver should arrive off the length of the segment, the receiver can easily extract the secret message from the encoded signal.
6. Discrete Fourier Transform is used for extracting the phase which holds the secret information. (Malviya et.al, 2012)
   Spread Spectrum

The spread spectrum (SS) method is the most effective method compared to other methods of audio Steganography. This is similar to the least significant bit replacement algorithm in which the secret information is spread across the frequency spectrum of the audio signal which is independent of the actual signal. As a result, the final signal occupies a higher bandwidth for transmission than the original signal. The spread spectrum is capable of contributing a better performance compared to other techniques such as LSB coding, spread spectrum, parity coding, and phase coding. The only disadvantage of the spread spectrum is noise creation into a sound file. It has a high level of robustness against the removal technique and good data transmission rate.

Steps in the Spread Spectrum method:

1. The secret message is encrypted using a symmetric key, k1.
2. Using low rate error-correcting code the encrypted message is encoded which helps to increase the overall robustness.
3. Using second symmetric key K2, the encoded message is modulated into the pseudorandom signal.
4. This resultant signal contains the secret message interleaved with the cover signal.
5. The new digital audio file is quantized which contains the message.
6. This process is reversed for message extraction on the receiver side.
   Echo Hiding

Echo hiding is another type of audio Steganography. In this method, the three parameters to be noted are initial amplitude, decay rate and offset. In inaudible echo, if the offset value is short then the echo which produced is subliminal in nature. Depends on the quality of recording the maximum delay without effect is I mile second. The initial amplitude and decay rate will be below the audible threshold of the human ear. In the encoding phase, the audio signal is divided into multiple windows. The hidden data is encoded using two delay times: Binary 0 encoded with delay = offset

Binary1EncodedWithDelay = offset + deltaValue

The delaying of the audio signal is done by a simple FIR filter equation.

$H(z) = 1 + g * z^{-d}$, Where g = initial amplitude, d = delay

Therefore, two impulses are used; one to copy the original signal and another is used to introduce an echo into the original signal

Final encoding process: In the final step of encoding the filtered original signal is separated through both binary "one" and "zero" filter. Using the mixer signal the ramping function is used to switch between 0 and 1 encodings.

In the decoding phase, the delay occurs before the echo is been identified. Initially, the cepstrum of the encoded signal is found. Since finding the cepstrum that makes the echo delay more pronounced and it is easier to detect.

$$F^{-1}(\ln(F(x))^2)$$

Then the autocorrelation of the cepstrum signal is found. This algorithm is mainly used to determine the thresholds of when the echo becomes perceivable, that's the type of music and the amount of delay (determine the amount of data that can be embedded into the cover file). It also helps to determine whether the mp3 compression process may destroy the hidden data. It also helps to detect whether it is easily detectable in the case of the spectrogram.

Video Steganography

There are various methods in video Steganography, (Febryan, Purboyo, & Saputra, 2017)

a)   Video steganography by LSB (least significant bit) substitution.
b)   Video steganography using vector quantization
c)   Video steganography using integer wavelet transform
d)   Video steganography using dynamic cover generation.
     Video Steganography by LSB Substitution

In this technique, the least significant bit is operated using different polynomial equations. These operated LSB bits of secret information are implanted into the carrier file. Thus the third party could not identify the existence of a secret message in the video file.

Video Steganography Using Vector Quantization

In vector quantization method a 32 *32 vector-matrix format is used for quantization. Process of Discrete Cosine Transform (DCT). Initially, the video is sliced into several frames. After slicing this video, all the sliced images are passed into 32 * 32-pixel management procedures which are followed by the quantitative LSB method. The secret message to be inserted is initially converted into ASCII; these bits are later implanted into the video file. The low-intensity bits are position were these bits of the secret message have been implanted, if they exist more in number then it is pinned into high-intensity bits. The implanting of a bit is done by Inverse Discrete Cosine Transform (IDCT).

Video Steganography Using Integer Wavelet Transforms

The Integer wavelet transform method is used handling high capacity video Steganography. The stego images obtained from the cover images using integer wavelet transform.

Video Steganography Using Dynamic Cover Generation

In the dynamic cover generation method, the cover message is created by the steganographic system instead of using the existing cover message. The secret message is then implanted into the cover message.

Image Steganography

Image Steganography is the process of hiding private information into digital images. (Bhallamudi, 2015). There are various methods available in image steganography, they are

1. Spatial domain Steganography (image-domain),
2. Transform domain Steganography (frequency domain),
3. Spread spectrum Steganography,
4. Model-based Steganography.
   Spatial Domain Steganography

   The spatial domain method is also called an image domain method. In the image domain, the secret information is inserted into the pixels of the original image and noise manipulation is done on the covered image. It includes, (Fkirin, Attiya, & El-Sayed, A. 2016)

1. LSB substitution method.
2. Gray level modification.
3. Pixel value differencing.
4. Quantization index modulation.
5. Multiple base notational systems.
6. Prediction based method.

○ *Least Significant Bit Substitution Method*

Replacing the least significant bit is the most common method used in the steganography model. A digital image is classified into a grayscale plane (8 bits) and colored plane (24 bits) depends upon the intensity of the pixels. The one pixel can be 1bit or 8 bits or 24 bits. Consider a digital image is assumed whose pixel value may be n bit, composed of n number of 1-bit planes from 0 to n-1-bit plane. For instance, consider a grey scaled image that contains the bit plane value from 0 to 7 since the greyscale image has a pixel value of 8 bits. This image is divided into 8 slices. These 8 slices are divided into 2 parts such most significant bits (MSB) and the least significant bits (MSB). Since LSB does not hold important data hence it is the perfect place for inserting the watermark bits. In the process of implanted the watermark bit of the important technique, the substitution method is used. The least significant bit is replaced by the watermark bits. LSB is used in this operation since it does not affect the quality of the image as well as the secret information cannot notice by the naked eye. LSB method holds some of the disadvantages such as lack of robustness, receptive to noise, scaling and cropping.

Image downgrading is also considered as the substitution system. In this system, both the cover and secret message are images in nature. For the high-security system, the image downgrading method is used for exchanging the secret information. The main objective of this technique is to transmit secret images in the same dimension of cover images. Any four least significant bits of the cover image has been selected and those bits are replaced by the most significant bits of the secret images. During extracting the secret images from the cover image the least significant bits of the embedded image holds the most significant bits of the secret image. The quality of the cover images does not degrade hence it cannot be noticed by the naked eye.

• *Gray Level Modification*

In a gray level modification, the grey level pixels are mapped to data pixels without embedding or hiding it and use the conception of even and odd numbers in mapping the data in the cover image. Mostly in gray level modification technique, even-numbered pixel values are mapped with zero and odd-numbered pixel values are mapped with one. The gray level modification method is characterized by its lower computational complexity and high capacity data transfer.

• *Pixel Value Differencing*

Pixel value differencing was initially developed by Da Chun et al in 2003. Initially, the cover image is divided into a non-overlapping block having two connecting pixels.

They are further modified into two block differences. They found that the larger the difference in original pixel value, there will be a greater the modification. They also found that the implanted secret information bits' number depends on the pixel case in the smooth area or pixel case in the edge area. The difference between adjacent pixels is less in the smooth area whereas it is more in the edge area. Thus, the data that is implanted into edge area pixels is more than implanted into the smooth area. This technique is better than LSB in watermarked image quality and imperceptibility. The PVD used for secure communication and to overcome attacks.

In this concept, the authors discuss how to secure communication and overcome attacks using PVD. There are various approaches such as the PVD method which is vulnerable to histogram analysis. He also discusses the benefits of a combination of modulus function and PVD (pixel value differencing).

- *Quantization Index Modulation (QIM)*

Quantization Index Modulation (QIM) technique is also called as host interference rejection method, as which host signal does not undergo the decoding process. It is based on embedding information in the cover message by first index modulation or through the embedded information. Then, the host signal is quantized with a quantizer or (sequence of quantizes). The quantization index modulation (QIM) technique is specialized for the ability to control robustness and high implanting capacity. This technique is mainly used in steganography purposes and also in digital watermarking.

- *Multiple Base Notational Systems (MBNS)*

Multiple Base Notational System (MBNS) steganography is based on converting secret data into symbols in a notational system that has multiple bases. Then, modifying the pixels of the host image, within which the remainders of values of the constituent that are divided by bases will be equal to symbols. Briefly, it is known that the binary number system (base 2) is the main basis of the computer. Most frequently the secret message used is in the type of binary stream and the important point to be noted is that each symbol is of one bit (in size). Therefore, to engraft extra knowledge into the busy areas, the message will appear as an integer number (by using a variable base system). That means the message will be reborn into a series of symbols that have {different /completely different} info carrying skills depends on different bases used. The greater base can cause additional data in the corresponding image. In this concept, the authors introduced a $(2n + 1)$ base system employing a methodology referred to as Exploiting Modification Direction (EMD). A unique strategy to cover information is an established supported mistreatment combination between VQ and MBNS. The MBNS (multiple base notational system) techniques are characterized by high payload capacity is achieved, better invisibility than PVD (pixel value differencing) and better PSNR than PVD.

- *Prediction Based Steganography*

In predication based steganography, a theme supported prediction based mostly steganography is developed. The prophetical cryptography approach is introduced as an answer to the matter of stego image distortion (which came from embedding data by modifying the values of the element directly), as 'prediction based mostly steganography' predicts element values using a predictor that estimates input image element values. The prediction-based mostly Steganography technique is characterized by high payload capability. This theme hide tree evidenced superior with nearly 99.85% capability of embedding.

Time Domain Method

Transform Domain applies image transformation and manipulation of the algorithmic rule. In remodel domain steganography, embedding the key needs transforming the image from the spatial domain to the frequency domain by victimization any of the transforms, for example, distinct circular function remodel (DCT), Discrete Wavelet remodels (DWT), and Singular Value Decomposition (SVD). Once the transformation process, the embedding method is drained correct transform coefficients. (Fkirin, Attiya, & El-Sayed, A. 2016).

- *Discrete Cosine Transformation*

Discrete trigonometric function remodels (DCT) relies on transforming signal or image from the spatial domain to the frequency domain. The DCT split the image into four up to spectral sub-bands (parts) of various significant concerning the visual quality of the image. Embedding positions Choices:

(i) Low-frequency coefficients: dangerous physical property, as a result of the human eye is sensitive to noise thereon because it contains the image visual components.
(ii) High-frequency coefficients: dangerous robustness, because the image may be corrupted through noise attacks or compression
(iii) Middle-frequency coefficients: sensible physical property and lustiness, therefore it's the best selection.

Assume that X is that the original greyscale image with size N1XN2, and also the watermark W with size M1XM2.

In W, the value of the marked pixels is ones, and also the price of others is zeros. The first image is described as:

$$X = \{zero \leq i < N1, zero \leq j < N2\}$$

Where, x (i, j) Î represents the intensity of the picture element x (i, j) and L represents the bits range of every pixel.

The watermark is diagrammatical as:

$$W = \{w(i, j), zero \leq i < M1, zero \leq j < M2\}$$

For each 8x8 image block for watermark embedding only (64x M1XM2 N1XN2) coefficients are employed. Where the amount of embedded data into the image is determined by the quantitative relation M1XM2 N1XN2.

Generally, to realize a lot of strength, the amount of embedded info ought to be reduced.

During the embedding method, the sender 1st splits the image into 8×8 blocks. Then, acting DCT on every block encodes one secret message bit. Next, choose a pseudorandom block that will code the message bit. After that, the watermark is embedded within the coefficients of middle band frequencies, as shown within the figure. Finally, apply inverse DCT (IDCT) to map back the coefficients to the space domain.

During the extraction method, initially, apply DCT to each watermarked image and the original image. Then, extract permuted knowledge by ultimately apply IDCT. The DCT is characterized by the foremost sturdy technique to lossy compression and Image visibility is protected. However, the drawbacks of this methodology are that Block impact image cropping impact.

- *Discrete Wavelet Transforms*

Wavelet rework is employed in a very big selection in signal processing applications and compression. It separates the signal to a line of basic functions that are called wavelets. Separate wave rework (DWT) is described as AN economical and extremely versatile methodology for decomposing signals sub-bands. In recent years, the JPEG committee releases a replacement customary of image secret writing is called 'JPEG-2000' that relies on DWT. DWT is employed in a very big selection in signal process applications, for instance, audio, video and image compression.

just in case of one-dimensional DWT, the image is rotten into four bands denoted by Low-Low (LL) level, poker (HL) level, Low-High (LH) level, and High-High (HH) level, as shown in Figure five (a). Where H is considered as high-pass filter (High frequency) and L is considered as low-pass filter (Low frequency).

In case of, Multi-Level separate wave rework. This represents the image when applying 3 times of DWT. The image consists of frequency areas of LL1, LH1, HL1, and HH1. The LL1 (low-frequency area) is rotten onto sub-level frequency area data of LL2, LH2, HL2, HH2. By applying the previous decomposition once more and once more the image will be rotten onto N level wave transformation. Once N decomposition is reached, it'll be 3N+1 sub-bands containing the multi-resolution sub-bands (LLN) and HLx, LHx and HHx, where, x has a limit from one to N. As the most essential a part of image is focused at LLx (lower frequency sub-bands), the embedding of the watermark during this sub-bands can cause a tangle because this might scale back the standard of the image significantly. Otherwise, HHx (high-frequency sub-bands) contains the textures and edges of the image and the changes on such sub-bands cannot be detected by human naked eyes. So, the embedding method is done on the coefficients of high-frequency sub-bands. Once implanting watermark, perform inverse discrete ripple Transformations (IDWT). These transformations are applied to get the watermarked image. To extract the watermark, first, execute N-level DWT on the watermarked image. Then, find the implanting locations. Finally, perform a comparison between the watermarked image and canopy image to obtain the watermark. The DWT is characterized by physical property and Robustness. However, the drawbacks of this methodology are that Long compression time, High procedure value, Noise/blur getting ready to edges of pictures.

- *Singular Value Decomposition (SVD)*

Singular Value Decomposition could be a mathematical technique supported an algebra theorem that declares that the oblong matrix (A) is analyzed into 3 matrices: U (Orthogonal matrix), S (Diagonal matrix), and V (Transpose of an orthogonal matrix)

The theory is given sometimes like:

$$A = USVT$$

For Embedding: Apply SVD to the first image:

$$A = USVT$$

Add watermark to the SVs of the square matrix of the first image equation may be the sum of S and kW,

$$D = S + kW$$

Apply SVD to the changed new matrix resultant from step2:

$$D = UWSWVWT$$

Get the watermarked image by mistreatment the modified matrix:

$$AW = USWVT$$

Where, A is that the original image, W is that the watermark image, AW is that the watermarked image, k could be an issue that controls the watermark strength.
For Extraction:
Apply SVD to the watermarked image.

$$AW^* = U * SW * V * T$$

Reason the matrix that contains the watermark.

$$D^* = UWSW * VWT$$ Acquire the watermark. $W^* = D^* - SK$

Where * could be a mark of potential corruption attributable to attacks. The SVD is characterized by resultant matrices size from SVD isn't mounted (square or rectangle) and Image singular values (SVs) that preserve image most energy, resist against attacks and having intrinsic algebraic image properties. However, the downside of this methodology is diagonal that may seem within the extracted watermark.

Spread Spectrum Steganography

In the spread spectrum method, the authors projected a ramification spectrum methodology based on spreading the narrowband information measure of a signal across a band of frequencies. In this, an approach depends on the unfold spectrum is given. In this approach, the key knowledge was embedded in GF (2m) Galois Field. The authors given correlation in addition to bit aware conception with unfold spectrum steganography. They projected 2 increased knowledge of hiding approaches. The unfold spectrum methodology is characterized by lustiness versus applied mathematics attacks.

Model-Based Steganography

Model-based mostly steganography could be a model that is presented to beat the weaknesses within the data activity embedding method such as issues that faces abstraction domain, Stego image distortions, and modifications. The authors projected 'model-based steganography' supported applied mathematics properties of the cover medium. This model is taken into account as statistics aware steganography or adjustive steganography. This new methodology helps to implant secret message taking care of overcoming previous drawbacks. During this methodology, the embedding method works as follows. The quilt image was divided into 2 halves: half that wasn't altered throughout embedding and therefore the different part was accustomed carry secret message while not modifying the quilt applied mathematics properties. The hidden message is meant to be a random uniform stream of bits. By mistreatment AN entropy decoder (which is chosen in line with chance conditional distribution), the hidden message was processed. For extracting, first, an entropy encoder was used. Then, the stego message was separated into 2 parts. After that, chance distribution was calculated; finally, the key message is obtained. AN adjustive steganography survey is introduced.

Sobel Operator Based Edge Adaptive Image Steganography based on LSBMR

The main feature of the image is the edges. Sobel edge detection techniques are used to obtain the edge. Based on secret data, the data hiding units that act as gradient image cover is selected. (Smitha & Baburaj, 2018)

Hybrid Technique

Some researchers mix 2 or additional approaches to the previous techniques to procedure a replacement technique. Due to this mix, the disadvantages of 1 method are going to be removed due to the result of the opposite used technique. Therefore, hybrid techniques are higher than individual previous techniques. In a hybrid watermarking technique combined fragile and sturdy techniques are introduced to boost authentication, verification, integrity and copyright protection at an equivalent time. In a hybrid DWT-SVD technique is projected by mistreatment human sensory system Model and compared with SVD solely. The comparison evidenced that the hybrid methodology is healthier in PSNR and BCR (Bit Correlation Rate). In a hybrid DCT-SVD technique is projected for copyright protection. This methodology is additional sturdy, conjointly achieves better PSNR and correlation. In a hybrid methodology combined of DWT, DCT and SVD are projected and compared with that used solely DWT and that used DCT and SVD. The comparison evidenced that the hybrid methodology is healthier in PSNR and correlation. In, a hybrid methodology combines the 3 techniques DCT, DWT and SVD are given and located that the results are improved. A hybrid technique combines DWT and DCT is projected whereas a hybrid technique that mixes DWT and SVD is developed in this way. In these ways, the PSNR price was improved and the lustiness was high. In this method a hybrid technique combines DWT, DCT and SVD are projected. The experimental results show that the image will overcome JPEG lossy compression and cropping of a picture. (Fkirin, Attiya, & El-Sayed, A. 2016)

LITERATURE REVIEW ON ENCRYPTION TECHNIQUE ON STEGANOGRAPHY

In 2011, S. Song et al. projected an innovative system which will mix the steganography and cryptography into one system. There'll be no separate computations for steganography and cryptography. Thence this method desires lesser computations than existing strategies, whereas maintaining the upper-security levels. The core of this method is the LSB matching technique and mathematicians operating in stream ciphers. For steganography, greyscale pictures are utilized and mathematician functions are applied for cryptanalytic purpose and to manage the pseudo-random increment and decrement of LSBs. Experimental results show that this method is extremely abundant safer from steganalysis attacks. (Singh, 2015)

In 2014, D. E. M. Ahmed and O.O. Khalifa in a gift away during which LSB image steganography is employed alongside Elliptic Curve Cryptography (ECC) to supply bigger security to knowledge. Within the projected work sender is allowed to settle on an appropriate cowl image and secret data. During this method, secret data is initial encrypted exploitation elliptic curve cryptography so this ciphered secret data is embedded into cowl image exploitation least vital bit image steganography technique. (Singh, 2015)

In 2014, Nouf A. Al-Otaibi et al. designed a replacement system known as a 2-layer security system for concealment sensitive data on personal computers. They divide the system into 2 layers particularly the cryptography layer and steganography layer. For the steganography layer, LSB algorithmic program is employed and for the cryptography layer, AES algorithmic program is employed. This method is meant on the visual basic platform. Authors have conjointly done a study on up hidden capability by conducted many tests. They use one to two bits of LSB to infix secret messages in cowl image. Thirty differing types of fastened size pictures are utilized in their study to explore the info dependency and security of this technique. They conclude that the result of 1LSB and 2LSB is lowest in stego image however with 3LSB, 4LSB, 5LSB, 6LSB and 7LSB the image is distorted to visible levels and have a terrible quality of stego image that isn't ideal for image steganography. (Singh, 2015)

In 2014, M. R. Islam et al projected a replacement improved version of LSB image steganography supported economical filtering technique exploitation standing a bit. Projected work conjointly uses the AES algorithmic program for cryptography proving further layer of security. In their work image pictures are used due to their uncompressed nature and image pictures are best suited to LSB based mostly steganography. During this technique, initial secret knowledge is encrypted exploitation AES algorithmic program so this encrypted knowledge is embedded into the image exploitation steganographic method. The improved steganographic technique is projected which may infix additional secret data exploitation filtering based mostly algorithmic program and for the filtering purpose savings bank of the image is employed. Projected work conjointly makes use of standing bit for checking insertion and extraction of secret messages. Experimental results demonstrate that this technique has high embedding capability than a basic LSB algorithmic program. PSNR values also are high due to high stego image quality. All the experimental results prove that this technique is additional economical than the ancient LSB technique for concealment of the info in image pictures. (Singh, 2015)

In 2014, S. Krishna Gopal et al. projected a system as a whole that contains the options of each steganography and cryptography. They create the use of Chaos-based mostly cryptanalytic strategies to develop a cryptography algorithmic program. Chaotic supply and cat maps are used as a base for his or her image cryptography algorithmic program. In their technique of image cryptography, the key secret is altered once encrypting each constituent of the image with the appliance of Arnold's Cat map. This idea of sterilization secret key once cryptography makes this method additional sturdy against varied attacks. Within the next part, encrypted image is embedded into cowl image exploitation image steganography. Simulation results are administrated on the idea of some parameters like SSIM index and PSNR. Results show that their system has zero.981 SSIM index worth and forty-seven.71 dB PSNR. Thus it generates excellent quality of stego image and it's additional economical and secure against attacks and may be used for real-time image cryptography and transmission. (Singh, 2015)

In 2015, D. Debnath et al projected a security theme within which steganography is employed at the side of cryptography to supply higher security to embedded knowledge. In their methodology, initial knowledge is encrypted then it's embedded into cowl image exploitation steganographic methodology. projected rule transforms any quite message into text with the assistance of manipulation tables, then carries out hill cipher strategies to that and eventually hides the info into red, blue, and inexperienced pixels of the duvet image. They use a range of image quality parameters like MSE, PSNR, AD, SC, NAE, and MD. (Singh, 2015).

APPLICATIONS OF STEGANOGRAPHY

1. Audio Steganography is used in both commercial and noncommercial sectors to prevent unauthorized persons from becoming aware of the existence of secret information.
2. In the business world, audio Steganography is used to secret information such as new chemical formulae, plans, and tactics.
3. In defensive sectors both the terrorists as well as military personnel use to keep their communications secret and to coordinate attacks on their opponent.
4. In the project ARTUS1, audio and video steganography techniques were used to implant animation parameters into audio and video content.

It is also used in the forensic department for inserting the hidden data into audio files and used in the authentication process, voice test / spoken words, music business for monitoring the songs over broadcast radio.

Current Applications of Steganography

Researchers at the University of Wisconsin-Madison and Amherst College are recently undergoing researches on Machine learning. A new form of Steganography is being applied in the domain of machine learning called "training set camouflage". Their framework has been published in a paper pre-published on arXiv, that's machine learning agent is used to hide the intention and its main goal is used to hide the information from third-party observers.

In this recent study, the researches at UW Madison specifically considers a scenario where the machine agent (Alice) acts as a sender, second agent (Bob) acts as a receiver and the secret information is the task to implement. Alice tries to send a message to Bob without eavesdropping third party agent (Eve); the message holds a secret classification task.

The Researches of UW Madison write in their paper, Consider Alice has a training set on illicit/illegal machine learning classification tasks. Alice wants Bob to learn the task without eavesdropping third-party agents such as Eve. Alice sends either the training set or the trained model to Bob.

In this scenario envisaged by the researchers at UW Madison, a third-party agent named Eve takes the role of data verification, that's monitoring the communication process between Alice and Bob. When Eve is dubious about what Alice is sending Bob, she can abort the communication process between them. And it refuses the process of data exchanges between Alice and Bob. Eve acts as an auditor who tries to figure out whether the training dataset is permissible before passing the dataset onto the learner (Bob).

Alice masquerades the communication for it to look prosaic to Eve while avoiding excessive coding tricks with Bob beforehand. Since if the private training set is sent, it would reveal Alice's intention; sending the model parameters direction will also raise suspicion, the researchers explain in their paper.

The Steganography approach devised by the researchers is to devise Alice to compute a secondary training set on an entirely different and seemingly amiable classification task, without raising Eve's suspicion. It does this by finding the dataset which seems to be applied to a particular task, while it can teach an agent to perform well in different task. By treating the secondary training set with a standard learning algorithm, Bob can approximately recover the classifier on the original task.

The Steganography approach devised by the researchers in the field of machine learning was a bit of coincidence, as it rose out as an unrelated project. The developed system should be able to create a series of teaching sets, this system encouraged them to investigate whether an agent (machine agent/ Alice) could teach another agent (Bob) to complete a task without masquerading with another task. The researches have carried out a series of experiments using the classification tasks and demonstrated the feasibility of this approach. This technique helps to hide a lot of information by simply leveraging the technique, several models can execute this type of technique. Further researches have been carried out in the steganography concept. Others, such as Scott Alfeld, are investigating adversarial settings in which an attacker unsettles the training instances rather than selecting a subset as in the case of training set masquerade. (Fadelli, 2019).

Security Algorithm

The security algorithm used for Steganography analysis is High Capacity and Steganography Security using a discrete wavelet transform model. (Reddy & Raja, 2009).

HCSSD Encoder

The most plans behind the planned algorithmic program are moving ridge primarily based fusion. It involves merging the moving ridge decomposition of the normalized version of each duvet image and therefore the payload into one united result. Social control is finished so the picture element varies of the image lies between zero.0 to 1.0 rather than the number varies (0, 255). Thus we tend to convert the number varies (0, 255) of pixels into floating purpose values between zero.0 and 1.0. This normalized picture element value is fed as input to the floating purpose filters which ends up in a reconstruction of the remodeled image with higher accuracy compared to direct number values of the pixels as input. social control could be a method on each duvet image and therefore the payload to ensure picture element worth don't exceed their most value of 1 thanks to modifying corresponding coefficients of the duvet image and payload throughout fusion. Each cowl image and payload are converting into the DWT domain. Further, apply DWT on the payload to extend the protection level. The one united resultant matrix is obtained, by the addition of moving ridge coefficients of the individual sub-bands of the duvet image and payload is given by the below equation.

$$F(x, y) = \alpha C(x, y) + \beta P(x, y)$$
$$\alpha + \beta = 1$$

Wherever F has changed DWT coefficients, C is that the original DWT coefficients and P is that the approximation band DWT coefficients of the payload. Also, alpha and beta area units are the embedding strength factors. Since alpha and beta area unit has chosen such the payload isn't preponderantly seen within the Stego image obtained within the spatial domain and conjointly for full utilization of the information measure of each the duvet Image and therefore the payload. Once fusion is finished, we tend to apply Inverse distinct moving ridge remodel (IDWT) followed by renormalization to induce the Stego image within the spatial domain.

HCSSD Decoder

It's used for retrieval of payload from the Stegoimage. The Stego image is normalized, and so DWT is taken. The extraction method involves subtracting the DWT coefficients of the initial cowl image from the DWT coefficients of the Stego image. It's then followed by the decipherment of the subtracted coefficients. Then beginning of IDWT on these coefficients is applied followed by the second IDWT solely with relevance the approximation band of the primary IDWT coefficients of the payload. Finally, denormalization is finished to induce back the payload in the spatial domain. (Reddy & Raja, 2009).

STEGANALYSIS

The process of analyzing the hidden message in the given carrier using different steganography techniques is called steganalysis. There may be various challenges in steganalysis, such as the suspect message may be encrypted, may/may not be inserted, the message may contain noise or irrelevant data and sometime the messages may be encrypted. There are various attacks in steganalysis such as stego-only-attack, known message attack, chosen stego attack, etc. There are various software tools for detecting digital forensic evidence. (Richer, 2003)

Steganalysis Attacks

There are four levels of steganalysis attacks based on the prior knowledge of the attacker gained in the learning phase.

Stego-Cover Only Attack (SCOA)

SCOA is that the primary level attack model wherever the steganalysis offender is assumed to own access solely to a collection of stego-covers. Whereas the offender has no channel providing access to the corresponding original cowl before knowledge concealing, all told sensible SCOA, the offender still has some data of the present natural covers. Within the learning part, the offender will use the applied mathematics analysis technique to model the distribution of the natural covers. The aim is to research the covers within the open channel so verify the presence of steganography. Equivalent to the case in point of fact, the offender might monitor all public channels. Once finishing the SCOA learning part, the offender enters the challenging part. (Douglas, Bailey, Leeney, & Curran, 2017)

Known Cover Attack (KCA)

KCA is an associate attack model for steganalysis wherever, additionally to the previous data beneath SCOA, the offender additionally has many pairs of the first cover and its corresponding stego version. The amount of pairs is finite inside the polynomial quality. Within the learning part, the offender can't solely do the educational in SCOA; however, additionally, learn from the pairs of the first cowl and their stego version. equivalent to the cases in point of fact, additionally to observation all open channels, the offender also can steal original samples by hacking into the steganography system or send spies to steal the first samples from the within. Once finishing the KCA learning part, the offender enters the challenging part. (Karampidis, Kavallieratou, & Papadourakis, 2018).

Chosen Cover Attack (CCA)

Additionally, to the previous data beneath the KCA, the offender also can invoke many times of embedding or extraction method of this steganography system. The amount of the invoking operation is finite inside the polynomial quality. (It ought to be noted that the embedding and extraction rule is already open, and therefore the invoking operation is to invoke many times of the key used for this secret communication whereas the key itself remains secret.) Within the learning part, additionally, to the KCA learning part, the offender will invoke the embedding or extraction method to be told the changes of the quilt. {The cowl | the duvet |the quilt} used for extraction is a stego-cover or a particular cast cover by the offender. equivalent to the cases in point of fact, the offender will remotely management the steganography system to implement knowledge embedding or extraction many times or instigate the user of the system to come to many operation results. Once finishing the CCA learning part, the offender enters the challenging part. (Ke, Liu, Zhang, Su & Yang, 2018)

Adaptive Chosen Cover Attack (ACCA)

Once the CCA challenges part, if the attack fails, the offender will still restart the CCA learning part on the targeted system and may repeat the educational and therefore the challenge phases many times till the attack succeeds. SCOA is considered the passive attack whereas the opposite higher level attacks area unit the active attacks. The higher than classification is especially supported the attackers' accesses to the quilt instead of their totally different usage rights of the key message, as a result of it's the covers that the offender will directly get within the channel, and therefore the steganography technology chiefly depends on the modification of the quilt to deliver further info. For the key message, the knowledge hider doesn't care regarding its content, and therefore the content doesn't offer attackers with abundant reference for future attacks as a result of the message is encoded or encrypted before embedding. If it's random-like, the influence on the quilt could also be indistinguishable. (Ke et.al, 2018)

SOFTWARE TOOLS TO IMPLEMENT STEGANOGRAPHY

There are various proprietary licensed and free software tools available to implement Steganography. (Kolla, 2017) Some of them are as follows

Camouflage

This tool hides any type of file within another file of your choice. The camouflaged seems to be the normal file i.e. not making any attention to it. For additional security, you can lock the camouflages file by a password. It will open only after the authentication successfully done. This tool is for Windows operating system. The limitations in this tool, camouflage files are open only with the help of this tool i.e. both sides of communication parties should have this tool.

S-tool

S-tool is an extremely simple tool to do steganography that can hide data within the various formats of image files. The user interface tool supports algorithms like IDEA, DES, and triple-DES, etc. A passphrase is used to reveal the hidden content in the image. Passphrase means a password. The passphrase must be the same on both sides to exchange passphrase is also an important thing here. Most of the place, the passphrase may be the filename or in some pattern. (Magee, 2018)

ADVANTAGE & DISADVANTAGES OF STEGANOGRAPHY

Though the Steganography is the strongest technique to secure data, it has its advantage and disadvantages because no systems are perfect.

Pros

1. As it hides data within another form of data, it is difficult to find whether the media contains any secret message or not.
2. It can be able applied to any other form of data like audio, video, binary files, protocol, etc.
3. To avoid tampering of data or media by intruder or attacker, hashing techniques are used to find whether the transmitted data has tampered or not i.e. At the sender side, a fixed hash value for the original message of variable size is encrypted and sends along with the message to be transmitted in the media. At the receiver side, the received message is decrypted and the hash from the

decrypted message is compared with the hash sent. If both are equal, it is surely no tampering occurs, else tampering occurs in the message transmitted (Rout & Mishra, 2014)
4. Steganography of the cryptographic message provides double security.

Cons

1. If the original file size is known or estimated, then it will be suspected whether the file is treated with some security techniques like Steganography to transmit a secret message
2. If the data embedded within the cover media exceeds its threshold capacity, then it leads the attacker to suspect because distortion happened in the stego media.
3. This technique is even often used by wrong people like terrorists, criminals to share information for an offensive purpose like attacks on people, etc, which can't be easily suspected or detected by people in defense which maybe leads to massive destruction. (Pawar, & Kakde, 2014). For example, the terrorist Osama bin Laden is said to have a message which is hidden in the pornographic web page and sports chat room by using steganography techniques along with cryptography. (Steganos, 2001)

CONCLUSION

In this chapter, the digitalized vision of Steganography is studied briefly. In the current period preserving secret messages is highly difficult in front of third parties. This can be easily achieved by modern steganography techniques. The term Steganography has many applications mainly used in forensics department for investigation of criminal cases, fraud detection, and illegal authorization and stealing of information, etc.

REFERENCES

Agarwal, M. (2013). *Text steganographic approaches: a comparison.* arXiv preprint arXiv:1302.2718

Bhallamudi, S. (2015). *Image Steganography* (Rep.). Retrieved https://www.scribd.com/document/377269663/EE7150-finalproject-Finalreport-Savitha-Bhallamudi-pdf#

Codr, J. (2009). *Unseen: An Overview of Steganography and Presentation of Associated Java Application C-Hide*. Citeseer.

Douglas, M., Bailey, K., Leeney, M., & Curran, K. (2017). An overview of steganography techniques applied to the protection of biometric data. *Multimedia Tools and Applications, 77*(13), 17333–17373. doi:10.100711042-017-5308-3

Fadelli, I. (2019). *A new approach for steganography among machine learning agents*. Retrieved from https://techxplore.com/news/2019-01-approach-steganography-machine-agents.html

Febryan, A., Purboyo, T. W., & Saputra, R. E. (2017). Steganography Methods on Text, Audio, Image and Video: A Survey. *International Journal of Applied Engineering Research, 12*(21), 10485–10490.

Fkirin, A., Attiya, G., & El-Sayed, A. (2016). Steganography Literature Survey, Classification and Comparative Study. *Communications on Applied Electronics, 5*(10), 13–22. doi:10.5120/cae2016652384

Jayaram, P., Ranganatha, H. R., & Anupama, H. S. (2011). Information hiding using audio steganography–a survey. *The International Journal of Multimedia & Its Applications, 3*(3), 86–96. doi:10.5121/ijma.2011.3308

Karampidis, K., Kavallieratou, E., & Papadourakis, G. (2018). A review of image steganalysis techniques for digital forensics. *Journal of Information Security and Applications, 40*, 217-235.

Ke, Y., Liu, J., Zhang, M. Q., Su, T. T., & Yang, X. Y. (2018). Steganography Security: Principle and Practice. *IEEE Access: Practical Innovations, Open Solutions, 6*, 73009–73022. doi:10.1109/ACCESS.2018.2881680

Kolla, A. (2017). *List of 10 Best Steganography Tools to Hide Data*. Retrieved from https://www.geekdashboard.com/best-steganography-tools/

Magee, K. (2018). *CISSP – Steganography, An Introduction Using S-Tools*. Retrieved from https://resources.infosecinstitute.com/cissp-steganography-an-introduction-using-s-tools/

Malviya, S., Saxena, M., & Khare, D. A. (2012). Audio steganography by different methods. *International Journal of Emerging Technology and Advanced Engineering, 2*(7), 371–375.

Olguin, J. (2016). Steganography... what is that? [Web log post]. Retrieved from https://www.trustwave.com/en-us/resources/blogs/spiderlabs-blog/steganography-what-is-that/

Pawar, S. S., & Kakde, V. (2014). Review on Steganography for Hiding Data. *International Journal of Computer Science and Mobile Computing*, *4*, 225–229.

Rani, N., & Chaudhary, J. (2013). Text Steganography Techniques: A Review. *International Journal of Engineering Trends and Technology*, *4*(7), 2231–5381.

Rathore, S. (2015). Steganography: Basics and Digital Forensics. *International Journal of Science. Engineering and Technology Research*, *4*(7), 2589–2593.

Reddy, H. M., & Raja, K. B. (2009). High capacity and security steganography using discrete wavelet transform. *International Journal of Computer Science and Security*, *3*(6), 462.

Richer, P. (2003). Steganalysis: Detecting hidden information with computer forensic analysis. SANS/GIAC Practical Assignment for GSEC Certification, SANS Institute, 6.

Rout, H., & Mishra, B. K. (2014). Pros and Cons of Cryptography, Steganography and Perturbation techniques. *IOSR Journal of Electronics and Communication Engineering*, 76-81.

Singh, S. (2015). *Literature Review On Digital Image Steganography and Cryptography Algorithms*. doi:10.13140/RG.2.1.1037.9124

Siper, A., Farley, R., & Lombardo, C. (2005). The Rise of Steganography. In *Computer Science and Information Systems*. Pace University. Retrieved from http://csis.pace.edu/~ctappert/srd2005/d1.pdf

Smitha, G. L., & Baburaj, E. (2018). Sobel edge detection technique implementation for image steganography analysis. *Biomedical Research*. doi:10.4066/biomedicalresearch.29-17-1212

Steganos. (2001). *Steganos responds to the current demands for a ban on cryptography and steganography* [Press release]. Retrieved from https://www.steganos.com/uploads/media/Steganos_Press_Release_2001-09-20_Steganography.pdf

ADDITIONAL READING

Doshi, R., Jain, P., & Gupta, L. (2012). Steganography and its applications in security. *International Journal of Modern Engineering Research*, *2*(6), 4634–4638.

Nissar, A., & Mir, A. H. (2010). Classification of steganalysis techniques: A study. *Digital Signal Processing*, *20*(6), 1758–1770. doi:10.1016/j.dsp.2010.02.003

Poornima, R., & Iswarya, R. J. (2013). An overview of digital image steganography. *International Journal of Computer Science & Engineering Survey, 4*(1), 23–31. doi:10.5121/ijcses.2013.4102

Saha, B., & Sharma, S. (2012). Steganographic techniques of data hiding using digital images. *Defence Science Journal, 62*(1), 11–18. doi:10.14429/dsj.62.1436

Swetha, V., Prajith, V., & Kshema, V. (2015). Data hiding using video steganography-a survey. International Journal of Science. *Engineering and Computer Technology, 5*(6), 206.

Varsha, R. S. (2015). Data Hiding Using Steganography and Cryptography. *International Journal of Computer Science and Mobile Computing, 4*(4), 802–805.

Wikipedia contributors. (2019, March 6). Cryptography. In Wikipedia, The Free Encyclopedia. Retrieved 10:08, March 16, 2019, from https://en.wikipedia.org/w/index.php?title=Cryptography&oldid=886442511

Wikipedia contributors. (2019). Steganography. In Wikipedia, The Free Encyclopedia. Retrieved 10:05, March 16, 2019, from https://en.wikipedia.org/w/index.php?title=Steganography&oldid=886442587

KEY TERMS AND DEFINITIONS

AES: A symmetric key algorithm in which the same key is used for encrypting and decrypting the message.

Cryptanalysis: The process of decrypting the message without using the private key.

HCSSD: High capacity and security steganography using discrete wavelet transform.

Line Shift Coding: Line shift coding is the process of changing a document by shifting the location of text in vertical direction.

Microdot: Microdot is a text or image that is reduced in size to prevent the detection by illicit recipients.

Steganalysis: The process of detecting the hidden message using steganography.

Word Shift Coding: This technique is to hide the information in text document by shifting the word slightly.

Chapter 10
Introduction to Email, Web, and Message Forensics

Mohammad Zunnun Khan
Integral University, India

Mohd. Shahid Husain
iD https://orcid.org/0000-0003-4864-9485
Ibri College of Applied Sciences, Oman

Mohd. Shoaib
Aligarh Muslim University, India

ABSTRACT

With the advent of information and communication technologies, e-mail is one of the prime tools for communication. Almost everyone uses emails for business communications as well as for sharing personal information. E-mail is vulnerable against cybercrimes. This chapter focuses on the basic concepts of web forensics and then provides an insight about the e-mailing policies, email architecture, and existing investigation techniques used by forensic investigators. Most of the organizations implement some standard e-mailing policies; however, it is not sufficient to handle and prevent the digital crimes. We need to monitor and investigate emails for proper check. This chapter discusses some prominent tools and techniques through which forensic experts can gather and analyze data about suspected email accounts for investigation and produce evidence in the court of law.

DOI: 10.4018/978-1-7998-1558-7.ch010

INTRODUCTION

In the current decade, it is very rare to find a device that cannot be used online. Today the internet has become ubiquitous. High-speed connections have given us 24x7 connectivity for activities like browsing, paying bills, sharing our personal life on social networks, entertainment with online audio and video streaming, working studying or even some sort of cybercrime is also committed using the internet (Suzuki S., 2005).

Every location, individual, industry or organization can be a target and the only actual requirement is being online at some point. Cybercrime has evolved and created a whole industry around it. And its budget reaches $2 trillion by 2019 and as per the Global Risk report 2016 from the world economic forum; this is simply a huge figure. Cybercrime is not just only related to money: there are a lot of online social predators, stalkers, pirates, bullies, identity thieves, etc. Well, there are so many people for investigating this sort of crime (Graham J., 1999).

Since it is not a simple task only experts can do these types of tasks. Those who want to become a certified digital professional, can acquire certification from one of the best certified cyber forensics professionals i.e. ISC (Tzerefos, 1997). These are various interesting topics; the CCFE needs Web, Email, and messaging forensics experts that can gather evidence which is strong enough to represent in the court of law.

WEB FORENSICS

If a crime is committed over the internet then that would be known as Web forensics. Perpetrators of hacking or cracking, child pornography and some sort of identity theft require delicate and expert skills with proper knowledge that can be traced back. The criminals can only be successfully penalized if a strong amount of evidence against them is found (Marwan Al-Zarouni, 2004) & (Crocker D., 2009). For these types of cases, history log of internet, server logs are most important. It is also a very interesting fact that most of the offenders search over the internet for advice on how one can conduct a crime. Evidences can be found on both the client-side (temp files, index.dat, cookies, favorites, list of the website visited, downloaded, files related to the registry) and also on server side (while analyzing server you may get precious registers like IP addresses, timestamps of the different visitor, etc.). Again, with proper tools and knowledge, if you can gather this sort of evidence; it is a great step towards building a strong case (Natarajan Meghanathan, 2009).

Mandiant Web Historian (Resnick P Ed., 2001) helps the user while reviewing URLs that are pre-stored in the computer history of most commonly used browsers. The tool helps the forensics examiner to judge how the intruder, where the intruder, what and when the intruder had visited the different websites. Parse version of specific web history or repetitively used searches can be used by Web Historians by giving a folder or drive path to retrieve browser's history.

A single report, generated by Web Historians, can be saved in different file formats. It contains all of the browser history and internet activity. Index.dat analyzer is a forensic tool to examine the contents of index files (in .dat format) (Marwan Al-Zarouni, 2004). The tool can help to browse history, cookies, and cache. The tool gives critical information about cookies (its key-value pair, web address, date and time of the first cookie was created and last used, etc.). It also supports the direct visit to those web addresses which are listed in the output of analyzer and open the uploaded/downloaded files of the website. As an added one to these tools, there are some specific tools such as total recall (AbusePipe), which can be used to enlist the hot and favorite web addresses available in the browser history.

EMAIL FORENSICS

Email communication is also on target. Because it is one of the most popular and commonalty used means of online communication, for both prospects individuals and businesses, emails are normally used by organizations to exchange most simple information, such as meeting schedules, document distribution and some sensitive information (Marwan Al-Zarouni, 2004).

While communicating with emails, the sender normally doesn't encrypt and also recipient rarely perform integrity checks, so the illegal use of emails are most common, and SMTP i.e. Simple Mail Transfer Protocol is widely used for email which doesn't include source authentication mechanism by default. Also, the Header of email metadata contains information about the sender and message path that can be manipulated quite easily.

Crimes related to Email are of different categories such as sending spam, cyber bullying, hate messages, child pornography distribution and online sexual abuse cases. Again the main issue is to find and preserve the strong evidence against criminals. The techniques for extracting data and identification of data are an essential step (Resnick P Ed., 2001). In most cases, the use of emails goes far beyond simple message exchange.

Servers are not just used to send/receive messages but also include databases, a repository for documents, log files and event manager for users. For an individual, it is the first and most important step to understanding the critical system first before collecting evidence.

To solve the dispute of sender over the message communication, the most essential requirement is to determine the receiver and sender attributes by reviewing the email's header, comparing information from fields like 'to', 'from' and 'cc' etc. for what information is on the logs of originating server.

Most of the emails spoofing cases are done using header manipulation and mail server do not enforce the user to authenticate the information normally, so it is the main challenge (Crocker D., 2009). Full non-repudiation, i.e. you can prove without a doubt that who the sender is, can be achieved by email signing with a digital signature. The signing process uses a PKI (public key infrastructure) based on asymmetric encryption, where the content of the message is hashed and then the hash is encrypted with the sender's private key. Sadly, email signing is not as massively implemented as it should be.

Encryption is the technique that can be used for protecting the contents of the email message: the public key of the recipient can be used to encrypt the content, and the message can only be read by the person who has the same set of the private key. So it will be easy to identify the person who leaks the information because it was first decrypted by the recipient (Marwan Al-Zarouni, 2004).

E-MAIL ACTORS, ROLES AND RESPONSIBILITIES

E-mail is a type of distributed service that involves several actors; each actor has a different role to achieve end-to-end mail exchange (Crocker D., 2009). These actors are as follows;

User Actors

This actor represents people or organizations or sometimes processes that serve as sources or sinks of messages. This actor can generate the message (also modify or look at the complete message). User Actors can be of four types:

Author- the creation of a message is the primary responsibility of the author. And the next responsibility of the author is to create its contents, and its list of Recipient addresses. The MHS transfers the message from the Author and delivers it to the Recipients. The MHS has an Originator role that correlates with the Author's role.

Recipient- the Recipient is a person or organization to whom the message will be delivered. The MHS has a Receiver role that correlates with the Recipient role. A Recipient is also responsible for closing the user-communication loop by either creating or submitting a new message that replies to the originator, for example, an automated reply is the Message Disposition Notification (MDN).

Return Handler- a special type of Recipient that provides notifications of completion in normal cases or failures in an exceptional case, generated by the MHS as it transfers or delivers the message. It is famously known as Bounce Handler.

Mediator- it works among author and recipient by receiving, aggregating, reformulating, and redistributing messages. It allows forwarding a message through a re-posting process. It shares several functionalities with the basic structure of MTA relaying, but with greater flexibility for both the addressing and content that is available to MTAs. It helps to maintain the integrity and originality of the original message that also includes the essential aspects of its beginning information. It does not support the creation of a new message that forwards an existing message, Reply or annotation.

Message Handling Service (MHS) Actors

These handlers are responsible for end-to-end messages transfer. These actors can generate or modify or look at only transfer data in the message. MHS Actors can be of four types. The validity of the message is ensured by MHS for posting and then submits it to a Relay. Mail Submission Agent's functionality is the responsibility of MHS. Post submission analysis is also performed that pertains to sending error and delivery notice. The Author only creates the message, but transmission issues with it are handled by the Originator.

Administrative Management Domain (ADMD) Actors

These are associated with other organizations that have their type of administrative authority, policies related to operation and decision making based on trust. ADMD Actors are of three types.

Relay

MHS-level transfer-service routing and store-and-forward functions are performed by transmitting and/or retransmitting the message to its Recipients. It also keeps the trace information but does not modify the semantics of message content.

Message contents can also be modified such as changing the form, encoding from text to binary or visa-versa. It is only based on requirements to meet the capabilities of the next hop in the MHS. As soon as a Relying is stopped to attempt to transfer a message; it converts to an Author because it sends an error in the form of a message to the original Return Address.

Gateway

It is a combination of different mail servers (syntax and semantics) of heterogeneous types. Without changing any components in the recipient/author's mail services, it can send a useful message to a recipient on the next side.

Receiver

The final delivery of a message is done by the receiver (or it sends the message to an alternate address). Filtering and other policies are enforced both before and after delivery.

E-MAIL ARCHITECTURE

E-mail system is an integration of several hardware and software components, services and protocols which provide interoperability between its users and among the components along the path of the transfer. The e-mail architecture specifies the relationship between its logical components for creation, submission, transmission, delivery and reading processes of an e-mail message.

Several communicating entities called e-mail nodes, which are essentially software units working on the application layer of the TCP/IP model, are involved in the process of e-mail delivery.

Nodes working on lower layers, such as routers and bridges, representing options to send e-mail without using SMTP are not considered in this architecture because almost all e-mail communication uses SMTP directly or indirectly. Further, proprietary nodes used for internal deliveries at sending and receiving servers are also not considered in this architecture.

E-MAIL FORENSIC INVESTIGATION TECHNIQUES

The study of E-mail forensics refers to the source and content of the e-mail as evidence to identify the actual sender and corresponding recipient of a message based on date/time of transmission, detailed record of e-mail transaction, etc. This study is based on an investigation of metadata, searching keywords, port scanning, etc. for authorship attribution and identification of e-mail scams.

Various approaches that are used for e-mail forensics are described in (Marwan Al-Zarouni, 2004) and are briefly defined below:

Header Analysis

Metadata of an email message is the forms of control information i.e. headers including headers in the message body contain information about the sender and/ or the path along of the message. Some of these may be spoofed to conceal the identity of the sender.

Bait Tactics

In this investigation, an email with HTTP: "<imgsrc>" tag at some computers having image source are monitored by the investigators and information is sent to the sender of e-mail under investigation containing a real (genuine) e-mail address. Email is opened and log entry with the IP address of the recipient. When the e-mail is opened, a log entry containing the IP address of the recipient is recorded on the http server hosting the image and thus sender is tracked. The IP address of the proxy server is recorded (of the recipient)

The sender of the email can be tracked using the log on the proxy server under investigation. If the proxy server's log is unavailable, then investigators may send the tactic email containing

a)   Embedded Java Applet that runs on the receiver's computer or
b)   Active X Object enabled HTML page.

These two techniques are used to extract the IP address of the receiver's end computer and email it back to the investigators.

Server Investigation

This particular type of investigation is done by investigating copies of delivered emails and server logs are also investigated by the team to identify the origin of that email message. On the request of the client, unintentionally purged e-mails from the clients whose recovery is impossible, may be done from Proxy servers or ISP providers as most of the store a backup copy of all email communication. Further, server logs are used to study and to trace the address of the responsible computer. But the server only stores all these for a limited period. And sometimes the investigator may face non-cooperation. Lastly, SMTP servers are used for identification of email sender. SMTP server stores sensitive data like credit card number and other data about the owner of a mailbox.

Network Device Investigation

Here, logs are maintained by the network devices (routers, etc.). The source of an email message can be investigated with the help of firewalls and switches. This investigation type is very complex and is used only when the logs of ISP or Proxy servers are unavailable for some unknown reason.

Software Embedded Identifiers

Information such as email creation including its initiator, files attached may be included along with the message by the software that is used by the sender for composing e-mail. This information may be included in the form of custom headers content as a Transport Neutral Encapsulation Format. Some vital information about the sender (like e-mail preferences) is also reviled by this type of Investigation. PST files Name and username of Windows, Machine Address, etc. of the client computer used to send e-mail messages are also investigated by this approach.

Sender Mailer Fingerprints

Identification of software handling e-mail at the server can be revealed from the Received header field and identification of software handling e-mail at the client can be ascertained by using a different set of headers like "X-Mailer" or its equivalent. These headers describe applications and their versions used at the clients to send an e-mail. This information about the client computer of the sender can be used to help investigators devise an effective plan and thus prove to be very useful.

E-MAIL FORENSIC TOOLS

There are a lot of tools which may help in investigation of emails. In this study, the source and content of email message are also examined so that an attack or the malicious intent of the intrusions may be easily investigated. These tools use GUI while providing easy to use browser format and automated reports generation, help to identify the origin and destination of the message, trace the path traversed by the message; identify spam and phishing networks, etc. This section introduces some of these tools.

eMailTrackerPro

This will analyse the headers of an e-mail to detect the logical address (IP) of the machine that is responsible for sending the message (Visualware Inc, 2014). Multiple e-mails can be traced at the same time and maintain the track easily. The geographical location, which can be traced for an IP address, works as key information for determining the threat level with the validity of an e-mail message. This tool helps pinpoint the location email source. It identifies the ISP of the email sender and contact information for the investigation purpose. The routing table will help find the actual path to the sender's IP address, also help to determine the additional location information of the sender's true location. One of the major features of this tool is reporting abuses profile and that can be sent to the ISP of the sender. On behalf of the report, ISP can then take steps to prosecute the account holder.

EmailTracer

EmailTracer (RCCF) was made by the Indian Cyber Forensics team named the Resource Centre for Cyber Forensics (RCCF), a premier centre for cyber forensics in India. It develops cyber forensic tools based on the requirements of law enforcement agencies. This tool helps trace the origination of IP address and related information from the email header, generates a detailed report of header analysis in HTML format, finds the city location details of the sender, graphically plots its route and displays the origination geographic location of the email. It also supports keyword-based searching on emails for its content.

Aid4Mail Forensic

Aid4Mail Forensic (FOOKES® Software, 2019) is e-mail investigation software that supports features like e-discovery and litigation support for forensic analysis. It supports email migration and conversion that has various mail formats including

Outlook, Windows Live Mail, m-box, etc. It can search based on date, header content and message body content in the email. Email folders and related files can be processed even when un-mounted from their email client including those stored on CD, DVD and USB drives. Special Boolean operations are also there. It can process un-purged e-mail from m-box files and can restore un-purged e-mail as well.

EnCase Forensic

EnCase Forensic (OpenText Corp, 2019) is a computer forensic tool that provides a privilege to the investigation team to preserve the drive-in image in a forensic manner using the EnCase evidence file format (LEF or E01). These digital evidence containers are accepted by courts worldwide. It is a full software suite that provides book marking and reporting features, includes any other network forensics investigations; also supports the Internet and e-mail investigations. It included the Instant Messenger toolkit for Microsoft Internet Explorer, Mozilla Firefox, Opera and Apple Safari.

FINALeMAIL

FINALeMAIL (AOS DATA Inc., 2019) is an email database recovers software and also locates the lost emails that haven't location information. FINALeMAIL can restore lost emails in its original state; recover email database files after a virus attack or accidental damage or loss due to formatting. It can recover Email messages and attachments emptied from the 'Deleted Items folder' in MS Outlook, Netscape Mail, and Eudora.

Forensic Investigation Toolkit (FIT)

Forensics Investigation Toolkit (FIT) (edecision4u) helps to read and analyse the content of the raw data over the Internet in Packet CAPture (PCAP) format. FIT provides security administrative officers and forensics investigator, provide the power to perform content analysis and reconstruction mechanism based on pre-captured Internet raw data from any communication medium (wired or wireless). Reconstruction is displayed in the readable format of all protocols and services that are analysed. Immediate parsing of raw data and its reconstruction is also a uniqueness of the FIT. It supports case management functions, detailed information including Date-Time, Source IP, Destination IP, Source MAC, etc., WhoIS and G-Map are integrated into it. Analysing and reconstruction of various Internet traffic types include POP3, SMTP, Webmail, IM, MSN, ICQ, Yahoo, Skype, Gtalk, FTP, P2P, Telnet, Content, Upload/Download, and Others SSL can be performed by it.

MESSAGING FORENSICS

Instant message applications are one of the most popular ways to exchange both messages and files such as images, audios, and videos, etc. Security is a primary concern in this and the security issues are quite similar to the email scenario: illegal/offensive use branding from various techniques like phishing and malicious code distribution, cyber bullying, sending hate messages/racial abuse content, unauthorized disclosure of sensitive information, distributing child pornography and other types of sexual stalking'(Simson L. Garfinkel, 2010).

Several protocols are supported by instant messaging, including IRC (Internet Relay Chat) which creates 'chat rooms' for multiple users. In the current era, Skype and yahoo messengers are popular and use either a proprietary protocol or Extensible Message and Presence Protocol, this standard is adopted by many popular IM clients like Facebook and Google Chat (Graham J., 1999).

While investigating the IMs' primary challenge is quite obvious: there are so many types of IM applications at the local level as well, each has its way of storing information and also stores that information at different places. An expert must know all the types and also all the places like registry or system folders, AppData, Program Files, etc. which depend on operating systems. Adding to this situation is the great variety of ways IMs indicate time: some may use Standard time and some use local time, but quite a few will have a particular (and not publically disclosed) way of time-stamping messages. This type of change also happens due to the constant updating in history format that may be changed each time an IM application is updated (Crocker D., 2009). Forming a strong case will be a question of knowing where to look for evidence and how to properly retrieve it.

CONCLUSION

E-mail is one of the highly distributed applications that are widely used by organizations. The email includes several actors as discusses in the chapter and each actor has its role. Hardware, software, service and related protocols are the actors which provide interoperability among its users and the rest of the components along the path of the transfer. Cyber criminals normally tire to forge e-mail headers or send it anonymously for illegitimate purposes which lead to several types of online and offline crimes and thus make e-mail forensic investigation crucial. This chapter portrays e-mail actors, roles and their responsibilities and also the web forensics and message forensics. Here logical architecture of e-mail and underlining various core components, modules and protocols has been discussed. It also shows the meta-data of an email message and various techniques used for e-mail forensics. This chapter also introduces several software related to e-mail, web and message forensic tools that have functionalities to automatically analyse web, message, and email and subsequently produces reports providing miscellaneous information related to it.

REFERENCES

Adcomplain. (n.d.). Retrieved from http://www.rdrop.com: http://www.rdrop.com/users/billmc/adcomplain.html

Al-Zarouni. (2004). *Tracing E-mail Headers. In Proceedings of Australian Computer* (pp. 16–30). Network & Information Forensics Conference.

AOS DATA Inc. (2019). *FINALeMAIL*. Retrieved from http://finaldata2.com

Arthur K. K. (2004). *An Investigation into Computer Forensic Tools.* Pretoria: Information and Computer Security Architectures (ICSA) Research Group.

Crocker, D. (2009). *Internet Mail Architecture.* RFC 5598.

edecision4u. (n.d.). *Forensics Investigation Toolkit (FIT).* Retrieved from http://www.edecision4u.com/FIT.html

FOOKES® Software. (2019). *Aid4Mail Forensic.* Retrieved from http://www.aid4mail.com/: http://www.aid4mail.com/

Garfinkel, S. L. (2010). Digital forensics research: The next 10 years. *Digital Investigation, 7,* 64–73. doi:10.1016/j.diin.2010.05.009

Geiger, M. (2005). Evaluating Commercial Counter-Forensic Tools. *Digital Forensic Research Workshop (DFRWS).*

Graham, J. (1999). Enterprise wide electronic mail using IMAP. *SIGUCCS '99: Proceedings of the 27th annual ACM SIGUCCS conference on User services: Mile high expectations.*

Kara Nance, B. H. (2009). Digital Forensics: Defining a Research Agenda. *42nd Hawaii International Conference on System Sciences.*

Natarajan Meghanathan, S. R. (2009). *Tools and Techniques For Network Forensic. International Journal of Network Security & Its Applications.*

OpenText Corp. (2019). *EnCase Forensic.* Retrieved from http://www.guidancesoftware.com

RCCF. (n.d.). *EmailTracer*. Retrieved from http://www.cyberforensics.in: http://www.cyberforensics.in/OnlineEmailTracer/index.aspx

Resnick, P. (Ed.). (2001). Internet message format. Internet Engineering Task Force (IETF); RFC 2822.

Suzuki, S. N. M. (2005). Domain Name System—Past, Present, and Future. *IEICE Transactions on Communications*, *E88-B*(3), 857–864. doi:10.1093/ietcom/e88-b.3.857

Tzerefos, S. S. (1997). A comparative study of Simple Mail Transfer Protocol (SMTP), Post Office Protocol (POP) and X.400 Electronic Mail Protocols. *22nd Annual IEEE Conference on Local Computer Networks*, 545–554. 10.1109/LCN.1997.631025

Visualware Inc. (2014). *eMailTrackerPro*. Retrieved from http://www.emailtrackerpro.com/: http://www.emailtrackerpro.com/

KEY TERMS AND DEFINITIONS

Bait Tactics: Header analysis various other approaches that can be used for e-mail forensics include bait tactics, server investigations, and network device investigation.

Email Forensics: Email forensics refers to analyzing the source and content of emails as evidence. Investigation of email related crimes and incidents involve various approaches.

Header Analysis: A detailed header analysis of a multiple tactic spoofed e-mail message is carried out.

Message Forensics: Investigation is quite obvious: there are several applications, each storing information in different areas.

Server Investigation: Part of header analysis.

Software-Embedded Identifiers: Also a part of header analysis.

Web Forensics: Web forensics relates to any sort of crime committed over the internet. With proper knowledge and expert skills, criminal activities like child pornography.

Chapter 11

Financial Statement Fraud Detection and Investigation in Digital Environment

Radiah Othman

iD https://orcid.org/0000-0002-9772-0439

Massey University, New Zealand

ABSTRACT

This chapter discusses some of the stages involved in detecting and investigating financial statement fraud in the digital environment. It emphasizes the human element aspects – the fraudster and the forensic investigator, their skills and capability. The explanation focuses specifically on the context of financial statement fraud detection and investigation which requires the accounting knowledge of the investigator. It also highlights the importance of the investigator to be a skeptic and have an inquiring mind of who had the opportunity to perpetuate the fraud, how the fraud could have been perpetrated, and the motive(s) to do so.

INTRODUCTION

The emergence of the Internet as a tool for global information exchange, accounting information systems, and the information they store and the process will increasingly fall victim to computer crime and fraud (Hurt, 2016, p. 197). Fraud is a deception that includes a representation about a material point that is false and intentionally or recklessly so, which is believed and acted upon by the victims to the victim's detriment (Albrecht, Albrecht, Albrecht, & Zimbelman, 2019). The essential characteristics of financial statement fraud are: 1) the misstatement is material and intentional, and 2)

DOI: 10.4018/978-1-7998-1558-7.ch011

Figure 1. Applying the forensic approach here

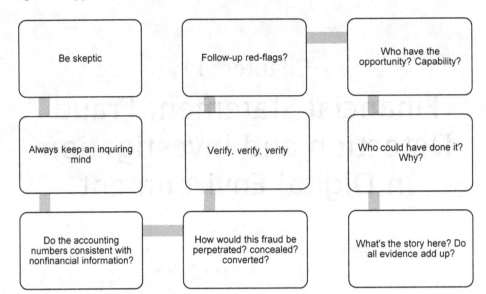

users of the financial statements have been misled. Often, the victims do not have access to information possessed by the perpetrators.

Financial statement fraud can be perpetrated by the management (e.g. earnings manipulation) or by the employees (e.g. billing fraud). The misstatement and misrepresentation can result from manipulating, falsifying, or altering accounting records in the accounting information systems. It is the most expensive type of fraud (Albrecht et al., 2019). Like any other fraud, this fraud involves intentional deceits and attempted concealment, so it is difficult to detect or takes a long time to investigate (Albrecht et al., 2019).

In investigating a fraud case, the investigators should incorporate qualities of skepticism, curiosity, and humility, and mix them with a deep understanding of human behavior and principles of fair play and forensic mindset (Schilit, Perler, & Engelhart, 2018, p. 287). Schilit et al., (2018) advise keeping the focus on key issues in investigating financial statement fraud. Figure 1 outlines some of the critical aspects that a forensic investigator needs to be aware of in investigating a fraud case.

Information technology (IT) is a double-edged sword in that it can be used to commit financial statement fraud, though IT can also be used to detect it by using computer forensics applications.

Computer forensics is the application of computer investigation and analysis techniques to determine perpetrated schemes and potential evidence (Taylor, Haggerty, Gresty & Lamb, 2011). In investigating financial statement fraud, forensic investigator's knowledge in accounting and information systems would be valuable (Huang, Lin, Chiu & Yen, 2016). In a digital environment, the investigator would emphasize electronic evidence in the absence of physical evidence (Solieri & Hodowanitz, 2016). However, interaction with the affected people such as interviews with witnesses, conspirators, and the suspects requires the investigator to have both computer and human-related skills. Financial statement fraud using a computer is people fraud as no computer system can perpetrate fraud without at least some human intervention (Hurt, 2016, p. 198).

According to (Kranacher, Riley, and Wells, 2019), investigations centered on the elements of fraud (act, concealment, and conversion) that include an indication of the fraud triangle have the greatest chances of being successful if grounded in the evidence. The well-known fraud triangle theory states that individual or group conducting fraud is motivated by pressure, opportunity, and rationalization. (Wolfe and Hermanson, 2004) introduce the fraud diamond theory, in which they includedthe capability element of the fraudster which is a trait that drives individuals to seek an opportunity and exploit such opportunities. Nonetheless, the need to understand the motives for the perpetration is paramount to any fraud investigation. The motives explain the reasons and if the investigator would be able to predict the motives and be supplemented with the evidence from the fraud detection process, he or she would be able to anticipate which accounts would be manipulated and what type of fraudhadpossibly beencommitted.

The proposed chapter aims to highlight how the emphasis on both the technology and the human aspects of a financial statement fraud detection and investigation focuses on the elements of pressure, opportunity, capability, and rationalization elements of the fraud triangle. It examines questions such as: Who could have committed such a crime? Is he/she acting alone or in collusion? How could he/she or they manage to circumvent controls in a digital environment? All these would need to be examined and a better understanding of the human side story could help investigators in their quest for the answers. To illustrate this, the chapter will use an example of Sam, a forensic investigator, investigating a financial statement fraud. Where necessary context and facts from a real financial statement fraud case, committed by Toshiba Corporation are also included. Toshiba, with more than 100-year-old history a 140-year-old history, was removed from the Dow Jones Sustainability World Index on August 3, 2015, after shocking earnings manipulation of more than US$2 billion.

WHAT IS FINANCIAL STATEMENT FRAUD?

Financial statement fraud or fraudulent financial reporting is part of financial reporting misconduct (Amiram, Bozanic, Cox, et al. 2018). An early definition refers

Figure 2. Financial Statement Fraud here

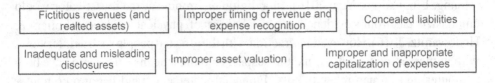

to it as intentional or reckless conduct, whether by act or omission, which results in materially misleading financial statements (The Treadway Commission, 1999). The misconduct includes misrepresentation, misreporting and other irregularities (Amiram et al. 2018), also known as "cooking the books" by using creative accounting (Skoda, Slavikova & Lajcin, 2016; Shi, Connelly, & Hoskisson, 2016; Stuart and Wang, 2015). Usually, financial statement fraud is undertaken to make the company's reported financial results look better than they are (Albrecht et al., 2019). Figure 2 lists some of the possibility of financial statement fraud.

The implications of financial statements fraud are substantial (Wei, Shaoyi, & Zhongju, 2018). It can negatively affect and erode investors' confidence in corporate financial statements (Perols, 2011; Jan 2018) thus poses a significant threat to the existence and efficiency of capital markets (Amiram, et al., 2018). Beasley, Carcello, Hermanson, and Lapides (2000) report that the average fraudulent firm's stock price dropped by 16.7% in response to the initial press disclosures of an alleged fraud; 28% of fraud firms were bankrupt or liquidated within two years; 47% were delisted from a national stock exchange; and 62% were affected by material asset sales. According to Albrecht et al., (2019), for every $1 of fraud, the net income of the firm is reduced by $1, which means more revenue is required to compensate for the loss. An example of a technique used by a fraudster would be the 'salami technique,' in which unnoticeable slices of a financial transaction are removed and transferred to another account (Hurt, 2016, p.199). The fraud is committed mainly to conceal true business performance, and to save the reputation of the individual senior management and the business as well as maintain personal wealth tight to salary, bonus or stock options.

The current business environment is experiencing an upsurge in financial accounting fraud (Omidi, Min, Moradinaftchali, & Piri, 2019). The number of corporate earnings restatements due to aggressive accounting practices, accounting irregularities, or accounting fraud has increased dramatically (Jan 2018; Kotsiantis et al., 2006). According to Perols (2011, p. 20) there are four distinguishing characteristics of firms perpetrating financial statement fraud: The ratio of fraud to nonfraud firms is small, which indicates there are many more nonfraud firms than fraud firms; it is more costly to classify a fraud firm as a nonfraud firm than to classify a nonfraud firm as a fraud firm; fraudster attempts to conceal fraud in such a way that fraud and nonfraud firms' attribute values look similar; and similar attribute values can signal both fraudulent and nonfraudulent activities. Even though these firms were audited by the independent auditors, it does not deter financial statement fraud. It also infers that a forensic investigator needs to possess skills beyond auditing.

Further, financial statement frauds are usually collusive, involving more than one perpetrator (Albrecht et al., 2019). There are three main groups of people who could potentially commit this fraud: senior management, middle-lower level management, and organized criminals (Kranacher et al., 2011). Of all, the management is the one that can override controls to manipulate accounting records and prepare fraudulent financial statements (Kassem, 2019; Kanapickienė & Grundienė, 2015). In the Toshiba case, the fraud revealed in 2015 was perpetrated by managers and three generations of its top executives since 2009 (IIC, 2015). The fraud typically starts with the intention of managing earnings, trying to buy time for their organization until conditions improve, but this would eventually lead to corporate malfeasance (Dorminey, Fleming, Kranacher, et al., 2012).

Acknowledging fraudsters as a human would enable forensic investigators to understand the human aspect of the investigation, anticipating their needs and thus, motives. Reviewing internal control vulnerabilities could also indicate opportunities they have at hand. This aspect of investigation could provide clues beyond what the technology can provide. As emphasized by Goldmann (2009), while some of the detection and prevention methods could be technological, a human element in the ðght will always be central to the war on such crimes. Kranacher et al., (2011, p. 266) also emphasized that fraud and forensic accounting professionals need to remain alert to the human side of fraud.

Fraud Detection vs. Fraud Investigation

Fraud investigation may be triggered by the observation of unusual behavior or discrepancies in the accounting system. This could involve various types of schemes, resulting in unexplained inventory shortages or adjustments, excess purchases, unreasonable expenses or reimbursements, and unusual relationships between financial statement items such as increased revenues with decreased inventory (Albrecht et al., 2019). In the Toshiba case, the corporation resorted to channel stuffing estimated to be JPY14.3b to overstate its profits in 2008 (IIC, 2015, p. 55). Channel stuffing is a practice that suppliers use to encourage customers to buy the extra inventory to increase current-period sales (Albrecht, et al., 2019). The internal and external auditors might have reported these, based on their audits, to those charged with governance. However, in the Toshiba case, the external auditor had been auditing the corporation for 60 years ("Japan Fines," 2015), so its independence from the management was questioned. An investigation could also be prompted by information obtained from other channels such as whistleblowing systems, tips, and complaints from internal and external stakeholders. Internal or external investigators might then be commissioned to investigate the concerns raised by these parties. In a recent study by Smaili and Arroyo (2019), most whistleblowers opt for external channels when they fail to receive an adequate response from management and seek media exposure.

The possibility of fraud is pursued in the fraud detection process. In this process, evidence was actively searched to discover the presence or existence of fraud. Fraud detection using technology-based search techniques is common. There are various statistical and machine learning algorithms that have been used and have the potential to be used in detecting financial statement fraud. These include logistic regression and artificial neural networks, support vector machines, decision trees and ensemble-based methods (Omidi et al., 2019; Jan, 2018; Hajek & Henriques, 2017; Perols, 2011; Kotsiantis et al., 2006; Spathis, 2002; Bell & Carcello, 2000, Green & Choi, 1997). Of recent, Wei et al. (2018) demonstrate the usefulness of user-generated content (UGC) on financial social media platform to automatically detect fraud.

Once the results of the analysis indicates that there is a possibility of financial fraud, Sam needs to focus on the 'how,' 'who,' and 'why' of financial statement fraud. The 'how' aspect requires Sam to ask questions like: 'How could financial statement fraud be committed?', 'How effective is the internal control environment?', and 'How susceptible is the company to management override?' The answers to the last two questions could indicate the answers to the first question.

Sam could start with understanding and reviewing the firm's accounting system. This stage is important for Sam to be able to understand the flow of transactions through business processes, identify where controls have been implemented, and identify the gaps and weaknesses. The existence of internal controls can have a deterrent effect only when the employee perceives that such a control exists and is intended for uncovering fraud (Kranacher et al, 2011, p. 13) but their weaknesses present opportunities to people who have the motives, are in the position to make use of the weaknesses, and have the access and the right set of capability and skills. In the Toshiba case, the Independent Investigation Committee concluded that Toshiba's internal control system had no force and correcting the situation was very difficult (IIC, 2015, p.56). Since the top management overrides the control system, it became non-operational (Dorminey, et al., 2012). However, by analyzing the weaknesses of the control system, Sam would be able to anticipate how they could be used to perpetrate financial statement fraud.

UNDERSTANDING AND REVIEWING THE ACCOUNTING SYSTEM

An accounting system is a system used by the company to manage the income, expenses, and other financial activities of the business. The understanding of the accounting system would enhance Sam's understanding of how it operates, what its potential weaknesses are, and most importantly, who has the opportunity and/or capability (and the motives) to exploit the weaknesses. Sam could refer to the report prepared by the external auditor as part of their annual audit or the internal audit department's report as part of their ongoing audit of efficiency and effectiveness of the operation.

Sam should also focus on the application controls as information manipulation can occur at any stage of information processing. Application controls are designed to address risks that threaten the processing and storage of data in these application areas (Kranacher et al., 2011, p. 265). For example, Nawawi & Salin (2018) investigate the weaknesses of internal control in expenditure claim procedures and fraud likelihood. By understanding the application control Sam would be able to identify who has the authority to initiate an accounting transaction and determine: Would that be somebody of internal or external to the organization with access to the accounting system?

Nowadays employees have the privilege to access their workplace accounting system without having to be physically present in their offices. Similarly, a potential fraudster with adequate capability and skills could exploit this for fraudulent actions remotely. Remote access means that the key evidence could potentially reside across several organization browsers' web history or caches. This would mean that collecting, collating, and verifying evidence is difficult and complex (Taylor et al., 2011). Though access log and exception report could be helpful, the evidence is limited by how skillful the fraudsters are in concealing the audit trails. To the prosecution team, evidence concerning logs of access, individuals who have control of the access, and the kind of access and permissions would be critical (Taylor et al., 2011, p. 6). It is common for financial statement fraud to be perpetrated by the insiders of the organization. In a digital environment, an increased risk of fraud could be expected in an organization with the following indicators (Kranacher et al., 2019, p. 119):

- Access privileges beyond those required to perform assigned job functions
- Exception reports not reviewed and resolved
- Access logs not reviewed
- Production programs run at unusual hours
- Lack of separation of duties in the data center.

Figure 3. Accounting System and Fraudulent Financial Statements here

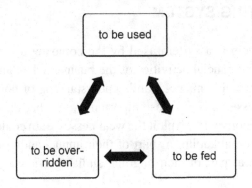

In terms of financial statement fraud, insider employees who have access to the computer could potentially abuse their position through input transaction manipulation schemes, unauthorized program modification schemes, or file alteration and substitution schemes (Goldmann, 2009). In this case, the computer is accessed with the intent to commit a fraudulent or criminal act. This use or abuse of the accounting system is depicted as 'playing the accounting system,' 'beating the accounting system,' and 'going outside the accounting system' (Kranacher et al., 2011). Figure 3 shows some of how fraudulent financial statement fraud could be perpetrated by misusing or abusing the accounting system.

An investigator with a good understanding of the accounting processes would know that the bottom-line figures such as sales, profit, and net income are summarized from all transactions that occurred for the year. Only the total amount would be reported in the financial statements. If the performance is not as what the management expects, there is a tendency for the amount to be altered. In a digital environment, the alteration can be challenging. There are at least two ways the management could resort to doing this.

Firstly, the management could instruct employees (or do it themselves by overriding the accounting system) to enter unusual, complex, and suspicious journal entries to reduce expenditures and liabilities with the intention, for example, to make a profit look higher than it should be. This is what Kranacher et al. (2011) call 'playing the accounting system.' In this way, the fraudster uses the accounting system as a tool to generate the desired results. In the Toshiba case, the monthly profits in the PC[1] business were in an abnormal state to the extent that the operating profit of the last months of the quarter sometimes exceeded the sales for that month (IIC, 2015). This input manipulation is probably the most common form of fraud since it is easy to perform, requiring only basic computer skills, and hard to detect (Hurt, 2016).

Second, in the 'beating the accounting system' approach, the fraudster feeds fictitious transactions into the accounting system to manipulate the results. Another way is through program manipulation, which involves the modification or insertion of specific functions into the accounting systems. This generally requires someone with advanced computer programming knowledge. In this way, the desired transaction and amount would be directly altered or entered into the accounting system. This would require someone with access and advanced IT skills. He or she either acts alone or in collusion with the management who can override the controls in the accounting system.

The last method is 'going outside the accounting system.' In this approach, the fraudster produces first the intended financial statements and works backward to generate transactions that make up the intended results. In this way, the accounting system is the back-end solution for the fraudster to feed the 'desired' numbers. Lenard, Petruska, Alam, et al. (2016) show that firms reporting weaknesses in internal controls exhibit higher levels of real activities manipulation. This manipulation involves the manipulation of real operations to increase short-term earnings and cash flows at the expense of future earnings.

Nonetheless, financial statement fraud may involve more than one method as the fraud grows (Kranacher et al., 2011).Being aware of all this information, the next step is for Sam to retrieve and review the documentation maintained by the organization concerning the accounting system. The understanding of the accounting system would indicate the extent to which the accounting system could be used and abused in producing fraudulent financial statements.

SYSTEM DOCUMENTATION

System flowchart is the graphical representation of the flow of data and represents the work process of the system. The system can be the sales, purchases, inventory, or payroll systems from which the data flows into the financial statements. Below is an example of the flowchart symbols used to capture the start of the ordering processes that are triggered when the sales clerk receives an order for a wedding cake from a customer.

Figure 4 depicts a system flowchart for the order processing of Sylvia Café. As shown in the above flowchart, the sales clerk takes an order from a client and then prepares an estimate. The estimate is filed in numerical order and a copy of it is sent to the customer. The customer reviews revise and finalize the estimate. The final estimate is sent back to Sylvia Café sales clerk, for which the process is depicted on p. 2. By reviewing these processes, Sam should notice that the estimate prepared by the sales clerk is not reviewed and approved by the sales manager. The sales clerk

Figure 4. System flowchart of the ordering process of Sylvia Café here

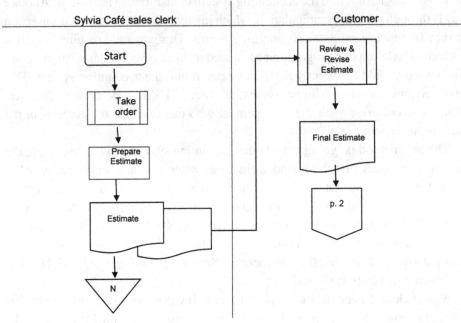

has the opportunity, to understate or overstate the sales order. This fraud possibility would not be visible to Sam if he were to directly assess the computerized accounting system to check the amount entered into the system.

Assuming, that the same amount is entered as per invoice amount issued to the customer, there is no fraudulent transaction occurred and this transaction would then be 'lost' among all other sales transactions for the year and never be red-flagged. Some of the potential weaknesses that could be observed from an accounting system applicable in a digital environment are listed in Table 1 below.

Therefore, by having a good understanding of the processes through the documentations, Sam would not only able to understand the processes involved before transactions being entered into the computerized accounting system but also be able to anticipate the loopholes that would otherwise 'invisible' when reviewing the sales transactions entered into the accounting system. Other types of documentation could be used, such as data flow diagram, document flowcharts, and REA diagram. Each has its strengths and weaknesses, which must be taken into consideration before a conclusion can be made about the weaknesses of the system.

Table 1. Potential Accounting System Weaknesses and Line of Inquiry

Potential control weaknesses	Fraud Line of Inquiry	
High possibility/ evidence of overriding of existing controls Lack of independent checks Lack of proper authorization Lack of segregation of duties	Who has the opportunity and/or capability?	Who could have the motives to do so?

Accounting System Assessment

Once the control weaknesses are identified, Sam could predict whether fraud is a possibility. The control weaknesses identified above (Table 1) could be extended to possible control risks. Examples of these risks are shown in Table 2 below. Not all risks could potentially lead to fraudulent actions. Therefore, Sam has to focus on which people have the opportunity and/or capability and motives to perpetrate fraudulent action.

The investigation of the 'how' aspect of the fraud would not complete without detecting the symptoms or red flags of financial statement fraud. The evidence to be obtained for this investigation could provide the most important element of a fraud investigation, that is, to establish a predication so that the investigation into 'who' and 'why' could then be pursued.

DETECTING RED FLAGS OF FINANCIAL STATEMENT FRAUD

Financial statement fraud is rarely obvious. As such, the symptoms or red flags must be determined and must be done with the management's approval. Regardless of the investigation being performed in a digital environment, Sam needs to have a good understanding of the red flags of financial statement fraud. Red flags are fraud indicators or symptoms. For example, in a situation where operating income is greater than expected, an earnings-based bonus plan is used, and debt covenants are restrictive, there is a higher likelihood of fraud (Church, McMillan, & Schneider, 2001). However, Sam must corroborate whether the symptoms resulted from actual fraud or were caused by other factors.

Missing documents might not be an issue in an environment where an on-line computerized accounting system would be used. In this environment, source documents would be automatically generated and sequentially numbered. However, these are some of the red flags or symptoms that Sam needs to be aware of. Nonetheless, Sam needs to make sure that they are not unintentional mistakes or

Table 2. Potential Risk in Sales Cycle and Line of Inquiry

Potential control weaknesses	Potential Risk	Fraud Line of Inquiry		Type of fraud?
High possibility/ evidence of overriding of existing controls Lack of independent checks Lack of proper authorization Lack of segregation of duties	Unauthorized granting of credit to certain customers Mishandling payment from customers Unauthorized extension of credit limit to customers in customer master file Unauthorized creation of new customer in customer master file without sales order Frequent delivery of goods to the same customers Unauthorized modification of customer's bank account in customer master file	Who has the opportunity and/ or capability?	Who could have the motives to do so?	Overstating sales? Premature recording of sales? Channel stuffing?

errors. Examples from Albrecht et al. (2019) are adapted in a digital environment and shown in Table 3.

GATHERING EVIDENCE BY ANALYZING ABNORMALITIES

Analyzing abnormalities and irregularities or ethical concerns as outlined above could be performed by using data analysis and other methods such as Benford's Law digital analysis (Benford, 1938), analytical review procedures, and financial statement analysis (Albrecht et al., 2019). This analysis could be performed, on-line and the results could be used as evidence in seeking admissions of guilt from the fraudsters through interviews.

Table 3. Red flags of Financial Statement Frauds and Investigator's Line of Inquiry

Red flags (adapted from Albrecht et al., 2019)	Investigator's Line of Inquiry	
<u>Electronic Source Documents</u> Common/repeated names of suppliers or customers in on-line purchases and sales invoices. Increased past-due accounts of customers and suppliers in online statements. Online supplier invoices indicate unapproved vendors. <u>Faulty Electronic Journal Entries</u> Unexplained adjustments made on-line to receivables, payables, revenues, or expenses. Journal entries made on-line by individuals who would normally make such entries. On-line journal entries made near the end of an accounting period. <u>Analytical Fraud Symptoms</u> Excess purchases than normal (possibility of kickback?). Too many debit or credit memos issues on-line by the same employee(s). Significant increases/decreases in on-line account balances, expenses (e.g. reimbursements). Unexplained relationships between accounts e.g., increased revenues accounts with decreased receivables.	Who has the opportunity and/or capability?	Who could have the motives to do so?

Data Analysis Software

Some of the data analysis software that could be used by Sam includes ACL Audit Analytics, CaseWare's IDEA, Microsoft Office + ActiveData. According to Albrecht et al. (2019), regardless of which software to be used, one principle that Sam must ensure is that he gets the right data in the right format during the right period. Another option is Open Database Connectivity (ODBC). According to Albrecht et al. (2019), ODBC is a standard method of querying data from a corporate relational database, which can retrieve data in real-time, allows use of the powerful SQL language for searching and filtering, allows repeated pulls for iterative analysis, and retrieves metadata like column types and relationships directly (p. 167). The use of the software would enable statistical tests and database queries to perform easily and effectively.

BENFORD'S LAW DIGITAL ANALYSIS (BENFORD, 1938)

According to Benford's Law, the first digit of random data sets will begin with a 1 more often than the other digits (refer to Table 4) below. Therefore, in reviewing, for example, invoices from suppliers, Sam would run the invoice numbers to determine whether the numbers follow Benford's distribution. The idea is that human-generated numbers usually do not conform to Benford distribution. For example, there are too many purchase invoices that started with digit 7, for example, 18%, when it should be 6% as per Benford's distribution.

The digits to be used can also depend on motivation. Firms wanting to make amounts appear higher would manage first digits up to the next 1 or 5 (Archambault & Archambault, 2011). Firms wanting to make an amount look lower would manage the first digit down to the previous 9 or 4 (Carslaw, 1988; Skousen, Guan, & Wetzel, 2004). For example, an analysis of 14 years' financial statements data using Benford's Law digital analysis revealed abnormalities and irregularities in Toshiba's various accounts, which started from 2002 and continued after the fraud was announced to the public (Othman, Ameer, & Laswad, 2019).

Busta and Weinberg (1998) suggest Benford's Law digital analysis is unaffected by the magnitude of error(s) and it is independent of the numbers' relationship to other data. It is also less sensitive to the pattern of contamination as it analyzes a data stream without regard to the time of the data, the location of the manipulation, or the comparison of the data to any cumulative totals. Benford's Law digital analysis can help alert auditors to possible errors, potential fraud, manipulative biases, or other irregularities (Nigrini, 1999a, 1999b). It must be cautioned that Benford's Law broadly red flags possible existence of fraud by narrowing down specific areas to be pursued, such as which invoice numbers should be thoroughly investigated. Table 4 shows the distribution of the first and second positions of numbers.

Table 4. Benford's Law Distribution

Digit	First Position (%)	Second Position (%)
0	Not applicable	12
1	30	11
2	18	11
3	12	10
4	10	10
5	8	10
6	7	9
7	6	9
8	5	9
9	5	9

Analytical Review Procedures

Analytical review procedures are performed to study the changes in accounting numbers to get an understanding of the factors that influence the company's performance and the environment in which it operates to achieve its predetermined goals. This can be performed by analyzing the changes in financial and nonfinancial information.

In a fraud investigation, the analytical procedures would enable Sam to identify outliers. Outliers can be a result of peculiar or unusual relationships between two or more accounts that do not match the norm. An example given in Figure 5 is an increase in revenue accounts with decreased receivables in a business that does not sell goods on a cash basis.

In this case, Sam might want to compare the information from other similar organizations operating in the same industry to ensure consistency between financial and non-financial information. For example, if the company under investigation seemed to perform better than the other companies operating within the same industry, this might red flag a possibility of fraud.

Graphical trend analysis over time of purchasing prices, purchasing quantities, revenues, expenses, and net income can reveal abnormalities. According to Albrecht et al. (2019), financial statements that contain large changes in account balances in comparison with previous periods are more likely to contain fraud than financial statements that contain small, incremental changes. For example, Figure 6 below shows that there was a sudden hike in sales in 2018. Fictitious sales transactions or channel stuffing could have been perpetrated. Channel stuffing is a deceptive

Figure 5. Sales and accounts receivable 2014 to 2019 here

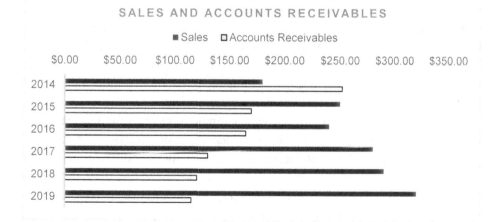

Figure 6. Sales trend analysis 2014 to 2019 here

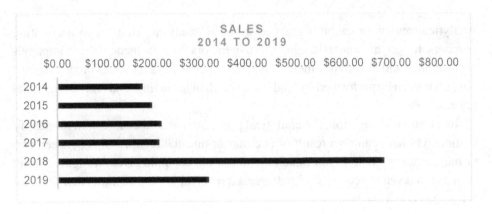

business practice used by a company to inflate its sales (and thus, profit figures) by deliberately sending customers more goods than they ordered and ensure the customers returned them after the year ended.

Also, nonfinancial information could be used to corroborate financial information at hand. Nonfinancial data includes the number of inventories held at the warehouse and the number of debtors to compare with the sudden increase in sales. Sales are the outcome of the selling price per unit X units sold to customers. If there is no sudden increase in selling price per unit, the number of units sold to customers can be verified by the shipping records to customers and inventory records. If nonfinancial data do not reconcile or correlate to financial data, Sam should consider this as a red flag.

Financial Statement Analysis

Another method of obtaining evidence of symptoms is to perform a financial statement analysis. Financial statement analysis summarizes all transactions in various accounts for a specific period. Sam should focus on unexplained changes by performing vertical or horizontal analysis. The vertical analysis compares numbers from one period to the next. For example, the balance sheet shows that the liabilities were significantly reduced in 2019, indicating the possibility of understatement of liabilities. Table 5 illustrates an extract of a balance sheet.

For horizontal analysis, Sam needs to calculate ratios to examine the reasonableness of the fluctuations. The common ratios are quick ratio, current ratio, debt-to-equity ratio, and profit margin. The debt-equity ratio formula is total liabilities/stockholders' equity. In Figure 5, the ratio for 2018 is 1,013/1,727 = 58.7%. For 2019, the ratio is 719/2,140 = 33.6%. The ratio is used to evaluate a company's financial leverage. It is a measure of the degree to which a company is financing its operations through

Table 5. Balance Sheet for the year ended 2018 and 2019

	FY-2018	FY-2019
	Prior Year ('000)	**Current Year ('000)**
Current Assets	1,962	2,115
Fixed Assets	758	714
Other Assets	20	30
Current Liabilities	983	717
Long-term Liabilities	30	2
Owner Equity	1,727	2,140
Total Assets	**2,740**	**2,859**
Total Liabilities & Stockholder Equity	**2,740**	**2,859**

debt as compared to owned funds, thus it reflects the ability of shareholder equity to cover all outstanding debts in the event of a business downturn.

As such, in this case, the management might want to portray a positive outlook to its shareholders that they have managed to improve its debt position. What Sam should do next is identify how the debts managed to be reduced so quickly by tracking any unusual adjustments made on-line on its accounting system and then following up by other inquiries such as reviewing contracts and agreements.

All evidence, digital or not, must be stored. The stored data as evidence could be used with data mining software such as Access, ACL, or IDEA to allow a large amount of evidence to be processed and evaluated as symptoms of fraud.

WHEN TO BEGIN THE INVESTIGATION?

Mere suspicion is not sufficient to justify a fraud investigation without adequate prediction. Predication refers to circumstances when taken as a whole, would lead a reasonable, prudent professional to believe fraud has occurred, is occurring, or will occur (Albrecht et al., 2019, p.78). Once symptoms are analyzed and predication threshold has been met, the next investigation should be targeted at the 'who' and 'why' aspect of financial statement fraud investigation Thus, the evidence obtained from the fraud detection investigation of the red flags provides credible information for Sam to decide whether a fraud has occurred, is occurring, and/or will occur. The next investigation is to determine the extent of the losses and the identity of the perpetrator(s). However, Albrecht et al. (2019, pp. 80–81) caution that the investigation:

- Must be undertaken only to 'establish the truth of the matter under questions.'
- Be conducted by individuals with experience and objectivity.
- Must ensure that only those who need to know are kept apprised of investigation activities.
- Must ensure that all information collected during an inquiry is independently corroborated and determined to be factually correct.
- Use techniques that are scientifically and legally sound and fair.
- Reports all facts fairly and objectively.

After narrowing down to the 'who' and the 'why' aspects of financial fraud the next step is concealment and conversion investigations. It would be more difficult for the alleged fraudsters to deny their fraudulent actions if concealment and conversion investigations implicate them with evidence. Therefore, Sam must understand that in perpetrating financial statement fraud, the management is more organized and deliberately equipped with more complex concealment schemes (Kranacher et al., 2011).

CONCEALMENT AND CONVERSION INVESTIGATION

The outcomes from concealment and/or conversion investigation provide credible evidence that links the alleged fraudster(s) to the fraud. In terms of financial statement fraud, the perpetrators typically deny that financial statements are fraudulently prepared. If the evidence reveals that the financial statements are fraudulent, this would provide credible evidence of concealment in itself as a whole. The very existence of the fraudulent financial statements, if proven, provides evidence of concealment and conversion. The company benefits from fraudulent financial statements by showing improved performance, getting more loans for financing and more investments from the shareholders. The perpetrators benefit from large bonuses or salary increments.

Specific concealment methods depend on individual financial statement components. For example, in terms of liability and expenses, they are concealed by not recording or disclosing them or by capitalizing the expenses so that they will not be deducted against a profit of the year. Fictitious sales are reversed in the next accounting period to help conceal the fraud. A bank loan, which should be recorded as a liability, is recorded as sales, that is, when cash is received, sales instead of liability (the bank loan) is credited. As both sales and liabilities are on the credit side, the double-entry rules of debit and credit are complied with. Fictitious assets could also be created, concealed by fictitious documents to support the existence of the assets, which are not physically available.

Who Could Have Done It?

As a fraud investigator, Sam needs to remain skeptical at every stage of the investigation to uncover who could have done it. Sam should be skeptical and have a questioning mind on the following: Who has the opportunity and/or capability? Who could have the motives to do so? According to Wolfe and Hermanson (2004), the person with capability has several essential traits: has the position with opportunity; smart enough to understand and exploit internal control weaknesses and to use position, function, or authorized access to the greatest advantage; has a strong ego and great confidence that he or she will not be detected, or believes that he or she could easily talk himself or herself out of trouble if caught; can coerce others to commit or conceal fraud; and lies effectively and consistently. In terms of financial statement fraudster, Figure 7 summarizes that this person has the power to influence subordinates and others, able to manipulate controls and people, and is persistent in his actions and lies.

The majority of the financial statement frauds are collusive (Albrecht et al., 2019). It is possible that the person with the above capability could convince or coerce others to participate in the fraud. According to French and Raven (1959), a conspirator's power over a potential co-conspirator depends on how the co-conspirator perceives the reward power, coercive power, expert power, legitimate power, and referent power of the conspirator. In terms of fraud, Albrecht et al., (2019) explain that it is perceived power rather than the actual power that affects the co-conspirator's decision to become involved or not, regardless of resistance. This person has the perceived reward, coercive, expert, and legitimate and referent power. In terms of financial statement fraud, the principal fraudster – the mastermind, has the view of or the belief that he or she is a person of status, superiority, supremacy, and stature.

Figure 7. Person with capability for fraud here

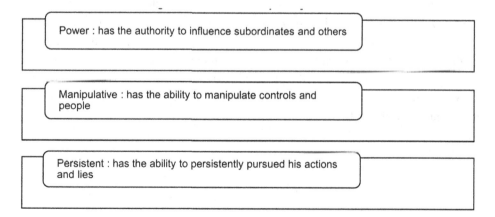

Figure 8. Perceived beliefs of the mastermind here

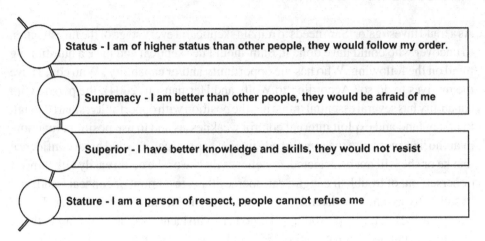

Without these beliefs, he or she would not have the confidence to influence and coerce the co-conspirator to collude. This is shown in Figure 8.

Regarding financial statement fraud, its concealment would require the collusion of various parties, from top management to employees and sometimes would involve third parties as well. This makes it more difficult for a forensic investigator to detect any wrongdoing. Perpetrating financial statement fraud is much easier when one or two individuals have primary decision-making power (Albrecht et al., 2019).

Nonetheless, many frauds would not have occurred without the right person with the right capabilities in place (Wolfe & Hermanson, 2004). They explain that opportunity opens the doorway to fraud, and incentive and rationalization can draw the person towards it, but the person must have the capability to recognize the open doorway as an opportunity and take advantage of it (p.38).

The investigationcan start with a series of questions, to identify who the fraudsters are by looking at who had the opportunity to commit fraud and his/her motivation. If the fraudster has the motivation but not the ability, he or she might recruit an insider or outsider to launch his or her attack/manipulation (conspirator) using his or her power of recruitment (Albrecht et al., 2019).

With the understanding of the above criteria, Sam can then start with the investigation of the 'why.'

Table 6. Common Reasons for Financial Statement Fraud by Senior Management adapted from Kranacher et al., 2011, p. 409)

Reasons for	
Overstating business performance	**Understating business performance**
To meet or exceed the earnings or revenue growth expectations of stock market analysts. To comply with loan covenants. To increase the amount of financing available from asset-based loans. To meet a lender's criteria for granting/extending loan facilities. To meet corporate performance criteria set by the parent company. To meet personal performance criteria. To trigger performance-related compensation or earn-out payments. To support the stock price in anticipation of a merger, acquisition, or sale of personal stockholding. To show a pattern of growth to support a planned securities offering or sale of the business.	To defer 'surplus' earnings to the next accounting period. To take all possible write-offs in one 'big bath' so future earnings will be consistently higher. To reduce expectations so future growth will be better perceived and rewarded. To preserve a trend of consistent growth and avoid volatile results. To reduce the value of an owner-managed business for purposes of a divorce settlement. To reduce the value of a corporate unit whose management is planning a buyout?

PRESSURES (MOTIVES)

Kranacher et al., (2011, pp. 409–410) summarize two situations in which the senior management perpetrated financial statement fraud: overstate or understate (Table 6 below).(

At the individual level, money and ego are the most common reasons (Kranacher et al., 2011, p. 266). Their ego of not wanting to lose reputation and the ideology of the betterment of the organization could push them into fraudulently reporting their performance in the financial statements (Rubasundram, 2015), or what Arnold & Bonython (2016) refer to as 'keeping up appearance.' Thus, Sam should pursue lines of inquiries such as Are the directors and management worth tied to the firm's performance? Are they under pressure to deliver and improve performance? Does the firm have debt covenants that need to be met?

The severity of cultural issues could also be examined. Culture could shape the perception of the larger community as to what constitutes as illegal or immoral. For example, in the Toshiba case, even though the employees were caught in a dilemma of either carrying out a directive that was wrong or disobeying an order, they lacked the courage and initiative to rectify the culture when they knew of no other option available to them (IIC, 2015). Obedience to authority occurs within a hierarchical structure in which the actor feels that the person above has the right to prescribe behavior (Hamilton & Sanders, 1995). These 'crimes of obedience' refer to acts in which subordinates obey authority by committing acts the larger community finds illegal or immoral (Kelman & Hamilton, 1989). Dishonest employees, especially those in the positions of authority within the organization, would eventually infect a portion of honest ones (Sutherland, 1983). The A-B-Cs of fraud: a bad Apple, a bad Bushel, and a bad Crop are introduced by Ramamoorti, Morrison, and Koletar (2009). A bad apple is an individual, a bad bushel suggests that certain group dynamics encourage or facilitate fraud (collusive fraud), and bad crop suggests a deficiency of morals at the top of the organization.

To implicate the co-conspirators, the investigation should target their communication with each other. Data mining software can then be used and the following procedures may be employed.

Review Emails

Corporate emails can reveal the recipient, sender, date, time and possibly the intent of the sender and the recipient, even the wider top management. Emails have served as evidence in a fraud investigation which includes the Enron Corporation. Debreceny and Gray (2011) have shown how data mining of emails (DME) techniques would be useful as audit evidence. As emails and their attachments can be created and stored in multiple devices and operating systems, this would provide an opportunity for Sam to recover or obtain them from other locations or storage. Goldmann (2009) urges that a request must be made for the attachments and storage conventions. Also, important to take note of is information such as who created the file (of the attachment), who modified the data, and when. The attachments can be files but can be other formats such as video, digital video, and recordings.

Analyze Social Media

Social media have become the most popular sites for people to share their daily activities. Holidays, traveling, achievements, and sorrows are shared through Twitter, Facebook, Instagram, etc. These are the gold mines for seeking evidence. For example, insurance companies have now turned to social media to find evidence of fraud (Millan, 2011). The aspects to be considered make sure that the evidence to be obtained is credible and of good quality.

Recover Instant Messages

Instant messages are the quickest way to communicate at the workplace without having to incur any additional costs such as messages using mobile phones. As the conversations are made using the office desktops, the history can be recoverable as they are preserved in the hard drive. The evidence must be relevant, material and competent (Kranacher et al., 2011). Evidence also must be authenticated and be shown it had not been altered since it was collected. In terms of mobile phones, Riadi, Umar & Firdonsyah (2017) report that mobile forensic methods can be applied in acquiring and analyzing instant messages recovered from Blackberry Messenger on Android smartphones using the Andriller tool. However, proper permission must be obtained to retrieve evidence from computers and network systems.

The next step is to get admission by interviewing with the alleged fraudsters, after interviewing witnesses and co-conspirators. Interviews must be planned properly and should only be conducted by experienced and trained investigators.

Rationalization

Rationalization is a precondition before a fraud crime took place. It is a part of the motivation for the crime (Kranacher et al., 2011). As such, it is an *ex post facto* means of justifying a fraudulent action (Cressey, 1973). Zourrig & Park (2019) suggest that there is a direct path between the perception of unfairness and fraud acceptance and the rationalization process was also found to contribute to shaping such acceptance. Nonetheless, a fraudster's rationalization often surfaced during the interview or interrogation session. By introducing evidence on how they have concealed and converted their fraudulent activities, the fraudsters often reveal various sorts of reasoning to rationalize their actions. In terms of financial statement fraud, the most common rationalizations include making the company look better for the sake of investors or complying with certain restrictions imposed by regulators or bankers.

Once the investigation is completed, a fraud report is usually prepared, which contains the evidence (findings), conclusions, and recommendations (if required). In this report, Sam should move from a world grounded in numbers to one where words carry the day in that he should be able to tell a complete and compelling story that explains who, what, where, when, how and possibly why (Kranacher et al., 2011, p. 31).

PUTTING IT ALL TOGETHER

When an organization is experiencing pressures and management rationalizes that the pressures are only short term and will correct themselves in the future, all that needed to commit financial statement fraud is, perceived opportunity (Albrecht et al., 2019). To prove fraud, the investigator must prove intent. If the investigator has evidence that the alleged perpetrator committed the act, benefitted from that act, and concealed his or her activities, it becomes more difficult for the accused to argue that they did not intend to cause harm or injury (Kranacher et al., 2011, p. 25).

REFERENCES

Albrecht, W. S., Albrecht, C. O., Albrecht, C. C., & Zimbelman, M. F. (2019). *Fraud examination*. Boston, MA: Cengage.

Amiram, D., Bozanic, Z., Cox, J. D., Dupont, Q., Karpoff, J. M., & Sloan, R. (2018). Financial reporting fraud and other forms of misconduct: A multidisciplinary review of the literature. *Review of Accounting Studies*, *23*(2), 732–783. doi:10.100711142-017-9435-x

Archambault, J. J., & Archambault, M. E. (2011). Earnings management among firms during the pre-sec era: A Benford's law analysis. *The Accounting Historians Journal*, *38*(2), 145–170. doi:10.2308/0148-4184.38.2.145

Arnold, B. B., & Bonython, B. (2016). Villains, victims and bystanders in financial crime. In M. Dion, D. Weisstub, & J. Richet (Eds.), Financial crimes: Psychological, technological, and ethical issues, (pp. 167–198). Springer. doi:10.1007/978-3-319-32419-7_8

Beasley, M. S., Carcello, J. V., Hermsanson, D. R., & Lapides, P. D. (2000, December). Fraudulent financial reporting: Consideration of industry traits and corporate governance mechanisms. *Accounting Horizons*, *14*(4), 441–454. doi:10.2308/acch.2000.14.4.441

Bell, T., & Carcello, J. (2000). A decision aid for assessing the likelihood of fraudulent financial reporting. *Auditing*, *9*(1), 169–178. doi:10.2308/aud.2000.19.1.169

Benford, F. (1938, March). The law of anomalous numbers. *Proceedings of the American Philosophical Society*, *78*(4), 551–572.

Busta, B., & Sundheim, R. (1992). *Tax return numbers tend to obey Benford's law* (Working Paper No. W93-106-94). Center for Business Research, St. Cloud State University.

Carslaw, C. (1988). Anomalies in income numbers: Evidence of goal-oriented behavior. *The Accounting Review*, *63*(2), 321–327.

Church, B. K., McMillan, J. J., & Schneider, A. (2001). Factors affecting internal auditors' consideration of fraudulent financial reporting during analytical procedures. *Auditing*, *20*(1), 65–80. doi:10.2308/aud.2001.20.1.65

Committee of Sponsoring Organizations of the Treadway Commission. (1999). *Fraudulent financial reporting: 1987-1997: An analysis of U.S. public companies*. Retrieved January 13, 2006, from http://www.coso.org/Publications.htm

Cressey, D. R. (1973). *Other people's money.* Montclair: Patterson Smith.

Debreceny, R. S., & Gray, G. L. (2011). Data Mining of Electronic Mail and Auditing: A Research Agenda. *Journal of Information Systems, 25*(2), 195–226. doi:10.2308/isys-10167

Dorminey, J., Fleming, A. S., Kranacher, M., & Riley, R. A. Jr. (2012). The evolution of fraud theory. *Issues in Accounting Education, 27*(2), 555–579. doi:10.2308/iace-50131

French, J., & Raven, B. (1959). The basis of social power. In D. Cartwright (Ed.), Studies in social power. Ann Arbor, MI: University of Michigan Press.

Goldmann, P. (2009). *Anti-fraud risk and control workbook.* Retrieved from https://onlinelibrary.wiley.com/doi/pdf/10.1002/9781119205654.app3

Green, B. P., & Choi, J. H. (1997). Assessing the risk of management fraud through neural network technology. *Auditing, 16*(1), 14–28.

Hajek, P., & Henriques, R. (2017). Mining corporate annual reports for intelligent detection of financial statement fraud – A comparative study of machine learning methods. *Knowledge-Based Systems, 128,* 139–152. doi:10.1016/j.knosys.2017.05.001

Hamilton, V. L., & Sanders, J. (1995). Crimes of obedience and conformity in the workplace: Surveys of Americans, Russians, and Japanese. *The Journal of Social Issues, 51*(3), 67–88. doi:10.1111/j.1540-4560.1995.tb01335.x

Huang, S. Y., Lin, C.-C., Chiu, A.-A., & Yen, D. C. (2016). Fraud detection using fraud triangle risk factors. *Information Systems Frontiers, 18,* 1–14.

Hurt, R. L. (2016). *Accounting information systems – Basic concepts and current Issues.* New York: McGraw Hill.

Independent Investigation Committee (IIC). (2015). *Investigation Report, 20 July 2015.* Available at https://www.toshiba.co.jp/about/ir/en/news/20151208_2.pdf

Jan, C. (2018). An effective financial statements fraud detection model for the sustainable development of financial markets: Evidence from Taiwan. *Sustainability, 10*(513), 1–14. PMID:30607262

Japan fines Ernst and Young affiliate $17.4 million over Toshiba audit. (2015). *Reuters.* Retrieved from https://www.reuters.com

Kanapickienė, R., & Grundienė, Ž. (2015). The model of fraud detection in financial statements by means of financial ratios. *Procedia: Social and Behavioral Sciences*, *213*, 321–327. doi:10.1016/j.sbspro.2015.11.545

Kassem, R. (2019). Understanding financial reporting fraud in Egypt: Evidence from the audit field. *Third World Quarterly*, *40*(11), 1996–2015. doi:10.1080/014 36597.2019.1626709

Kelman, H. C., & Hamilton, V. L. (1989). *Crimes of obedience*. New Haven, CT: Yale University Press.

Kotsiantis, S., Koumanakos, E., Tzelepis, D., & Tampakas, V. (2006). Forecasting fraudulent financial statements using data mining. *International Journal of Computational Intelligence*, *3*(2), 104–110.

Kranacher, M., Riley, R., & Wells, J. T. (2010). *Forensic accounting and fraud examination*. Wiley.

Lenard, M. J., Petruska, K. A., Alam, P., & Yu, B. (2016). Internal control weaknesses and evidence of real activities manipulation. *Advances in Accounting*, *33*, 47–58. doi:10.1016/j.adiac.2016.04.008

Millan, L. (2011, March 25). Insurers and Social Media: Insurers' use of social networks impinges on privacy rights. *The Lawyers Weekly*. Retrieved from https://www.google.com/search?q=http%3A%2F%2Fwww.lawyersweekly.ca%2Findex.php%3Fsection%3Darticle%26articleid%3D908&ie=&oe=

Nawawi, A., & Salin, A. (2018). Internal control and employees' occupational fraud on expenditure claims. *Journal of Financial Crime*, *25*(3), 891–906. doi:10.1108/JFC-07-2017-0067

Nigrini, M. (1999a). Adding value with digital analysis. *The Internal Auditor*, *56*, 21–23.

Nigrini, M. (1999b, May). I've got your number. *Journal of Accountancy*, *187*(5), 79–83.

Omidi, M., Min, Q., Moradinaftchali, V., & Piri, M. (2019). The Efficacy of Predictive Methods in Financial Statement Fraud. *Discrete Dynamics in Nature and Society*, *2019*(4), 1–12. doi:10.1155/2019/4989140

Othman, R., Ameer, R., & Laswad, F. (2019). *Strategic camouflage: Toshiba's deception tactics 2019*. Asia-Pacific Interdisciplinary Research in Accounting Conference, AUT, Auckland, New Zealand.

Perols, J. (2011). Financial statement fraud detection: An analysis of statistical and machine learning algorithms. *Auditing, 30*(2), 19–50. doi:10.2308/ajpt-50009

Ramamoorti, S., Morrison, D., & Koletar, J. W. (2009). *Bringing Freud to fraud: Understanding the state-of-mind of the C-level suite/white collar offender through "A-B-C" analysis* (Working paper). Institute of Fraud Prevention.

Riadi, I., Umar, R., & Firdonsyah, A. (2017). Identification of Digital Evidence On Android's Blackberry Messenger Using NIST Mobile Forensic Method. *International Journal of Computer Science and Information Security, 15*(5), 155–160.

Rubasundram, G. A. (2015). *Perceived "tone from the top" during a fraud risk assessment.* 7th International Conference on Financial Criminology 2015, Oxford, UK.

Schilit, H. M., Perler, J., & Engelhart, Y. (2018). Financial shenanigans – How to detect accounting gimmicks and fraud in financial report (4th ed.). New York: McGraw-Hill.

Shi, W., Connelly, B. L., & Hoskisson, R. E. (2017). External corporate governance and financial fraud: Cognitive evaluation theory insights on agency theory prescriptions. *Strategic Management Journal, 38*(6), 1268–1286. doi:10.1002mj.2560

Skoda, M., Slavikova, G., & Lajcin, D. (2016). Fraud accounting in Slovakia after times of financial crisis. *International Journal of Economic Perspectives, 10*(4), 139–146.

Skousen, C., Guan, L., & Wetzel, T. (2004). Anomalies and unusual patterns in reported earnings: Japanese managers round earnings. *Journal of International Financial Management & Accounting, 15*(3), 212–234. doi:10.1111/j.1467-646X.2004.00108.x

Smaili, N., & Arroyo, P. (2019). Categorization of Whistleblowers Using the Whistleblowing Triangle. *Journal of Business Ethics, 157*(1), 95–117. doi:10.100710551-017-3663-7

Solieri, S. A., & Hodowanitz, J. (2016). Electronic Audit Confirmations: Leveraging technology to reduce the risks of fraud. *Journal of Forensic & Investigative Accounting, 8*(1), 68–74.

Spathis, C. (2002). Detecting false financial statements using published data: Some evidence from Greece. *Managerial Auditing Journal, 17*(4), 179–191. doi:10.1108/02686900210424321

Stuart, T., & Wang, Y. (2016). Who cooks the books in China, and does it pay? Evidence from private, high-technology firms. *Strategic Management Journal, 37*(13), 2658–2676. doi:10.1002mj.2466

Sutherland, E. H. (1983). *White collar crime: The uncut version*. New Haven, CT: Yale University Press.

Taylor, M., Haggerty, J., Gresty, D., & Lamb, D. (2011, March). Forensic investigation of cloud computing systems. *Network Security*, *2011*(3), 4–9. doi:10.1016/S1353-4858(11)70024-1

Wei, D., Shaoyi, L., & Zhongju, Z. (2018). Leveraging Financial Social Media Data for Corporate Fraud Detection. *Journal of Management Information Systems*, *35*(2), 461–487. doi:10.1080/07421222.2018.1451954

Wolfe, D. T., & Hermanson, D. R. (2004). The fraud diamond: Considering the four elements of fraud. *The CPA Journal*, *74*(12), 38–42.

Zourrig, H., & Park, J. (2019). The effects of cultural tightness and perceived unfairness on Japanese consumers' attitude towards insurance fraud: The mediating effect of rationalization. *Journal of Financial Services Marketing*, *24*(1-2), 21–30. doi:10.105741264-019-00061-w

KEY TERMS AND DEFINITIONS

Conceal: Way in which the alleged fraudsters hide their fraudulent action.

Control: Mechanism established to prevent or minimize error or fraud.

Digital Environment: An environment in which computer and other technological apparatus and systems are used to prepare and produce financial statements.

Financial Statements: The statements required to be produced at the end of the accounting period which includes balance sheet, income statement, and cash flow statement.

Fraud: An action perpetrated with intent to the detriment of the victim(s).

Fraud Diamond Theory: An extension of the fraud triangle theory to include the capability element of the fraudster.

Fraud Triangle Theory: A theory that explains the elements of fraud perpetration, that is, pressure (motive), opportunity, and rationalization.

Investigation: A systematic process of investigating an alleged fraud.

ENDNOTE

[1]   Personal Computer.

Chapter 12

A Compendium of Cloud Forensics

Mohd. Akbar
Integral University, India

Mohammad Suaib
Integral University, India

Mohd. Shahid Husain
🆔 https://orcid.org/0000-0003-4864-9485
Ministry of Higher Education, Oman

Saurabh Shukla
University Teknologi of Petronas, Malaysia

ABSTRACT

The cloud computing environment is one of the most promising technologies in the development of computing resources. The cloud service providers provide almost every resource for computing to their users through the internet. With all its advantages, cloud computing has major security issues. Especially in the case of public clouds, anyone can misuse the services for performing unlawful activities. The traditional approaches used for cyber forensics and network forensics are not adequate for the cloud environment because of many technical constraints. There is a need for setting up effective countermeasures that can help an investigator to identify and track unlawful activities happened in a cloud environment. Cloud forensics is an emerging area of research where the researchers aim to provide effective digital forensic techniques that help in the investigation of digital crimes in a cloud environment. The cloud environment helps to extract data even from devices that are not physically accessible. However, cloud forensics is not as easy as it seems; a lot of the success depends on the cloud service model implemented in

DOI: 10.4018/978-1-7998-1558-7.ch012

the context. Getting the support of cloud service providers in accessing the potential sources of evidence necessary for investigation is also a major concern. Another critical aspect of cloud forensics is dealing with legal issues. This chapter discusses the basic concepts of cloud forensics, its challenges, and future directions.

INTRODUCTION

Cloud computing has emerged as one of the most transformative computing technologies. Cloud computing is drastically changing the information technology business. Organizations, specifically startups, are now looking for low-cost solutions for creating, delivering, accessing and managing IT services. Gartner (Gartner Forecasts, 2019) predicts that the worldwide public cloud services market will grow by 17.5 percent in 2019 from 2018. With the expansion of the cloud services market, digital forensic cases are also increasing exponentially. According to Roussev et. al. (V. Roussev, 2009), we need sophisticated methods to deal with cloud forensic because the amount of data that must be processed in expanding the cloud environment is outgrowing the ability to process it in time.

The emergence of cloud computing technologies not only intensifies the issue of extracting data from various sources and analyzing the large volume of data but also scale up digital crime activities (Verma, 2018). This opens up a new frontier for cyber-crime investigations. The forensic experts must develop more sophisticated tools to counter the challenges in cloud computing environments. Likewise, cloud service providers, as well as customers using cloud services, have to implement measures that can help in reducing cloud security risks.

CLOUD FORENSIC

Cloud forensic is an interdisciplinary science where more sophisticated digital forensic techniques are incorporated to identify and investigate any illegal activity in the cloud computing environment. According to NIST (Grance, 2011), Cloud computing can be defined as a shared collection of configurable networked resources (e.g., networks, servers, storage, applications, and services) that can be reconfigured quickly with minimal effort. Digital forensics is the application of computer science principles to recover electronic evidence for presentation in a court of law (K. Kent, 2006).

A forensic investigation of networks is commonly called Network forensic. The backbone of cloud computing is the internet and hence cloud computing is based on broad network access. In that sense cloud forensic is a kind of network forensic. Therefore, in cloud forensic one has to go through the same stages of network forensic but with the incorporation of techniques customized to the cloud computing environments.

Cloud computing is a budding paradigm with certain characteristics. Due to these characteristics, it reduces the IT cost dramatically and business and government are rapidly adopting it. Cloud service providers need to maintain multiple data servers at different locations. Data is replicated on these servers as a backup in case of any failure. However, the replication of data on multiple servers ensures service availability also increases the risk of data security. The role of cloud service providers and customers concerning forensic depends on the cloud service model implemented in the context. Similarly, how the users sharing the same cloud resource communicate with each other depends on the deployment model being employed.

Cloud forensic faces additional legal challenges due to the intrinsic characteristics of multiple jurisdictions and multi-tenancy. Most of the cloud forensic investigations require sophisticated communications between all the entities involved, sharing of resources by multiple users (multi-tenancy) and collaborative support from international law enforcement agencies.

TECHNICAL ASPECTS OF CLOUD FORENSIC

We know that the traditional forensic approach is not effective in the cloud environment due to the intrinsic characteristics of cloud computing. Hence there is a need for tailored methods and tools to help investigators to perform the forensic process in a cloud computing environment. The process includes a collection of forensic data, live forensic, evidence segregation, investigation in virtualized environments and taking proactive measures.

The first step in forensic investigation is identifying the resources/media and extracting the data which helps in further investigation and can be used as evidence. These data resources can be located in the provider infrastructure or it can of clients. Different cloud service models (Husain, 2017)provides a different level of access and authority to the users and service providers. Based on the service model we need to implement data extraction methods that help in maintaining the data integrity and confidentiality of other users in the multi-tenancy environment without compromising rules and regulations of the jurisdictions from where data is extracted.

One of the basic characteristics of cloud computing is multi-tenancy (Husain, 2017). It helps in minimizing the cost by sharing resources. According to the NIST, the Resources are dynamically assigned and reassigned according to consumer demand from a pool of resources to serve multiple users simultaneously in a multi-tenancy environment. The process of evidence segregation in the cloud environment is a complex one. To separate forensic data between multiple tenants, it requires the incorporation of tailored tools and techniques in various cloud deployment models and cloud service models.

The tools and techniques for cloud forensic need to be elastic. As we know rapid elasticity is one of the key features of cloud computing i.e.to adapt the changing workload, cloud resources can be provisioned and de-provisioned on demand. Hence large-scale static and live forensic tools are required for data acquisition & recovery (including volatile data collection), evidence examination and evidence analysis.

Virtualization is a key technology that is used to serve multiple cloud service users simultaneously. In virtualization, multiple users access a single resource with full transparency. This is implemented by the virtual machines called the hypervisor. There is a need for developing procedures that can be used for investigating hypervisors. Due to this virtualized environment tools and techniques must be developed to physically locate forensic data with specific timestamps while taking into consideration the jurisdictional issues. It is advised to take some proactive measures that can significantly help cloud forensic investigations in case of some illegal activity. These proactive measures may include saving snapshots of storage on regular intervals, making a log of activities, constantly tracking authentication and access control, and performing object-level auditing of all accesses.

ENTITIES INVOLVED IN CLOUD FORENSIC

There are two main entities involved in a cloud environment. a) Cloud service provider; provides different services on demand to the customers based on the cloud service model implemented. b) Customers; users of cloud services on pay per usage concept.

However, in many cases, there are other entities involved like third party vendors and other cloud service providers. In the case of cloud forensic, the investigator has to track all the entities involved and the success of the investigation depends on the support and coordination of all the entities. If the investigator misses any entity involved or there is a lack of coordination of responsibilities between all the entities involved parties, it will create serious problems in the investigation of the case.

Collaboration and communication in case of forensic activities can be effectively aided by service level agreements (SLAs) and well laid Organizational policies. For the investigation of the forensic cases, the investigators need effective means of collaboration and communication with not only services providers, customers, and law enforcement agencies but also with third-party vendors and experts from academia. The role of vendors and third parties can be very helpful in assisting investigators in auditing and compliance processes while academic experts can play a vital role in case of an investigation by providing technical expertise in improving the efficiency and effectiveness of the investigations.

For the implementation of effective cloud forensic measures, there should be effective communication and collaboration between cloud service providers, customers, and third-party vendors. There is also a need for proper assistance from academia and the research community for the development of sophisticated measures against crimes. Hence there are different entities/personals involved and there should be proper distribution of roles and responsibilities among them.

Investigators

Investigators are professionals having experience in identifying and tracing the unlawful activities. Investigators have to collaborate with other entities like law enforcement agencies, cloud service providers, customers, third party venders and an expert from academia & research. Investigators are responsible for probing a case, tracing down the activities and finally preparing the case report based on legal and technical parameters.

Incident Handlers

In a distributed system like cloud there may be a variety of security issues such as unauthorized data access, data leakage or loss, breach of tenant confidentiality, illegal use of systems, malicious code attacks, insider attacks and denial of service attacks. Every cloud entity should have a well-planned module to identify and counter any incident which compromises the security of the cloud system. Incident handlers are used to monitor the cloud system and in case of any security incidents, it takes countermeasures or notifies the administrators.

IT Professionals

They are the skilled professionals in the area of ethical hacking, network and cloud system security. They provide expert knowledge and technical support to the investigators in getting details of the crime and also help them in retrieving relevant data from various sources and analyzing it.

Legal Advisors

The cloud environment is a global computing environment that can be accessed without any geographical boundary. Hence cloud is a multi-jurisdictional computing environment providing services to multiple users simultaneously. Investigators involved in probing any cyber forensic case needs help from a legal professional who can assist the investigators to investigate the case in multi-jurisdiction without violating any rule and help in assuring the confidentialities of the users sharing the same resources. These legal advisors also help in preparing service level agreements and play a role in getting collaboration with external law enforcement agencies in investigating cases.

External Entities

To investigate any case cooperation and collaboration is required with not only internal staff but also with external parties. The system should have well defined transparent policies and guidelines with the consent of internal staff and external parties. These guidelines help the external parties to perform their roles as per the law enforced in the jurisdiction.

LEGAL ASPECTS

One of the key characteristics of the cloud computing environment is facilitating multiple users simultaneously (Multi-tenancy) across the globe (multi-jurisdiction). This vital feature is one of the reasons behind the success of cloud computing but at the same time, it is one of the major legal concern especially in investigating a cloud forensic case this issue aggravates.

With the advice of legal experts, and with the consent of all the cloud entities, a transparent legal document is created called service level agreement (SLA). All the entities are bound to follow this agreement. This SLA clearly defines the legal aspects and the roles each entity must play to support the investigation in case of any crime.

It is also required to implement proper regulations to monitor the investigation activities to ensure the confidentiality and privacy of the customers sharing the same resource. Because of the multi-jurisdiction environment, the investigators have to be aware of the international laws and should be careful during the investigation that no law should be violated.

CHALLENGES OF CLOUD FORENSIC

Due to its key characteristics, Cloud computing has many advantages but these features also open new avenues for the crime. Investigators have to perform many activities during the probe of any crime like identification of resources, extracting the required data, analysis of the retrieved data for tracing the illegal activities, segregation and classification of the data, prediction and making case reports. To perform these activities the investigators, need to collaborate with internal and external entities, law enforcement agencies, Information Technology professionals and academia. Some of the challenges an investigator may face in different stages during the case investigation are as follows:

Data Collection

The collection of data related to an activity is the basic step to start any investigation. Access of data depends on the cloud deployment model as well as the cloud service model being implemented. In general, customers don't have any information about the physical location of their data and hence have no control over it, especially in the case of SaaS (Software as a Service) model. To provide backup service providers need to maintain multiple copies of data at a different location and hence they intentionally hide the physical locations of data from customers.

While drafting SLAs the CSPs generally ignore to incorporate terms for data usage that can help forensic investigators in data collection. For example, SaaS providers may not provide IPlogs of client accesses, and IaaS providers may not provide recent virtual machines and disk images. Even most of the customers don't have access to log files and they cannot perform real-time monitoring on their own.

Live Forensic

As discussed in previous section, extracting the relevant data is the first step in forensic investigation. The success of the crime investigation depends on the analysis of the data recovered from various sources. Hence it is very crucial to gather all the data related to a case in time. To seize and analyze the relevant data from multiple sources we need to follow standard operating procedures following the legislation.

Due to the increase of RAM size in modern computer systems, the volume of volatile data is also increased. Volatile data means the digitally stored data having a high probability of being deleted or altered. Investigators aim to identify the relevant data, recover it, preserve it and present the facts after analyzing the data that might become evidence in a trial.

Live forensic deals with capturing the data which is volatile and can be altered or lost if the system gets off. Volatile data is even more crucial in the case of cloud forensic. Live forensic helps in recovering deleted data, identifying the ownership of the deleted data (a vital aspect in the case of multi-tenancy) by extracting the traces of data from memory snapshots (Amazon, n.d.). These recovered data from traces are used to reconstruct the scenario of the event in the cloud.

Evidence Segregation

Because of the multi-tenancy feature of the cloud computing environment, multiple users share the same physical resources simultaneously. This is a transparent approach where each user thinks he is the only one using the resource. However, instead of a physical resource, they have access to only virtual copies of the resources. The service providers maintain an audit log to store the data and activities of multiple users sharing the same physical resource. While the investigation of a case, it is a challenge for investigators to identify and segregate the resources and data required for the case without compromising the confidentiality and privacy of the other customers sharing the same resource.

Cloud computing is a budding area and to attract more customers, most service providers have a very simple (and insecure) registration system. Anyone across the globe can easily register for cloud services anonymously and access them. Criminals make use of this feature by registering with unknown identities to perform illegal activities. It is very difficult for investigators to identify and trace the perpetrators in such situations.

The segregation policies and the process should be incorporated in service level agreements (SLA) with the consent of service providers, cloud customers, and law enforcement agencies.

To separate data from multiple cloud users sharing the same resource, encryption techniques are used by most of the cloud service providers. It is recommended to the users of cloud service, that they should upload the sensitive data on the cloud in encrypted form as sometimes the encryption feature is not provided by the CSP or it's a week.

The procedure for encryption key management should also be formalized between the service providers and service users by the legal standards.

Virtualization

To provide reliability and to facilitate multiple users simultaneously, cloud computing maintains data and computational redundancy by making replicas of resources (Mishra, 2015). Virtualization is a key characteristic of a cloud computing environment where multiple users access the virtual replicas of the resources. These virtual copies of resources are run, provisioned and monitored by the module called 'hypervisor'. There is a lack of formal policies and procedures to investigate the hypervisors, and that makes hypervisor a soft target for criminals.

For backup and increased reliability, mirroring (replication) of data is done on multiple servers in different locations across the globe. Lack of information about real physical location, the investigators may unknowingly violate laws and regulations because they do not have clear information about data storage jurisdictions (ENISA, 2009).

Lack of Experts

Until recently, cloud forensic investigations are also carried by traditional digital forensic experts. In this era of rapidly-evolving cloud technologies, conventional forensic tools and techniques are not effective. There is a need for professionals having expertise in sophisticated techniques concerning the cloud computing environment to deal with various technical and legal challenges involved in cloud forensic.

Participation of Third Party/Vendors

To provide customize facilities to the customers, the service providers collaborate with third parties or vendors. Also, many of the log files are maintained by these external entities. During the investigation of a crime, the investigators have to identify the external entities that may involve and get support from them. For the successful investigation, proper coordination and communication are required between all the parties (including internal and external entities). There is no standard policy or procedure that can assist the investigators to investigate the third parties.

Multiple Jurisdictions

The cloud computing environment is expanded across the globe. This creates a lot of problems for investigators as different regulations are enforced by different jurisdictions for data privacy and security. There is no central body to standardize laws worldwide for accessing and recovering data for investigation purposes.

SLA (Service Level Agreements)

Service level agreements are an important document that defines the terms and conditions on which the service provider and the cloud customer are agreed. Most of the customers are not aware of the issues that may arise in a cloud forensic investigation and their significance. Service providers also neglect many terms which are important regarding forensic investigation from SLAs, they don't have the legal and technical expertise to deal with such issues. So there is an urgent need for some international rules and regulations to monitor such activities and provide transparency in SLAs.

DRIVING FORCES BEHIND CLOUD FORENSIC

Although cloud forensic is currently facing a lot of challenges, there are several factors that motivate the experts in the field of cloud forensics.

Cost-effectiveness

Just like other services, forensic capabilities can also be offered as a service in a cloud environment which can help enterprises to afford forensic services at a low cost.

Data durability

To deal with volatile data, Amazon S3 and Amazon Simple DB ensure object durability by storing objects multiple times in multiple availability zones on the initial write. Subsequently, they further replicate the objects to reduce the risk of failure due to device unavailability and bit rot (Amazon, n.d.).

Robustness

Techniques like on-demand cloning of virtual machines and provision for storing version of every object stored has increased the robustness of the forensic system. Like in case of any illegal activity, customers himself can take a clone of the live virtual machine and perform offline forensic analysis in less time. Also, this process can be speedup by concurrently analyzing multiple clones.

Scalability

One of the key characteristics of cloud computing is scalability. The service provider's provision or de-provision the resources based on the demand of the customers. This also provides flexibility to the customer, they can demand the services based on the current requirement and pay per usage. This feature can help in the forensic investigation by getting all the resources required for investigation activities like storage for maintaining logs and other resources for searching, extracting and processing data.

FUTURE DIRECTIONS

In the recent past, some prominent work has been done in the field of cloud forensics. The concept of security as a service is emerging in cloud computing. Research has demonstrated the advantages of cloud-based anti-virus software (J. Oberheide, 2008) and cloud platforms for forensic computing (V. Roussev, 2009). Cloud forensic is still in the early stage and there are a lot of areas where researchers, experts, and academicians can contribute. Some of the opportunities/areas where one can focus on are:

- Securing cloud computing
- Defining forensic policies and standards about cloud forensic keeping in mind the multi-jurisdiction.
- Tenant's confidentiality and privacy in the multi-tenant environment.
- Protected virtualization by implementing tools and techniques to secure hypervisor.
- Security as a service
- Forensic as a service

CONCLUSION

Nowadays, with most of our company's critical data moved to Cloud service providers, one of our major concerns is dealing with security matters. That includes being able to quickly respond to and report events that may lead to legal issues such as lawsuits and, in extreme instances, even involve law enforcement. This is by no means an easy task and matters are further complicated by the fact that we have to trust our Cloud provider's ability to deliver digital forensics data in the case of any legal dispute (either civil or criminal) during cyber attacks or even if a data breach occurs. Cloud forensics combines Cloud computing and digital forensics, which mainly focuses on the gathering of digital forensic information from a Cloud infrastructure.

Cloud forensics is an emerging need to counter cybercrime. The traditional tools and techniques of digital forensic are not capable enough to counter sophisticated crimes done in the cloud environment. Many of the intrinsic features of the cloud computing environment help the criminals and post vital challenges for forensic investigators. However, these features can also be utilized for strengthening cloud forensic.

Not having standard guidelines and a lack of a worldwide authority to deal with legal issues is one of the major concerns in cloud forensic.

Nevertheless, cloud forensic provides various areas of research that can significantly advance and improve cyber forensic.

REFERENCES

Amazon. (n.d.). *AWS Security Center*. Retrieved from aws.amazon.com/security

ENISA. (2009). *Cloud Computing Risk Assessment*. Retrieved from www.enisa. europa.eu/act/rm/files/deliverables/cloud-computing-risk-assessment

Gartner Forecasts. (2019, April). Retrieved from Gartner: https://www.gartner. com/en/newsroom/press-releases/2019-04-02-gartner-forecasts-worldwide-public-cloud-revenue-to-g

Grance, P. M. (2011). *The NIST Definition of Cloud Computing. Special Publication 800-145 (Draft)*. Gaithersburg, MD: National Institute of Standards and Technology.

Husain, M. S. (2017). Cloud Computing in E-Governance: Indian Perspective. In Securing Government Information and Data in Developing Countries (pp. 104-114). IGI Global.

Kent, K. (2006). *Guide to Integrating Forensic Techniques into Incident Response. Special Publication 800-86*. National Institute of Standards and Technology.

Mishra, N. S. (2015). A compendium over cloud computing cryptographic algorithms and security issues. *BVICA M's International Journal of Information Technology*, 810.

Oberheide, J. E. C. (2008). CloudAV: N-version antivirus in the network cloud. *Proceedings of the Seventeenth USENIX Security Conference*, 91–106.

Roussev, V. L. W. (2009). A cloud computing platform for large-scale forensic computing. In Advances in Digital Forensics V (pp. 201-214). Springer.

Verma, A. A. (2018). Analysis of DDOS attack Detection and Prevention in Cloud Environment: A Review. *International Journal of Advanced Research in Computer Science*.

KEY TERMS AND DEFINITIONS

Cloud Computing: Cloud computing is the use of hardware and software to deliver a service over a network (typically the internet). With cloud computing, users can access files and use applications from any device that can access the internet.

Cloud Forensics: Cloud forensics is cross-discipline between cloud computing and digital forensics.

Digital Forensics: Computer forensics, also known as digital forensics, on the other hand is a much more specific discipline, which involves the analysis of computers and other electronic devices in order to produce legal evidence of a crime or unauthorized action.

ICT: Information and communication technology, which makes use of digital systems for storing, retrieving, and sending information.

Live Forensics: Live data forensics is one part of computer forensics which is a branch of digital forensic science pertaining to legal evidence found in computers.

Network Forensics: Network forensics is a sub-branch of digital forensics relating to the monitoring and analysis of computer network traffic.

Chapter 13
Application of Machine Learning In Forensic Science

Mohammad Haroon
Integral University, India

Manish Madhava Tripathi
Integral University, India

Faiyaz Ahmad
Integral University, India

ABSTRACT

In this chapter, the authors explore the use of machine learning methodology for cyber forensics as machine learning has proven its importance and efficiency. For classification and identification purposes in forensic science, pattern recognition algorithms can be very helpful.

INTRODUCTION

Machine learning is the application of artificial intelligence, and it's a very important area of computer science, in which a computer can learn from raw data and machine draw its conclusion. The machine can decide by own experience, it cannot be programmed. Machine learning technologies are used in different fields across the world in these days. In these days a large amount of data is created day by day and with the help of machine learning technology, machine analyses the data and infer the conclusion. In context of data analysis, this technique i.e. gathering of data, analyzing of data and generating information from that is commonly known as data mining. Developing machine learning algorithms is a complex task. The application

DOI: 10.4018/978-1-7998-1558-7.ch013

of machine learning to find pattern and interpret data without involvement of human, is very efficient and powerful technique. The use of machine learning is increasing in the last couple of years. In forensic science, machine learning techniques are playing a significant role. Crime detection, pattern recognition and similar tasks can easily performed by machine learning.

Data is created day by day with rapid rate. Now massive data is available these days. But most of the data are noisy. By applying machine learning and signal processing techniques, we can get quality data for processing. With the advent of the IoT system, many types of medical data are sampled by machine learning methods and signal processing techniques (M. F. S. Ana Azevedo. Kdd, semma and crisp-dm, 2008).

Machine learning helped several data scientists across the world to perform various studies on such kind of huge data; every data analyst has come across very noisy data. Hence to properly feed the data in a processing model, data preprocessing must be performed.

Machine learning is the field of artificial intelligence, in which machines can take decision without any specific programming. All programs can learn from its own experiences when machine solved a problem, its knowledge base gets updated and hence its performance. Machine learning is broadly categorized into two different parts; one is supervised learning another is unsupervised learning (P. J. S. W. Anne H. Milley James D, 1998).

MACHINE LEARNING

Machine learning is the application of artificial intelligence. Arthur Samuel describes machine learning as a field where the computer learns without any explicit program. A more formal definition of machine learning can be given as: computer trying to learn from its input and output pattern. In general, the machine automatically designs an algorithm with the help of input and output data. Traditionally we design the algorithm then we submit the input data then after we get the result, but in machine learning, first, we trained the machine by submitting input as well as output then machine design the algorithm. Tom Michel provides a more modern definition of machine learning, a computer program is said to learn from own experience during the solving of any task, and the performance of the computer program must be improved with respect to experience like in checker playing game.

E = the experience of playing such game
T= the task of playing game
P= the probability that the program will win the game.

The machine-learning broadly categorized as into main domain

1: supervised learning
2: unsupervised learning

SUPERVISED LEARNING

In these methods, the learning process will be complete under the supervision of any instructor, means all the output data are already given along with input data set. The system learns on the idea that there is a relationship between input and output data sets.

Supervised learning is further categorized into two subdomains, first is regression and second is classification. In regression Problem, we try to predict the result with the help of continuous function. Meaning that, we're trying to map input variable to some continuous function, in classification problem we trying to map input variable to some discrete function (S. H. B. S. R. Bulkley, 1999).

UNSUPERVISED LEARNING

This kind of learning is Agent-based learning, in this learning agent try to learn by own effort. In this learning there is no training data, we are simply put in the input, and based on the knowledge base of the system the input will be processed into an output. We are driving the structure of data where we don't necessarily know the effect of a variable, in unsupervised learning, there is no feedback.

In clustering suppose we are going to group millions of different records like genes, first, the clustering machine understand the data characteristics means gene life span, gene location, gene role etc. On the basis of above parameters, similar genes whose life span is approximately equal they can be arranged in a single group similarly the gene whose location matches they arrange in another group by the help of these policies the geans can be arranged into number of groups that group is known as Cluster (P. C. et. al. Crisp-dm 1.0, 2010).

In non-clustering we cannot arrange the entire sample into a number of a group based on the similar parameter, like in Cocktail party it's not easy to identify the individual voice and music from a mess of sound.

MODEL REPRESENTATION

For making a model for machine learning, we give sample data X_i as an input, and we are also putting the corresponding output, Y_i. Now the pair (Xi, Yi) is known as training data, or data set by which machine can be trained. The variable X and Y are known as the input space variable and output space variable.

In supervised learning, our goal is to give a training set of X and Y to learn a function H(X): Y so that H(X) is known as a good predictor of the output value y for any given x.

Here this function is called a hypothesis.

The target variable that we are trying to predict is continuous; we call the above problem as regression problem.

Figure 1. Machine Learning Training Process

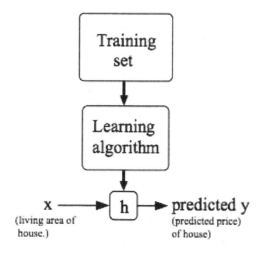

COST FUNCTION

We can check the accuracy of our hypothesis by using a cost function. We can take the average difference of all the result of hypothesis with input from X and the actual output y.

The cost function is calculated by the given formula

J (theta0-theta1) =1/2m å from i=1to m (h (theta $(X_i$-$Y_i)$/2

Visually all training data are scattered on the XY plane, so we try to make a straight line between our skeletal training data on the XY plane. Our object is to find the best line in XY plane so that the mean error should be minimized (I. C. e. a. Fidel, 2016).

In the case of classification, we are going to classify our input data into different classes. Like in decision tree, we perform a different kind of diffusion-based approach on every decision-making node. In the learning process we perform branching on the basis of examples and based on their outcome we are taking a decision. But in case of an uncertain situation, we will not be able to decide based on current data.

ARTIFICIAL NEURAL NETWORK

An artificial neural network is analogous to the human neural network. In artificial neural network we are using neuron, a Processing Unit. These neurons are interconnected. We are getting the data from the dendrite that is also known as an input device of the neural network, the result is produced from the output device that is known as the axon and in between we may have n number of layers. Artificial neural network is very complex, how your input is going to proceed from the input layer to the hidden layer, and hidden layer to the output device, and how your input is going to be converted to an output, all the process was very complex. The processing of neurons in artificial intelligence is fully dependant on the input and the weight we are applying.

In general artificial neural network is complex to implement. Whatever input we give to the artificial neural network that particular input is being computed by some linear and nonlinear function. The connections of artificial neural networks are known as the edge. We assign some initial weight for each edge; these weights are updated in the learning process. In Artificial neural network another parameter that is being used is known as the threshold, if the value of function of input as well as the weight applied on the neurons is greater than the value of Threshold it means neurons will perform the computing action.

APPLICATION AREA OF MACHINE LEARNING

We are using the machine learning concept in various fields, like in Robo-war, robotic surgery, horticulture, agriculture.

Some of the machines learning applications are given as under

Web Searching

Maximum search engine on the website is based on the machine learning concept, how to tag our keyword with the search engine this concept is learned by the machine.

Photo Tagging

When we are uploading a photograph on social media services like Facebook at that moment, learning algorithms behind the web page provide suggestions to tag my friends and relative in the photograph.

Spam Detection

We regularly receive collection of email messages on our email accounts like Google but how Google account recognises which is the real mail and which is the Spam on the basis of mail tag directory. So here the machine learning concept comes into picture to filter the mail and send the unusual and unimportant mail to my spam folder and important mail to my mailbox folder.

Data Analysis

In these days' majorities of companies are using machine learning concept to detect whether the business is going to be increase or decrease as per the market survey. Politicians are also using machine learning concept to predict their winning probability as well as losing probability as per that initial situation. We are also using machine learning concept for natural language understanding, digital image processing, to understand the concept of pattern recognition, to understand the concept of database design and algorithms. A variety of data is being created these days; which data is important and which data is not important that particular thing can be categorized by the concept of data mining. In medical automation we have so many medical records and based on those records we build a system which helps doctors in practicing and better treatment of their patients.

APPLICATION THAT CANNOT BE PROGRAM

There are applications which cannot be programed, in that situation we are using a machine learning concept to carry out the decision like in natural language processing understanding of questions and applying out a question to the respective output is not easy by the machine. So in this situation, artificial intelligence systems are going to use the concept of machine learning. We also need to design a suitable algorithm. Some applications which cannot be solved using traditional methods are face recognition, handwriting recognition, natural language processing, computer vision, common sense perception, forecasting, driving an autonomous car etc. These kind of applications are not easy to program. In the case of mundane tasks that cannot be programmed easily, we are using machine learning concept to program the system automatically.

LEARNING

Machine learning is also analogous to human learning like we have long-term memory; we build knowledgebase from our experience, from the environment, from the tutor, from our colleagues, from our parents. In the same way machine can learn by which it can solve any kind of problem. Machines can learn from the environment and all the data can be stored inside the knowledge base of the machine so that machine uses that particular knowledge to solve the problem in future. Machine learning is fully based on the concept of making the account of its input data. And with the help of a machine learning concept, the size of the knowledge base keeps on increasing.

Some of the machines learning concepts are given as under:

Machine Learning and Medium

Suppose you are working in any real estate agency, so it's very easy for you to predict the house prices. Reason being, you have some historical data and you know that the house has been sold about this expected cost. And you are much familiar with the current market prices. Based on some parameters like area construction, material, floor of the house etc, you can easily predict the price of new house. The parameter we are using like area, floor, and construction material are known as indicators in terms of machine learning.

But when the system size is bigger, the sample size is also bigger; a lot of indicators, lots of attributes are also given, and in this situation decision is complex. In this situation, we use the concept of machine learning. By using machine learning concept, we can easily make decision or predict the output.

In machine learning approach, there is not a single algorithm to perform the computation of any given problem. No algorithm works best for every problem and it especially relevant in context of machine learning. For example, every time neural network is not the best approach to perform all the calculation and make the decision, sometime decision tree and other algorithms performs significantly better than neural network. There are many factors depend on the performance of any machine learning approach like data structure, data set and the size of data etc.

We try different algorithms to solve the problem, and evaluate the result we got

Figure 2. Linear Regression

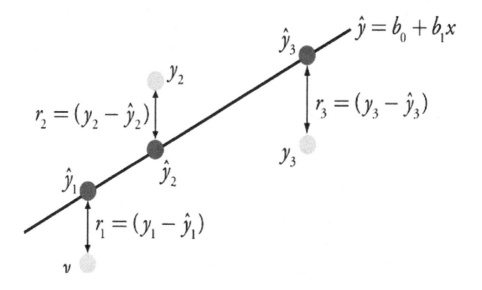

from different algorithms. We choose the best algorithm among all in context based on execution time, efficiency and throughput of the algorithm.

THE BIG PRINCIPLE

Machine learning is the implementation of algorithm to learn by the target function. By the machine learning concept, we try to map our input data to some of the function $y = f(x)$, where x is the input variable and $f(x)$ is the function by which we are predicting the respective output y.

Linear Regression

Predictive modeling is primarily concerned to minimize the error of a model, or making the most accurate predictive result for the given problem. Linear Regression is the best way to map input variable to the output variable. All the input variables are applied to the linear regression model with sum weight known as coefficient of the input. The given representation is a straight line in which input and output will meet with a coefficient value of B

Logistic Regression

Logistic reasoning is another technique adopted by machine learning from the field of statistics. It is used in binary classification. Logistic regression is like linear regression that goes to find the value of coefficient that is weight of each input variable. Unlike the linear regression, this will be calculated by nonlinear function called the Logistic function.

Figure 3. Logistic Relation sample

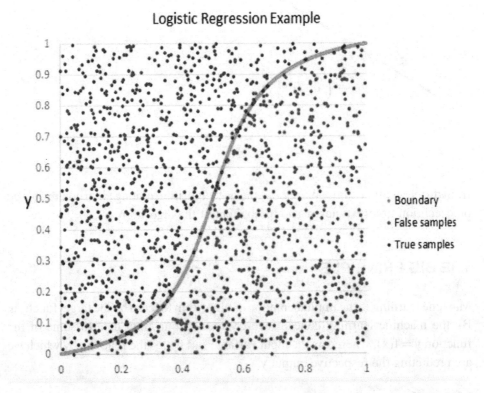

Classification and Regression Trees

The decision tree is the important learning algorithm. A decision tree is going to help us to decide whether this work will be going to be performed or not. This tree is also helping us for predictive modelling. The decision tree has several types like binary decision tree and general decision tree.

The leaf node of the decision tree is known as the classified node. Root node and intermediate nodes are known as decision-making node. All the decisions will start from the root node and it will go to the leave node. The value of the leaf node shows the result of the decision tree.

Naive Bayes

Naive Bayes is a powerful algorithm for predictive modeling. This approach we use in the case of un-sampled data. This model is fully based on probability that cannot be calculated directly from the training data. For taking a decision, we calculate the probability of each class individually, after that we are in the position to take the decision. In Naive Bayes, all the input data is treated as an independent variable, after the calculation of the probability of all the individual variables we will take the decision.

K-Nearest Neighbors

KNN approach is a very simple and very effective approach. We use this model for the training of the system. With the help of the KNN, machine will take the right decision and may predict output based on the training data set. Here K signifies the training set of data. For regression, K might be the mean of data. For classification might be the mode of data. The method how to determine the dissimilarity between two different data items, the simplest way is the use of Euclidean distance.

Figure 4. Decision tree in Machine Learning Algorithm

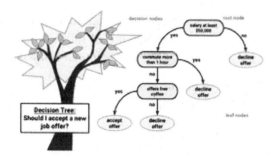

Learning Vector Quantization

Learning vector quantization algorithm is a machine learning algorithm. By learning vector quantization algorithm all the training data can be categorized, instances having the same distance, can be grouped into the same cluster for quantization purposes.

CONCLUSION

Machine learning constitutes an important area of computational intelligence dealing with the ability of computer machines to learn through knowledge representation, processing and storing. Machine learning gives a solution to a complex problem like mathematical problems and medical problems. Machine learning enable machines to work like a human, it's like a human brain. Machine learning is important in these days because of the diversity of data. Different kinds of data like audio data, video data, image data, time-series data, so we required an intelligent storage system for storing various data. Overall the computation is done by the machine learning algorithm.

These approaches can help in cyber forensics like face recognition problem. For face recognition, advance principal constituent analysis method is proposed that employs the local particular information enclosed in face image patches. Exclusive research on two standard face data set showed the routine of the planned method for PCA similar algorithms.

REFERENCES

Ana Azevedo, M. F. S. (2008). A parallel overview. *IADIS European Conference on Data Mining*.

Chao Zhang, G. Z., & Huang, Y. (2010). Study on the application of knowledge discovery in data bases to the decision making of railway track safety in china. *Management and Service Science (MASS) International Conference*.

Crisp-dm 1.0, (2018). *Step-by-step data mining guide*. Retrieved from https://www.the-modeling-agency.com/crisp-dm.pdf

I. C. e. a. Fidel Reb_on. (2015). An antifraud system for tourism smes in the context of electronic operations with credit cards. *American Journal of Intelligent Systems*.

Milley & Seabolt. (1998). *Data mining and the case for sampling solving business problems using sas R enterprise minertm software*. SAS Institute Inc.

Srivastava, S., Haroon, M., & Bajaj, A. (2013). Web document information extraction using class attribute approach. *4th International Conference on Computer and Communication Technology (ICCCT)*, 17-22. 10.1109/ICCCT.2013.6749596

KEY TERMS AND DEFINITIONS

Digital Forensics: Computer forensics, also known as digital forensics, on the other hand is a much more specific discipline, which involves the analysis of computers and other electronic devices in order to produce legal evidence of a crime or unauthorized action.

Human Learning: Human learning generates knowledge, residing in the brain.

KNN: KNN is the distance-based algorithm K-nearest neighbor.

Linear Regression: Linear regression is used when your response variable is continuous.

Logistic Regression: Logistic regression is used when the response variable is categorical in nature.

Machine Learning: Machine learning is an application of artificial intelligence (AI) that provides systems the ability to automatically learn and improve from experience without being explicitly programmed.

Naive Bayes: This classifier is statistical based Naïve Bayes classifier.

Supervised Learning: In supervised learning, you train the machine using data which is well "labeled." Supervised learning allows you to collect data or produce a data output from the previous experience.

Unsupervised Learning: Unsupervised learning is a machine learning technique, where you do not need to supervise the model.

Chapter 14
Digital Forensics and Data Mining

Mohammad Suaib
Integral University, India

Mohd. Akbar
Integral University, India

Mohd. Shahid Husain
iD https://orcid.org/0000-0003-4864-9485
Ministry of Higher Education, Oman

ABSTRACT

Digital forensic experts need to identify and collect the data stored in electronic devices. Further, this acquired data has to be analyzed to produce digital evidence. Data mining techniques have been successfully implemented in various applications across the domains. Data mining techniques help us to gain insight from a large volume of data. It helps us to predict the pattern, classify the data, and other various aspects of the data based on the users' perspective. Digital forensics is a sophisticated area of research. As the information age is revolutionizing at an inconceivable speed and the information stored in digital form is growing at a rapid rate, law enforcement agencies have a heavy reliance on digital forensic techniques that can provide timely acquisition of data, zero fault data processing, and accurate interpretation of data. This chapter gives an overview of the tasks involved in cyber forensics. It also discusses the traditional approach for digital forensics and how the integration of data mining techniques can enhance the efficiency and reliability of the existing systems used for cyber forensics.

DOI: 10.4018/978-1-7998-1558-7.ch014

INTRODUCTION

Digital forensics is the process that applies state of the art technologies to collect and analyze data stored on electronic media to produce evidence, which is crucial and admissible to cyber investigations.

A digital forensic investigation is an examination of the questionable or unusual activities in the Cyberspace. Figure 1 shows the complete phases of Digital Forensic investigation processes defined by (K. Kent, 2006).

a) **Collection phase:** The first step in the forensic process is to identify potential sources of data and acquire forensic data from them. Major sources of data identified by (Song, 2008) are desktops, storage media, Routers, Cell Phones, Digital Camera, etc. The forensic experts have to decide and plan to acquire data from these sources according to their importance, volatility and other parameters like how much effort is required to collect data.

b) **Examination phase:** In the next phase, the acquired data is examined. This phase consists of assessing and extracting the relevant pieces of information from the data acquired in phase 1.

c) **Analysis phase:** The relevant data, extracted in the previous phase has been analyzed in this phase. The objective of data analysis is to produce evidence related to a certain unwanted or illegal activity performed in the cyberspace. This is the most important phase of the investigation. Investigators have to analyze the acquired data from a different perspective. For example finding the relation between gathered data and the activities, classification or grouping of data, predicting the trends based on the existing data/activities and finding out the unusual activities which are not expected in a system.

d) **Reporting phase:** this is the final stage where a proper document is prepared to report the outcomes of the analysis stage.

Figure 1. The digital forensic investigation processes (K. Kent, 2006)

DATA MINING FOR DIGITAL FORENSICS

Digital forensics is a branch of forensic science that focuses on the recovery and investigation of material found in digital devices, about digital crime. The objectives of Digital forensics, is to answers the when, what, who, where, how and why concerning a crime conducted employing electronic media or devices. While investigating a digital crime, forensic experts have to solve the following questions:

- 'when' i.e. the time interval during which the activities took place.
- 'what' i.e. the illegal/unwanted activities performed.
- 'who' i.e. the person(s) accountable for these activities.
- 'where' i.e. the sources from where the data for the evidence can be extracted.
- 'how' i.e. how these activities were performed.
- 'why' i.e. seeks to determine the motives behind these activities.

Since the 1980s, the development of a variety of specialist commercial and freeware tools for cyber forensics began. A lot of tools have been developed and available as software to assist forensic investigators. These tools ensure that the digital evidence required concerning a cybercrime is acquired and preserved properly. These tools also confirm the accuracy of the results obtained by the processing and analysis of digital evidence (Albert Marcella, 2007).

Based on Literature survey, we can categorize these Computer Forensics Tools as follows:

- **General forensic tools:** these tools assist in a wide variety of investigations, particularly keyword searching on digital media.
- **Specialist forensic tools:** these tools are used to study and analyze a specific piece of forensic material for investigation purposes like images, or internet artifacts. These tools take input from the results generated by the general forensic tools.
- **Case Management tools:** These specific tools are used for the management of cases, like tracking, auditing and preparing reports.

Most of the Computer forensic tools available are used for extracting data from various sources; they have very limited features to assist the investigators in the analysis of the acquired data. With the growing sizes of online data and the development of sophisticated methods of crime, the presentation of data offered by computer forensic tools is deceptive at times. The forensic investigators still have to examine the presented data and draw conclusions.

Analyzing large volumes of data from various sources involved in criminal and terrorist activities post a challenge for law enforcement agencies.

The formal steps involved in data mining include (Padhraic Smyth, 2001):

a)   Define the nature of the data and how to represent the data sets.
b)   Determine the methods to quantify the data and to evaluate how well different representation structures fit the data.
c)   Evaluate and select the algorithmic process for the optimization of the scoring function
d)   Determine the required data management principles for implementing the algorithms effectively.

For the analysis of data recovered from various sources, different tasks have to be performed by the analyst. The traditional computer forensic tools are not ideal for these tasks and there is a growing need for seamless integration of data mining techniques with digital forensic science. The data mining techniques will help in boosting up the performance of the cyber forensic systems and enhance the reliability of investigations of the cases. Data mining techniques can assist an investigator in the following tasks:

a)   **Entity extraction:** for the investigation purpose the experts have to retrieve data from different media or sources. Entity extraction techniques have been used to automatically extract login ID, Password, ID no, IP of the system used, and personal properties from reports or logs for unique identification of persons may involve in an activity.

b)   **Clustering:** Clustering is a data mining technique to arrange the data into different clusters or groups for analysis purposes. Clustering techniques such as "concept space" can be used to automatically associate different objects (such as persons, organizations, hardware systems) in crime records (Justickis, 2010). The use of clustering helps in finding and visually presenting groups of facts previously unknown or left unnoticed. Most commonly used clustering techniques are K-means algorithm, EM algorithm, Hierarchical clustering

c)   **Association rules:** association rule mining is an effective method to generate rules describing the frequent patterns based on the relation between different data items. Data Mining incorporates a variety of Association techniques that can help identify correlations among the data extracted from different sources concerning a case. Association Rule Mining Algorithms like Apriori Algorithm can be effectively used to ascertain the relationship between different activities over some time, or among the data sets.

d) **Classification:** classification techniques are used to discover and group the data elements based on some similarity measures. The data recovered from different media can be classified by using classification techniques like decision tree, SVM, Bayesian classification, neural networks, etc.

e) **Forecasting:** this data mining technique is used to discover patterns and data that may lead to reasonable predictions. It can be incorporated to predict the users' behavior based on their activity logs.

f) **Anomaly detection:** the concept behind these methods is to discover unexpected data or activities in a system. These methods have been applied in various application domains like fraud detection, network intrusion detection, and other crime analyses that involve tracing unusual activities.

g) **Visualization:** by employing visualization techniques, the investigators can discover information that is critical in context more efficiently with ease. Visualization of data (from a different perspective) also helps investigators to identify the next steps in their search so that digital evidence recovery is carried out more efficiently and effectively. (George Forman, 2005)

Table 1. Basic digital forensic tasks where data mining techniques can be incorporated

Digital Forensic Techniques	Data Mining Techniques	Tool
Data Recovery, Data generation and pre-processing	Statistical Test Analysis Bartlett's test of sphericity Kaiser-Meyer-Olkin (KMO)	Recuva FTK Encase Sleuth kit/Autopsy ProDiscover
Data Analysis	Clustering – K-means, EM, Hierarchical Clustering Classification – Supervised learning - Decision Tree, Neural Networks, SVM, Naïve Baiyesian Unsupervised learning – PCA, Karnohuen Map Frequent Pattern Mining/Association rule Mining - Apriori, Eclat Named Entity recognition Visualization Statistical Analysis and Anomaly Detection Phishing	Weka Weka Weka LingPipe CyberForensic TimeLab EMT/MET Invisible Witness

EXISTING TOOLS AND DATA MINING
TECHNIQUES FOR DIGITAL FORENSIC

During the investigation, an expert has to extract data from different media, has to pre-process it and then has to analyze the data from different levels of granularity. Most of the common tools available for cyber forensic are not capable of effective data analysis. The investigators have to data analysis manually. Researchers have implemented Data mining techniques in various application domains with reasonable success. Hence, a variety of data mining techniques can also be incorporated to assist digital forensic experts in their cases. The following table summarizes different digital forensic tasks, where data mining techniques or tools can be used effectively:

Some prominent research has been done in the area of cyber forensic wherein solving different crime cases, data mining techniques are implemented effectively. Most of the research has been done in the area of intrusion detection, credit card fraud, financial statement fraud, telecommunication fraud, medical data fraud, cellular phone fraud, etc. Based on the study we can summarize Case-specific use of Data mining techniques for digital forensic (Phua, 2010), (Mieke Jans, 2011), (W. Lee, 1998), (Cahill, 2002), (Bolton, 2002), (Fanning, 1998):

Table 2. Sample of specific data mining techniques used in digital forensic cases

Case	Data Mining Technique	Approach
Mobile phone networks intrusion detection and financial statement fraud	Neural Network	Pattern recognition to make predictions from historical data.
Financial Reporting	Fuzzy Neural Network	Use association rules
Medical Insurance Fraud	Hybrid-Based System	Expert Knowledge is incorporated with statistical methods
Cellular clone fraud	MADAME	Mining Audit Data for Automated Models for Intrusion Detection
Telecommunication Fraud	Pattern Identification (Fraud Signature)	A signature (pattern) is derived to concisely describe the caller's behavior.
Credit Card Fraud	Rule-Learning Decision Tree Analysis	Generating valid rules for decision making A predictive model that is based on a sequence of decision
Telecommunication Fraud	Anomaly detection	Identification of significant deviation from an account's usual behavior

CONCLUSION

During the investigation of any cyber-crime, the tasks performed by the forensic experts can be broadly categorized as:

- Identification of various sources/media and data extraction from these sources.
- Data analysis for reporting evidence and deciding the next steps for investigation.

Currently many tools available in the form of software which can assist in the first step i.e. recovering/extracting data from media/sources. But these tools are not very much helpful to support effective analysis of gathered data.

Seamless integration of Data mining techniques with traditional cyber forensic methods has produced encouraging results. Use Data mining techniques, like pattern recognition, association, classification, clustering, anomaly detection, and data visualization enhances the efficiency of cyber forensic investigators.

REFERENCES

Albert Marcella, J. D. (2007). *Cyber Forensics: A Field Manual for Collecting, Examining, and Preserving Evidence of Computer Crimes* (2nd ed.). Auerbach Publications. doi:10.1201/9780849383298

Bolton, R., Hand, D. J., Provost, F., Breiman, L., Bolton, R. J., & Hand, D. J. (2002). Statistical fraud detection: A review. *Statistical Science*, *17*(3), 235–255. doi:10.1214s/1042727940

Cahill, M. H. (2002). Detecting fraud in the real world. In *Handbook of massive data sets* (pp. 911–929). Boston, MA: Springer. doi:10.1007/978-1-4615-0005-6_26

Fanning, K., & Cogger, K. O. (1998). Neural network detection of management fraud using published financial data. *International Journal of Intelligent Systems in Accounting Finance & Management*, *7*(1), 21–41. doi:10.1002/(SICI)1099-1174(199803)7:1<21::AID-ISAF138>3.0.CO;2-K

George Forman, K. E. (2005). Finding similar files in large. In *Proceeding of the eleventh ACM SIGKDD international* (pp. 394-400). New York: ACM. 10.1145/1081870.1081916

Justickis, V. (2010). Criminal Datamining. In Security Handbook of Electronic Security and Digital Forensics. Academic Press.

Kent, S. C. (2006). *Guide to Integrating Forensic Techniques into Incident Response.* NIST SP800-86 Notes.

Lee, W. (1998). Data Mining Approaches for Intrusion Detection. *Proceedings of the 7th USENIX Security Symposium.*

Mieke Jans, J. M. (2011). A business process mining application for internal transaction fraud mitigation. *Expert Systems with Applications, 38*(10), 13351–13359. doi:10.1016/j.eswa.2011.04.159

Padhraic Smyth, D. H. (2001). *Principles of Data Mining.* MIT Press.

Phua, C. L. (2010). *A comprehensive survey of data mining-based fraud detection research.* arXiv preprint arXiv:1009.6119

Song, S. K. (2008). Computer Forensics: Digital Forensic Analysis Methodology. *Computer Forensics Journal, 56*(1), 1–8.

KEY TERMS AND DEFINITIONS

Anomaly Detection: In data mining, anomaly detection is the identification of rare items, events or observations which raise suspicions by differing significantly from the majority of the data.

Data Mining: Data mining is the process of discovering patterns in large data sets involving methods at the intersection of machine learning, statistics, and database systems.

Data Recovery: Data recovery is the process of restoring data that has been lost, accidentally deleted, corrupted, or made inaccessible.

Digital Crime: Digital crime begins when there is illegal activity. These activities are done to data or information on computers or networks.

Digital Forensic Tool: Specialized digital forensic tools existed, and consequently investigators often performed live analysis on media, examining computers from within the operating system using existing system admin tools to extract evidence.

Forecasting: Forecasting is the process of making predictions of the future based on past and present data and most commonly by analysis of trends.

Legal Advisors: Legal advisors are lawyers who are employed by the government, large companies and other organizations to provide legal advice and services to the organization and its employees.

Phishing: Phishing is the fraudulent attempt to obtain sensitive information such as usernames, passwords and credit card details by disguising oneself as a trustworthy entity in an electronic communication.

Chapter 15
Forensic Case Studies

Faiyaz Ahmad
Integral University, India

M. Z. Khan
Integral University, India

ABSTRACT

In this chapter, the authors collected and defined different types of case studies based on cyber forensics. They tried to gather the latest as well as the oldest case studies. This chapter will help those who want to study different categories of cyber care and their forensics studies. The following scenarios are specific examples of the problems that have been faced by various organizations in the past. For reasons of client confidentiality and legal sensitivity, actual names have been changed.

INTRODUCTION

Computer technology is the major integral part of everyday human life, and it is growing rapidly, as are computer crimes such as financial fraud, unauthorized intrusion, identity theft, and intellectual theft. To counteract those computer-related crimes, Computer Forensics plays a very important role. "Computer Forensics involves obtaining and analyzing digital information for use as evidence in civil, criminal or administrative cases (Nelson, B., et al., 2008)". We are categorizing these case studies as follows:

DOI: 10.4018/978-1-7998-1558-7.ch015

GENERAL CASE STUDIES

Case Study 1

X, the sales manager of Company A gives 4 weeks' notice. Soon after he leaves, Company A receives advice from several clients that they received emails from an unknown Hotmail account containing defamatory information about Company A.

Computer Forensics NZ Ltd (CFNZ) is instructed to search for evidence on X's PC that the emails originated from it. During the briefing, CFNZ suggests that the PC be examined for any evidence of any confidential data being copied to removable external media during the preceding 4 week7safe, (2013) s.

Every bit and byte on the PC's hard disk is acquired and preserved using rigorous procedures as employed by NZ Police, the Serious Fraud Office, NZ Customs, etc. The data is then meticulously analyzed and various data (deleted) and system files are recovered showing that email data was created at the date and time that X was known to be operating the PC.

Detailed analysis also shows that during the last 3 days of X's employment 1 MYOB data file and 1 Microsoft Access file were copied to a USB drive. The files and detailed reports are provided to Company and appropriate discussions are held with the company's legal advisors for recommended action.

Case Study 2

It was noticed by her manager that C's work output had been dropping over the previous 3 weeks, which coincided with the provision of broadband Internet to her department. It is visually established that she is spending many hours Internet 'surfing', which is specifically banned under her terms of employment ACPO (2013).

She is cautioned appropriately but she continues with the unauthorized activity. Workmates also note that pornographic images are seen on her PC after the second caution.

The company subsequently dismisses her and within 14 days the company receives formal advice that it would be served with a charge of unjustified dismissal.

The manager convinces Management that all correct procedures were followed and that the Internet use was clearly beyond any amount or type that could be considered reasonable. Management decides to contest the action, especially as a significant amount of money is at risk, and instructs CFNZ to analyze her PC for evidence of excessive Internet activity and deliberate entry to pornographic sites.

Analysis of her PC by CFNZ shows that incontestable evidence exists proving that the company's assertions were correct. Finally, costs are awarded to the employer.

Case Study 3

Employee M is discovered stealing products from Finished Goods Store during lunch break. M is told to collect his personal effects from his office and report to the accountant in 30 minutes for final pay reconciliation Adams, R., (2012).

The next day his company laptop is inspected and the PC is found to have been formatted. Unfortunately, M's PC contained important time-sensitive company data that was in My Documents and not part of the regular network backup. CFNZ is contacted and briefed as to the types of files required and queried as to whether it would be possible to determine the actual time that the disk was formatted.

Within seven days CFNZ has successfully recovered the complete suite of data and has ascertained that the formatting took place when M was known to be in the office collecting personal items.

The company seeks legal advice regarding the appropriate action to take because of the malicious deletion activities Aquilina, M.J., (2003).

Case Study 4

Employee F suddenly resigns from company G and establishes a company in direct competition of the ex-employer.

CFNZ conducts a detailed briefing session with management and legal counsel of company G. The PC previously used by employee F is delivered to CFNZ and an evidential copy of all data on the hard disk drive is made and preserved Carvey, H., (2005).

The deleted file area undergoes detailed analysis and evidence is found of Company G's confidential marketing data sent as email attachments to a private email account. F deleted the draft of a business plan for the new competitive company is also recovered PwC (2010).

A full report is presented to the management of company G and the ex-employee F makes appropriate reparation.

Case Study 5

A major organization was facing a crisis when a very senior member of staff was under suspicion of downloading thousands of pornographic images from the internet. He vehemently denied it all, but the case against him looked very serious.

Our detailed and sustained analysis of internet use and traffic pinpointed a clash of IP addresses on the system. The evidence started to point towards the organization's system administrator, but he denied it Dave, P., (2013).

As we dug deeper, we proved that it was the administrator who'd been using his local desktop system to access numerous pornographic websites. Over three months, he had visited 1200 pornographic websites and downloaded over 15,000 images. To cover his tracks, and in an attempt to frame a senior manager, he had been altering his local system IP address so the trail led to his senior manager colleague.

Our expertise in computer forensics and incident response meant we were able to unravel the mystery. It saved an innocent person's job and a good name and uncovered the real culprit. The senior manager was cleared of all involvement, and his reputation was restored.

Before our involvement, the system administrator had claimed he knew nothing at all about the downloading of pornography. But in the end, he had to confess, confronted with the evidence we uncovered Dave, P., (2013). He no longer works for the organization.

Case Study 6

After a local dairy was robbed at gunpoint, it was found that the media file located on the hard disk drive of the Digital Video Recorder linked to the store's CCTV system was corrupted and provided authorities with no clue as to the identity of the perpetrators Fowler, K., (2007).

We were able to successfully recover the media file and repair it to a state where it could be replayed on an ordinary computer system. This helped with the identification of the offenders as well as providing incontestable evidence as to their involvement in the crime. The pair is now serving a 12-year prison term.

INTELLECTUAL PROPERTY, BRAND PROTECTION AND CIVIL SEIZURE BASED CASE STUDIES

Case Type – Computer Forensics, Electronic Auditing, Email

Environment – Desktops, Laptops, Distribution Software and Sales Management System. GDF supported attorneys, private investigators and US Marshalls on a civil seizure. The client's intellectual property, in this case, garments, were being counterfeited and sold throughout the United States. GDF supported the seizure team by locating additional locations during the seizure, as well as gathering digital evidence onsite, eliminating the need to remove and return computers and other electronic devices, ensuring that the terms of the order were adhered to and the gathering of evidence was expedited Han, D.R., (2012).

Case Study – Banking, Corporate Fraud SOX Auditing

Case Type – Computer Forensics, Environment – Complex Network, Mainframe, Banking Industry Specific Software, Email, Voice Mail

A large accounting firm was hired to audit certain activities related to loans to individuals on the board of directors of medium size, publicly-traded bank (the "Bank"). During the audit, the auditors needed to examine several computer systems used by certain Bank employees, as well as by certain board members. GDF's digital forensic examiners were immediately dispatched and sent in to arrange for the forensic analysis of the computer systems and to search for corroborating evidence in support of the audit team's suspicions and findings. The systems GDF analysts forensically analyzed included laptop computers issued to managers in the loan origination department and desktop systems used by managers and board members. Email (Exchange) servers, as well as voicemail systems, were examined Hunt, R., (2012).

Case Study – Drug Diversion, Brand Protection, Counterfeiting, and International Fraud

Case Type – Computer Forensics, Law Enforcement Support, Criminal
   Environment – Email, Desktops, Laptops, Blackberries (BES and Handhelds), Foreign Language Data

A pharmaceutical company began receiving complaints from its representatives in certain geographical areas that sales of normally high volume drugs were slowing down considerably. The company's internal security department, as well as the security departments of its major distributors, began an investigation ISO/IEC 17799:2005, (2005). The results of the investigations led the security professionals to believe a significant amount of the company's product was being diverted from foreign countries into the United States and sold through smaller distributors who specialized in sales to local, privately owned pharmacies and dispensaries within nursing homes. The diversion activities were immediately reported to the local authorities in the regions, as well as to the FDA. An investigation was immediately launched and millions of dollars of diverted drugs and repackaging equipment were seized from several locations, including the warehouses of fully licensed pharmaceutical distributors. Along with the diverted product, computers and other electronic equipment were also seized. The seizure went smoothly and the company was satisfied, as were investigators from the FDA and local law enforcement. However, the case was severely hindered by the fact that the majority of communications between the principals of the distribution companies (foreign nationals) and the foreign suppliers were conducted by email ISO/IEC 17799:2005, (2005). There were also virtually no paper records on-site. While the local authorities and the FDA had access to computer forensic labs, both faced similar roadblocks in their investigations; the labs were severely backlogged and the systems were encrypted and fairly complex, as well as being in a foreign language.

CASE STUDIES FROM INDIA

Case - 1: Blackmailing (Mumbai)

The first faults are theirs that commit them; the second faults are theirs that permit them. - Thomas Fuller

The accused posed to be a young girl living in Kolkata and lured a non-resident Indian (NRI) working in Dubai (the complainant) to enter into an e-mail correspondence. Subsequently, the accused began corresponding with the complainant using different e-mail IDs, under the guise of different female names which made the complainant believe that he was corresponding with different girls Kendall, K, (2007).

Having won the confidence of the complainant, the accused asked him for money and gifts. The complainant complied with the requests in the hope of receiving sexual favors from the 'girls' he was corresponding with. However, after some time, when these favors were not forthcoming the complainant stopped this correspondence.

The accused then resorted to blackmailing the complainant by referring to the e-mail exchanges that had taken place earlier. Besides, the accused led the complainant to believe that one of the girls had committed suicide and that the complainant was responsible for it. The accused also sent fake copies of the letters from CBI, High Court of Calcutta, New York Police and Punjab University, etc. Kent, K, and Grance, T., (2006).

The complainant lived in constant fear of being arrested in connection with the suicide over a year and a half. He paid the accused a sum of INR 12.5 million ostensibly to bribe the officials that were supposedly investigating the suicide and to compensate the victim's family for the loss of her income. The complainant was continuously under the threat of being arrested by the police. Given the huge strain upon his financial resources as well as the mental agony faced by him, the complainant himself contemplated suicide.

Investigation

The complainant handed over all the e-mail correspondence to the police. Many of them had masked headers and therefore the police could not investigate them any further. Moreover, no e-mail could be traced to Kolkata where the accused was staying as per the complainant's version. However, the investigating team was able to trace some of these e-mails to the corporate office of a large cement company and a residence in Mumbai. A raid was conducted at these premises.

In the raid one computer, two laptops, seven mobile phones, and a scanner were seized. The computer equipment that was recovered was sent to the office of the forensic examiner, who found all the evidence of e-mails, chatting details, etc in the laptops and the computer.

During the investigation, property worth INR 0.9 million was seized, along with cash worth INR 0.3 million. The total flow of the extorted money was traced from the bank in Dubai to the account of the accused person Kent, K, and Grance, T., (2006).

Case-2: Credit Card Fraud (Tamil Nadu)

The environment that the organization worries about is put there by the organization. - Weick

Background

The assistant manager (the complainant) with the fraud control unit of a large business process outsourcing (BPO) organization filed a complaint alleging that two of its employees had conspired with a credit card holder to manipulate the credit limit and as a result cheated the company of INR 0.72 million Khanuja, H.K., and Adane, D.S., (2011), .

The BPO facility had about 350 employees. Their primary function was to issue the bank's credit cards as well as attend to customer and merchant queries. Each employee was assigned to a specific task and was only allowed to access the computer system for that specific task. The employees were not allowed to make any changes in the credit card holder's account unless they received specific approvals.

Each of the employees was given a unique individual password. In case they entered an incorrect password three consecutive times then their password would get blocked and they would be issued a temporary password.

The company suspected that its employees conspired with the son (holding an add-on card) of one of the credit cardholders. The modus operandi suspected by the client is as follows.

The BPO employee deliberately keyed in the wrong password three consecutive times (so that his password would get blocked) and obtained a temporary password to access the computer system. He manually reversed the transactions of the card so that it appeared that payment for the transaction has taken place. The suspect also changed the credit card holder's address so that the statement of account would never be delivered to the primary cardholder.

Investigation

The investigating team visited the premises of the BPO and conducted a detailed examination of various persons to understand the computer system used. They learned that in certain situations the system allowed the user to increase the financial limits placed on a credit card. The system also allowed the user to change the customer's address, blocking and unblocking of the address, authorizations for cash transactions, etc Swanson, M., (2001).

The team analyzed the attendance register which showed that the accused was present at all the times when the fraudulent entries had been entered in the system. They also analyzed the system logs that showed that the accuser's ID had been used to make the changes in the system.

The team also visited the merchant establishments from where some of the transactions had taken place. The owners of these establishments identified the holder of the add-on card.

Case-3: Hosting Obscene Profiles (Tamil Nadu)

Nothing has happened until it has been recorded. - Virginia Woolf

Background

The complainant stated that some unknown person had created an e-mail ID using her name and had used this ID to post messages on five Web pages describing her as a call-girl along with her contact numbers Swanson, M., (2001).

As a result, she started receiving a lot of offending calls from men.

Investigation

After the complainant heard about the Web pages with her contact details, she created a username to access and view these pages.

Using the same log-in details, the investigating team accessed the Web pages where these profiles were uploaded. The message had been posted on five groups, one of which was a public group.

The investigating team obtained the access logs of the public group and the message to identify the IP addresses used to post the message. Two IP addresses were identified.

The ISP was identified with the help of publicly available Internet sites. A request was made to the ISPs to provide the details of the computer with the IP addresses at the time the messages were posted. They provided the names and addresses of two cyber cafes located in Mumbai to the police Swanson, M., (2001)

The investigating team scrutinized the registers maintained by the cyber cafes and found that in one case the complainant's name had been signed into the register.

The team also cross-examined the complainant in great detail. During one of the meetings, she revealed that she had refused a former college mate who had proposed marriage.

Given the above, the former college mate became the prime suspect. Using this information the investigating team, with the help of Mumbai police, arrested the suspect and seized a mobile phone from him. After the forensic examination of the SIM card and the phone, it was observed that the phone had the complainant's telephone number that was posted on the internet. The owner of the cyber cafes also identified the suspect as the one who had visited the cyber cafes. Based on the facts available with the police and the sustained interrogation the suspect confessed to the crime.

Case - 4: Illegal money transfer (Maharashtra)

The present contains nothing more than the past, and what is found in the effect was already in the cause. - Henri Bergson

Background

The accused in the case we're working in a BPO that was handling the business of a multinational bank. The accused, during the course of their work, had obtained the personal identification numbers (PIN) and other confidential information of the bank's customers. Using these accused and their accomplices, through different cyber cafes, transferred huge sums of money from the accounts of different customers to fake accounts Swanson, M., (2001).

Investigation

On receiving the complaint the entire business process of the complainant firm was studied and a systems analysis was conducted to establish the possible source of the data theft.

The investigators were successful in arresting two people as they laid a trap in a local bank where the accused had fake accounts for illegally transferring money.

During the investigation, the system server logs of the BPO were collected. The IP addresses were traced to the Internet service provider and ultimately to the cyber cafes through which illegal transfers were made Swanson, M., (2001).

The registers maintained in cyber cafes and the owners of cybercafes assisted in identifying the other accused in the case. The e-mail IDs and phone call print outs were also procured and studied to establish the identity of the accused. The e-mail accounts of the arrested accused were scanned which revealed vital information to identify the other accused. Some e-mail accounts of the accused contained swift codes, which were required for internet money transfer.

All the 17 accused in the case were arrested in a short period. The charge sheet was submitted in the court within the stipulated time. In the entire wire transfer scam, an amount to the tune of about INR 19 million was transferred, out of this INR 9 million was blocked in transit due to timely intimation by police, INR 2 million was held in balance in one of the bank accounts opened by the accused which was frozen. Also, the police recovered cash, ornaments, vehicles and other articles amounting to INR 3 million.

During the investigation, the investigating officer learned the process of wire transfer, the banking procedures and weakness in the system. The investigating officer suggested measures to rectify the weakness in the present security systems of the call center. This has helped the local BPO industry in taking appropriate security measures.

Case-5: Fake Travel Agent (Mumbai)

Background

The accused in this case was posing to be a genuine railway ticket agent and had been purchasing tickets online by using stolen credit cards of nonresidents. The accused created fraudulent electronic records/ profiles, which he used to carry out the transactions.

The tickets so purchased were sold for cash to other passengers. Such events occurred for a period of about four months Shiner, D.L.D., and Cross, M., (2002).

The online ticket booking service provider took notice of this and complained about the cybercrime investigation cell.

Investigation

The service provider gave the IP addresses, which were used for the fraudulent online bookings, to the investigating team. IP addresses were traced to cyber cafes in two locations.

The investigating team visited the cyber cafŽs but was not able to get the desired logs as they were not maintained by the cyber cafŽ owners. The investigating team was able to shortlist the persons present at cyber cafes when the bookings were made. The respective owners of the cyber cafes were able to identify two persons who would regularly book railway tickets.

The investigating team then examined the passengers who had traveled on these tickets Shiner, D.L.D., and Cross, M., (2002). They stated that they had received the tickets from the accused and identified the delivery boy who delivered the tickets to them. Based on this evidence the investigating team arrested two persons who were identified in an identification parade.

Case-6: Creating Fake Profile (Hyderabad)

Life is the art of drawing sufficient conclusions from insufficient premises. - Samuel Butler

Background

The complainant received an obscene e-mail from an unknown e-mail ID. The complainant also noticed that obscene profiles along with photographs of his daughter had been uploaded on matrimonial sites.

Investigation

The investigating officer examined and recorded the statements of the complainant and his daughter. The complainant stated that his daughter was divorced and her husband had developed a grudge against them due to the failure of the marriage.

The investigating officer took the original e-mail from the complainant and extracted the IP address of the same. From the IP address, he could ascertain the Internet service provider. The IP address was traced to a cable Internet service provider in the city area of Hyderabad. The said IP address was allotted to the former husband sometime back and his house was traced with the help of the staff of ISP Swanson, M., (2001).

A search warrant was obtained and the house of the accused was searched. During the search operation, a desktop computer and a handicam were seized from the premises. A forensic IT specialist assisted the investigation officer in recovering e-mails (which were sent to the complainant), using a specialized disk search tool as well as photographs (which had been posted on the Internet) from the computer and the handicam respectively. The seized computer and the handicam were sent to the forensic security laboratory for further analysis.

258

The experts of the forensic security laboratory analysed the material and issued a report stating that: the hard disk of the seized computer contained text that was identical to that of the obscene e-mail; the computer had been used to access the matrimonial websites on which the obscene profiles were posted; the computer had been used to access the e-mail account that was used to send the obscene e-mail; the handicam seized from the accused contained images identical to the ones posted on the matrimonial Websites. Based on the report of the FSL it was established that the accused had: created a fictitious e-mail ID and had sent the obscene e-mail to the complainant; posted the profiles of the victim along with her photographs on the matrimonial sites.

Current Status

Based on the material and oral evidence, a charge sheet has been filed against the accused and the case is currently pending trial.

Case-7: Intellectual Property Theft (Bangalore)

Unfortunately, problems do not come to the administrator carefully wrapped in bundles with the value elements and the factual elements neatly sorted. - Herbert Simon

Background

The complainant (a software company based in Bangalore) alleged that some of the company's former employees had accessed the company's IT system and tampered with the source code of the software under development.

Investigation

The investigating team visited the complainant's premises and scanned the logs of e-mails. They identified the IP address and using tracing software traced the ISP and the address of the place where the e-mails had been sent Swanson, M., (2001).

This address was of a Hyderabad based company. On visiting the company the investigating team found 13 computers and a server. Using specialized forensic tools the disks were imaged and analyzed by the team. The analysis revealed that the source code, as well as its tampered version, had been stored from these systems.

Case-8: Obscene E-mails (Mumbai)

It requires a very unusual mind to undertake the analysis of the obvious. - Alfred North Whitehead

Background

The complainant received an e-mail stating that the sender had in his possession some objectionable/ morphed/ obscene photographs of the complainant. The accused in this case demanded to meet the complainant. Failing to do so, the accused threatened to put these on the Internet and circulate these among her friends and relatives Swanson, M., (2001).

Investigation

Upon receiving the complaint, the investigating team extracted the e-mail header to trace the IP address. This IP address was tracked down to a company.

Using system logs, the exact computer used and its user was identified. The accused was arrested. The investigating team also seized the computer and some photographs of a look-alike of the victim from the accused. This evidence was sent to the forensic sciences laboratory, which confirmed that the seized computer contained evidence that implicated the accused in the incident.

Case-9: Online Railway Ticket Fraud-I (New Delhi)

It isn't that they can't see the solution. It is that they can't see the problem. - G K Chesterton

Background

The complainant, an online railway ticket booking Website, complained that some unknown people had used the Internet ticket booking facility to book more than 50 railway tickets using stolen credit cards. They had taken the delivery of the tickets at different places. The company received a chargeback from credit card companies for the transactions causing huge financial losses.

Investigation

During the investigation, a 'patch program' was installed in the department's system to give an alert on any further booking done by the accused using existing user IDs, credit card details or place of delivery. The IP addresses retrieved from the computer server of the company handling Internet booking was traced to multiple locations. They all belonged to different cyber cafes.

In the meantime, the patch program installed in the department's system signaled an alert that the accused had used one of the existing twelve user-IDs again for booking of two more railway tickets and had sought the delivery at Hyderabad. The accused was arrested from Hyderabad while receiving the railway tickets by courier Shiner, D.L.D., and Cross, M., (2002).

Stolen credit card details of various banks were found with the accused which he used to make fraudulent bookings. Also, more than 25 flight tickets were recovered during the search of his residence.

Case-10: Obscene Phone Calls (Bangalore City)

Nothing has the power to broaden the mind as the ability to investigate systematically and truly all that comes under thy observation in life. - Marcus Aurelius

Background

A written complaint was submitted by the complainant stating that she had been receiving obscene phone calls on her mobile and landline numbers. The complainant learned from the callers that a doctored profile of hers had been posted on a Website. The profile stated that the complainant loved sex and when the viewers were in Bangalore, they should contact her. The profile also gave out victim's landline and mobile phone numbers Shiner, D.L.D., and Cross, M., (2002).

Investigation

The investigating officer obtained call details of the perpetrator's number from the cellular service provider and observed that the most frequent incoming and outgoing calls were from two other mobile numbers. The investigating officer also obtained the IMEI addresses for these numbers from the mobile service provider Shiner, D.L.D., and Cross, M., (2002).

The investigating officer sent out letters to the Website on which the obscene profile of the complainant had been hosted to obtain details of the date, time of the profile creation, the IP address used for the creation, the access details for the profile and any other details that the Website would be able to provide regarding the profile and the e-mail ID.

The investigating officer then contacted the outlet from where the mobile connection had been purchased and learned that one of the SIM cards used was a demo card that had been issued to a dealership. Upon further investigation, it was found that the other SIM card was allotted to a college student and was being used by his friend. The investigating officer got suspicious and on further inquiry found that the college student was of dubious character.

The investigating officer obtained a search warrant and raided the residence of the college student. Using disk imaging and analysis tools, the team recovered the obscene profile that was posted on the internet from the student's computer. The partners of the accused were also examined in the presence of the complainant. The accused admitted that he was guilty.

It later transpired that the college student was a close family friend of the complainant and that he was suffering from a personality disorder, secondary depression, and poor self-esteem.

CONCLUSION

Digital forensic investigation is a challenging process because every incident differs from other incidents. A computer forensic investigator must be competent enough in Technical and Legal to conduct the investigation. Since the evidence which is provided by a computer forensic investigator can be an important part of the case, the investigation report must be precise and in detail.

REFERENCES

ACPO. (2013). *Good Practice Guide for Computer-Based Electronic Evidence V4.0*. ACPO.

Adams, R. (2012). Evidence and Digital Forensics. *Australian Security Magazine*. Available at http://www.australiansecuritymagazine.com.au/

Aquilina, M. J. (2003). *Malware Forensics, Investigating and Analysing Malicious Code*. Syngress.

Carvey, H. (2005). *Windows Forensics and Incident Recovery*. Boston: Pearson Education Inc.

Casestudies.(2010).*PwCCybercrimeUSCenterofExcellence*.PricewaterhouseCoopers LLP. Retrieved from http://www.pwc.com/us/en/forensic-services/assets/cyber-crime-data-breach-case-studies.pdf

Dave, P. (2013). *SQL – A Career in Database Forensics!* Available at http://blog. sqlauthority.com/2013/12/24/sql-a-career-in-database-forensics/

Fowler, K. (2007). *Forensic Analysis of a SQL Server 2005 Database Server.* Available at https://www.sans.org/reading-room/whitepapers/application/forensic-analysis-sql-server-2005-database-server-1906

Han, D. R. (2012). SME Cyber security and the Three Little Pigs. *ISACA Journal, 6.* Available at www.isaca.org/journal

Hunt, R. (2012). New Developments. In *Network Forensics – Tools and Techniques* (pp. 377–381). IEEE.

ISO/IEC 17799:2005. (2005). *Information technology — Security techniques — Code of practice for information security management.* Available at http://www. iso.org/iso/iso_catalogue/catalogue_ics/catalogue_detail_ics.htm?csnumber=39612

Kendall, K. (2007). *Practical Malware Analysis.* Mandiant Intelligent Information Security. Available at http://www.blackhat.com/presentations/bh-dc-07/Kendall_McMillan/Paper/bh-dc-07-Kendall_McMillan-WP.pdf

Kent, K., & Grance, T. (2006). *Guide to Integrating Forensic Techniques into Incident Response.* Available at: http://csrc.nist.gov/publications/nistpubs/800-86/SP800-86.pdf

Khanuja, H. K., & Adane, D. S. (2011). Database Security Threats and Challenges in Database Forensic: A Survey. In *IPCSIT* (Vol. 20). Singapore: IACSIT Press.

Kruse, W. G. II, & Heiser, J. G. (2010). *Computer Forensics: Incident Response Essentials* (14th ed.). Indianapolis, IN: Pearson Education.

Nelson, B. (2008). *Guide to Computer Forensics and Investigations* (3rd ed.). Course Technology.

Nelson, M., Wright, A., Lowry, R. G., & Mutrie, N. (2008). Where is the Theoretical Basis for Understanding and Measuring the Environment for Physical Activity? *Environmental Health Insights, 2,* 111–116. doi:10.4137/EHI.S1048 PMID:21572837

7. safe. (2013). *Good Practice Guide for Computer-Based Electronic Evidence.* Available at: http://www.7safe.com/electronic_evidence/ACPO_guidelines_computer_evidence.pdf

Shiner, D. L. D., & Cross, M. (2002). *Scene of the Cybercrime* (2nd ed.). Burlington: Syncress.

Swanson, M. (2001). *NIST Security Self-Assessment Guide for Information Technology Systems*. Available at http://www.itl.nist.gov/lab/bulletns/bltnsep01.htm

KEY TERMS AND DEFINITIONS

BPO: Business process outsourcing is the contracting of business activities and functions to a third-party provider.

Corporate Fraud: Corporate fraud refers to activities undertaken by an individual or company that are done in a dishonest or illegal manner and are designed to give an advantage to the perpetrating individual or company.

Digital Forensics: Computer forensics, also known as digital forensics, on the other hand is a much more specific discipline, which involves the analysis of computers and other electronic devices in order to produce legal evidence of a crime or unauthorized action.

ISP: An internet service provider (ISP) is a company such as AT&T, Verizon, Comcast, or Bright House that provides Internet access to companies, families, and even mobile users.

Compilation of References

Abdullah, M. T., Mahmod, R., Ghani, A. A. A., Abdullah, M. Z., & Sultan, A. B. M. (2008). Advances in computer forensics. *International Journal of Computer Science and Network Security, 8*(2), 215–219.

Abhineet Anand, A. G. (2017). Ethical Hacking and Hacking Attacks. *International Journal of Engineering and Computer Science.*

ACPO. (2013). *Good Practice Guide for Computer-Based Electronic Evidence V4.0.* ACPO.

Adams, R. (2012). Evidence and Digital Forensics. *Australian Security Magazine.* Available at http://www.australiansecuritymagazine.com.au/

Adcomplain. (n.d.). Retrieved from http://www.rdrop.com: http://www.rdrop.com/users/billmc/adcomplain.html

Agarwal, M. (2013). *Text steganographic approaches: a comparison.* arXiv preprint arXiv:1302.2718

Albert Marcella, J. D. (2007). *Cyber Forensics: A Field Manual for Collecting, Examining, and Preserving Evidence of Computer Crimes* (2nd ed.). Auerbach Publications. doi:10.1201/9780849383298

Albrecht, W. S., Albrecht, C. O., Albrecht, C. C., & Zimbelman, M. F. (2019). *Fraud examination.* Boston, MA: Cengage.

AlFahdi, M. (2016). *Automated Digital Forensics & Computer Crime Profiling* (Ph.D. thesis). Plymouth University.

Allemang, D. H. J. (2011). *Semantic web for the working ontologist: effective modeling in RDFS and OWL.* Elsevier.

Alzaabi, M. J. A. (2013). An ontology-based forensic analysis tool. *Proceedings of the Conference on Digital Forensics, Security and Law.*

Al-Zarouni. (2004). *Tracing E-mail Headers. In Proceedings of Australian Computer* (pp. 16–30). Network & Information Forensics Conference.

Amazon. (n.d.). *AWS Security Center.* Retrieved from aws.amazon.com/security

Ami-Narh, J. T., & Williams, P. A. H. (2008). Digital forensics and the legal system: A dilemma of our times. *6th Aust. Digit. Forensics Conf.*, 30–40.

Amiram, D., Bozanic, Z., Cox, J. D., Dupont, Q., Karpoff, J. M., & Sloan, R. (2018). Financial reporting fraud and other forms of misconduct: A multidisciplinary review of the literature. *Review of Accounting Studies, 23*(2), 732–783. doi:10.100711142-017-9435-x

Ana Azevedo, M. F. S. (2008). A parallel overview. *IADIS European Conference on Data Mining.*

Anthony trial. (2011). *Chloroform searched on computer.* Retrieved from http://edition.cnn.com/2011/CRIME/06/08/florida.casey.anthony.trial/

Antwi-boasiako, A., & Venter, H. (2017). A Model for Digital Evidence Admissibility Assessment. *Adv. Digit. Forensics XIII, 511*, 23–38. doi:10.1007/978-3-319-67208-3_2

AOS DATA Inc. (2019). *FINALeMAIL.* Retrieved from http://finaldata2.com

Aquilina, M. J. (2003). *Malware Forensics, Investigating and Analysing Malicious Code.* Syngress.

Archambault, J. J., & Archambault, M. E. (2011). Earnings management among firms during the pre-sec era: A Benford's law analysis. *The Accounting Historians Journal, 38*(2), 145–170. doi:10.2308/0148-4184.38.2.145

Ariely, G. (2007). Knowledge Management, Terrorism and Cyber Terrorism. *Terrorism*, 10.

Armstrong, H., & Russo, P. (2004). *Electronic forensics education needs of law enforcement.* Available from http://www.ncisse.org/publications/cissecd/Papers/S4P02.pdf

Arnold, B. B., & Bonython, B. (2016). Villains, victims and bystanders in financial crime. In M. Dion, D. Weisstub, & J. Richet (Eds.), Financial crimes: Psychological, technological, and ethical issues, (pp. 167–198). Springer. doi:10.1007/978-3-319-32419-7_8

Arthur K. K. (2004). *An Investigation into Computer Forensic Tools.* Pretoria: Information and Computer Security Architectures (ICSA) Research Group.

Aucsmith, D. (2016). Disintermediation. Counterinsurgency and Cyber Defense. Academic Press.

Ayers, D. (2009). A second generation computer forensic analysis system. *Digital Investigation, 6*, S34–S42. doi:10.1016/j.diin.2009.06.013

Bapna & Hua. (2012). How can we deter Cyber Terrorism? *Information Security Journal: A Global Perspective, 21*(2).

Bapna, S. (2013). The economic impact of cyber terrorism Jian Hua. *The, 22*(2), 175–186.

Baryamereeba, V., & Tushabe, F. (2004). The Enhanced Digital Investigation Process Model. *Proceeding of Digital Forensic Research Workshop.*

Baryamureeba, V., & Tushabe, F. (2004). The Enhanced Digital Investigation Process Model. *Digital Forensics Research Workshop.*

Beasley, M. S., Carcello, J. V., Hermsanson, D. R., & Lapides, P. D. (2000, December). Fraudulent financial reporting: Consideration of industry traits and corporate governance mechanisms. *Accounting Horizons*, *14*(4), 441–454. doi:10.2308/acch.2000.14.4.441

Beebe, N. L., & Liu, L. (2014). Clustering digital forensic string search output. *Digital Investigation*, *11*(4), 314–322. doi:10.1016/j.diin.2014.10.002

Bellovin, S. M., Landau, S., & Lin, H. (2017). Limiting the Undesired Impact of Cyber Weapons: Technical Requirements and Policy Implications. *Journal of Cybersecurity*, *3*(1), 59–68.

Bell, T., & Carcello, J. (2000). A decision aid for assessing the likelihood of fraudulent financial reporting. *Auditing*, *9*(1), 169–178. doi:10.2308/aud.2000.19.1.169

Benford, F. (1938, March). The law of anomalous numbers. *Proceedings of the American Philosophical Society*, *78*(4), 551–572.

Benredjem, D. (2007). *Contributions to cyber-forensics: processes and e-mail analysis* (Doctoral dissertation). Concordia University.

betanews. (2018). *Banking Trojan Attacks Up By 16 Percent In 2018*. Retrieved from https://betanews.com/2019/03/07/banking-trojan-attacks-2018/

Bhallamudi, S. (2015). *Image Steganography* (Rep.). Retrieved https://www.scribd.com/document/377269663/EE7150-finalproject-Finalreport-Savitha-Bhallamudi-pdf#

Boddington, Hobbs, & Mann. (2008). *Validating digital evidence for legal argument*. Australian Digital Forensics Conference, Edith Cowan University, Perth, Australia.

Bolton, R., Hand, D. J., Provost, F., Breiman, L., Bolton, R. J., & Hand, D. J. (2002). Statistical fraud detection: A review. *Statistical Science*, *17*(3), 235–255. doi:10.1214s/1042727940

BrianC. (2019). *Autopsy Features*. Retrieved from https://sleuthkit.org/autopsy/features.php

Buchholz, F. S. E., & Spafford, E. (2004). On the role of file system metadata in digital-forensics. *Digital Investigation*, *1*(4), 298–309. doi:10.1016/j.diin.2004.10.002

Burney A., A. M. (2016). Forensics Issues in Cloud Computing. *Journal of Computer and Communications*, 63-69.

Busta, B., & Sundheim, R. (1992). *Tax return numbers tend to obey Benford's law* (Working Paper No. W93-106 94). Center for Business Research, St. Cloud State University.

Cahill, M. H. (2002). Detecting fraud in the real world. In *Handbook of massive data sets* (pp. 911–929). Boston, MA: Springer. doi:10.1007/978-1-4615-0005-6_26

CAINE. (2018). *CAINE 10.0 "Infinity" Computer Aided Investigative Environment*. Retrieved from https://www.caine-live.net/

calyptix. (2017). *Biggest Cyber Attacks 2017: How They Happened*. Retrieved from https://www.calyptix.com/top-threats/biggest-cyber-attacks-2017-happened/

Carrier & Spafford. (2003). Getting Physical with the Digital Investigation Process. *International Journal of Digital Evidence, 2*(2).

Carslaw, C. (1988). Anomalies in income numbers: Evidence of goal-oriented behavior. *The Accounting Review, 63*(2), 321–327.

Carvey, H. (2005). *Windows Forensics and Incident Recovery*. Boston: Pearson Education Inc.

Case studies. (2010). *PwC CybercrimeUS Center of Excellence*. PricewaterhouseCoopers LLP. Retrieved from http://www.pwc.com/us/en/forensic-services/assets/cyber-crime-data-breach-case-studies.pdf

Case, A. C. A., Cristina, A., Marziale, L., Richard, G. G., & Roussev, V. (2008). FACE: Automated digital evidence discovery and correlation. *Digital Investigation, 5*, S65–S75. doi:10.1016/j.diin.2008.05.008

Casey, E. (2004). *Digital Evidence and Computer Crime* (2nd ed.). Amsterdam: Elsevier Academic Press.

Casey, E. (2011). *Digital Evidence and Computer Crime: Forensic Science, Computers and the Internet*. London: Academic Press.

Casey, E. (2011). *Digital evidence and computer crime: Forensic science, computers, and the internet*. Academic press.

Chao Zhang, G. Z., & Huang, Y. (2010). Study on the application of knowledge discovery in data bases to the decision making of railway track safety in china. *Management and Service Science (MASS) International Conference*.

Chhabra, G. S., &. S. (2015). Distributed Network Forensics Framework: A Systematic Review. *International Journal of Computers and Applications*.

Christa Miller. (2019). *Career Paths In Digital Forensics: Practical Applications*. Retrieved from https://articles.forensicfocus.com/2019/07/31/career-paths-in-digital-forensics-practical-applications/

Church, B. K., McMillan, J. J., & Schneider, A. (2001). Factors affecting internal auditors' consideration of fraudulent financial reporting during analytical procedures. *Auditing, 20*(1), 65–80. doi:10.2308/aud.2001.20.1.65

cisecurity. (2019). *Top 10 Malware January 2019*. Retrieved from https://www.cisecurity.org/blog/top-10-malware-january-2019/

Codr, J. (2009). *Unseen: An Overview of Steganography and Presentation of Associated Java Application C-Hide*. Citeseer.

Colarik. (2006). *Cyber Terrorism: Political and Economic Implications*. Academic Press.

Committee of Sponsoring Organizations of the Treadway Commission. (1999). *Fraudulent financial reporting: 1987–1997: An analysis of U.S. public companies.* Retrieved January 13, 2006, from http://www.coso.org/Publications.htm

Computer Forensics Services. (2018). Retrieved from https://www.kroll.com/en/services/business-intelligence-and-investigations/forensic-accounting

Cressey, D. R. (1973). *Other people's money.* Montclair: Patterson Smith.

Crisp-dm 1.0, (2018). *Step-by-step data mining guide.* Retrieved from https://www.the-modeling-agency.com/crisp-dm.pdf

Crocker, D. (2009). *Internet Mail Architecture.* RFC 5598.

Das, R. (2019). *tool-comparison.* Retrieved from https://resources.infosecinstitute.com/category/computerforensics/introduction/commercial-computer-forensics-tools/tool-comparison/

Das, R. (n.d.). *An Introduction to computer forensics.* Retrieved 2019, from infosecinstitute.com: https://resources.infosecinstitute.com/category/computerforensics/introduction/#gref

Daubert v. Merrell Dow Pharmaceuticals, Inc., 509 U.S. 579 1993

Dave, P. (2013). *SQL – A Career in Database Forensics!* Available at http://blog.sqlauthority.com/2013/12/24/sql-a-career-in-database-forensics/

Dayalamurthy, D. (2013). Forensic Memory Dump Analysis And Recovery Of The Artifacts Of Using Tor Bundle Browser- The Need. *Australian Digital Forensics Conference.*

Debreceny, R. S., & Gray, G. L. (2011). Data Mining of Electronic Mail and Auditing: A Research Agenda. *Journal of Information Systems, 25*(2), 195–226. doi:10.2308/isys-10167

Digital forensics: An Analytical Crime Scene Procedure Model (ACSPM) Forensic Science International. (2013). Retrieved from https://corporate.findlaw.com/litigation-disputes/top-ten-things-to-do-when-collecting-electronic-evidence.html

digitalguardian. (2019). *A History of Ransomware Attacks: The Biggest and Worst Ransomware Attacks of All Time.* Retrieved from https://digitalguardian.com/blog/history-ransomware-attacks-biggest-and-worst-ransomware-attacks-all-time

Dorminey, J., Fleming, A. S., Kranacher, M., & Riley, R. A. Jr. (2012). The evolution of fraud theory. *Issues in Accounting Education, 27*(2), 555–579. doi:10.2308/iace-50131

Douglas, M., Bailey, K., Leeney, M., & Curran, K. (2017). An overview of steganography techniques applied to the protection of biometric data. *Multimedia Tools and Applications, 77*(13), 17333–17373. doi:10.100711042-017-5308-3

edecision4u. (n.d.). *Forensics Investigation Toolkit (FIT).* Retrieved from http://www.edecision4u.com/FIT.html

Embar-Seddan. (2002). *Cyber terrorism: Are We Under Siege?* Academic Press.

Emiliogarcia. (2014). *The Importance of Computer Forensic Investigations*. Retrieved from https://www.smgconsultingservices.com/the-importance-of-computer-forensic-investigations/

EncryptionW. I. (n.d.). Retrieved from http://web.deu.edu.tr/doc/oreily/networking/puis/ch06_02.htm

ENISA. (2009). *Cloud Computing Risk Assessment*. Retrieved from www.enisa.europa.eu/act/rm/files/deliverables/cloud-computing-risk-assessment

Erbacher, R. F. (2010). Validation for Digital forensics. *Conference Paper*, Army Research Laboratory.

Fadelli, I. (2019). *A new approach for steganography among machine learning agents*. Retrieved from https://techxplore.com/news/2019-01-approach-steganography-machine-agents.html

Fahey, R. (2019). *forensic-techniques-part-1*. Retrieved from https://resources.infosecinstitute.com/category/computerforensics/introduction/areas-of-study/digital-forensics/forensic-techniques-part-1/#gref

Fanning, K., & Cogger, K. O. (1998). Neural network detection of management fraud using published financial data. *International Journal of Intelligent Systems in Accounting Finance & Management*, *7*(1), 21–41. doi:10.1002/(SICI)1099-1174(199803)7:1<21::AID-ISAF138>3.0.CO;2-K

Febryan, A., Purboyo, T. W., & Saputra, R. E. (2017). Steganography Methods on Text, Audio, Image and Video: A Survey. *International Journal of Applied Engineering Research*, *12*(21), 10485–10490.

Fkirin, A., Attiya, G., & El-Sayed, A. (2016). Steganography Literature Survey, Classification and Comparative Study. *Communications on Applied Electronics*, *5*(10), 13–22. doi:10.5120/cae2016652384

FOOKES® Software. (2019). *Aid4Mail Forensic*. Retrieved from http://www.aid4mail.com/: http://www.aid4mail.com/

Forbes. (2019). *Four Phishing Attack Trends To Look Out For In 2019*. Retrieved from https://www.forbes.com/sites/forbestechcouncil/2019/01/10/four-phishing-attack-trends-to-look-out-for-in-2019/#17dddc404ec2

Forensics, O. (n.d.). *Oxygen forensic® detective features*. Retrieved from https://www.oxygen-forensic.com/en/products/oxygen-forensic-detective

Fowler, K. (2007). *Forensic Analysis of a SQL Server 2005 Database Server*. Available at https://www.sans.org/reading-room/whitepapers/application/forensic-analysis-sql-server-2005-database-server-1906

French, J., & Raven, B. (1959). The basis of social power. In D. Cartwright (Ed.), Studies in social power. Ann Arbor, MI: University of Michigan Press.

Frye v. United States, 293 F. 1013 D.C. Cir. 1923.

Furnell, S. M., & Warren, M. J. (1999). Computer hacking and cyber terrorism: The real threats in the new millennium. *Computers & Security, 18*(1), 28–34. doi:10.1016/S0167-4048(99)80006-6

Garfinkel, S. (2007). Anti-forensics: Techniques, detection and countermeasures. *2nd International Conference on i-Warfare and Security*, 77-84.

Garfinkel, S. L. (2010). Digital forensics research: The next 10 years. *Digital Investigation, 7*, 64–73. doi:10.1016/j.diin.2010.05.009

Gartner Forecasts. (2019, April). Retrieved from Gartner: https://www.gartner.com/en/newsroom/press-releases/2019-04-02-gartner-forecasts-worldwide-public-cloud-revenue-to-g

Gartzke, E., & Lindsay, J. R. (2015). *The Cyber Commitment Problem and the Destabilization of Nuclear Deterrence*. Academic Press.

Geiger, M. (2005). Evaluating Commercial Counter-Forensic Tools. *Digital Forensic Research Workshop (DFRWS)*.

George Forman, K. E. (2005). Finding similar files in large. In *Proceeding of the eleventh ACM SIGKDD international* (pp. 394-400). New York: ACM. 10.1145/1081870.1081916

Gholap, P. M. (2013). Information Retrieval of K-Means Clustering For Forensic Analysis. *International Journal of Science and Research*.

Giordano, J. C. (2002). *Maciag Cyber forensics: a military operations perspective*. Available from: http://www.utica.edu/academic/institutes/ecii/publications/articles/A04843F3-99E5-632B-FF420389C0633B1B.pdf

Goldmann, P. (2009). *Anti-fraud risk and control workbook*. Retrieved from https://onlinelibrary.wiley.com/doi/pdf/10.1002/9781119205654.app3

gomindsight. (2018). *History of Cyber Attacks From The Morris Worm To Exactis*. Retrieved from https://www.gomindsight.com/blog/history-of-cyber-attacks-2018/

Gordon, S. (2002, November). Cyber Terrorism: An Overview. *Computers & Security, 21*(7), 636–647. doi:10.1016/S0167-4048(02)01116-1

Graham, J. (1999). Enterprise wide electronic mail using IMAP. *SIGUCCS '99: Proceedings of the 27th annual ACM SIGUCCS conference on User services: Mile high expectations*.

Grance, P. M. (2011). *The NIST Definition of Cloud Computing. Special Publication 800-145 (Draft)*. Gaithersburg, MD: National Institute of Standards and Technology.

Green, B. P., & Choi, J. H. (1997). Assessing the risk of management fraud through neural network technology. *Auditing, 16*(1), 14–28.

Gregg, M. (2004). *The certified computer examiner certification*. Available from: http://www.gocertify.com/article/certifiedcomputerexaminer.shtml

Grimm, H. O. N. P. W. for Authenticating Digital Evidence. (2016). *Hot-car death highlights key role of digital evidence.* Retrieved from https://edition.cnn.com/2014/07/02/tech/web/digital-evidence/index.html

Gross, M. L., Canetti, D., & Vashdi, D. R. (2018). Cyber Terrorism: Its Effects on Psychological well being, Public Confidence and Political Attitudes. In *Bytes, Bombs and Spies: The Strategic Dimensions of Offensive Cyber Operations.* Brookings Institution Press.

Guo, H., Jin, B., & Huang, D. (2010, November 11). *Research and Review on Computer Forensics.* Retrieved from https://link.springer.com/chapter/10.1007/978-3-642-23602-0_21

Guo, H., Jin, B., & Huang, D. (2011). Research and review on computer forensics. *Lect. Notes Inst. Comput. Sci. Soc. Telecommun. Eng., 56,* 224–233. doi:10.1007/978-3-642-25255-6_29

Gupta, Singh, Kaur Arora, & Mahajan. (2011). Digital Forensics- A Technological Revolution in Forensic Sciences. *J Indian Acad Forensic Med., 33*(2).

Hailey, S. (2003). *What is Computer Forensics.* Retrieved from http://www.cybersecurityinstitute.biz/forensics.htm

Hajek, P., & Henriques, R. (2017). Mining corporate annual reports for intelligent detection of financial statement fraud – A comparative study of machine learning methods. *Knowledge-Based Systems, 128,* 139–152. doi:10.1016/j.knosys.2017.05.001

Hamilton, V. L., & Sanders, J. (1995). Crimes of obedience and conformity in the workplace: Surveys of Americans, Russians, and Japanese. *The Journal of Social Issues, 51*(3), 67–88. doi:10.1111/j.1540-4560.1995.tb01335.x

Han, D. R. (2012). SME Cyber security and the Three Little Pigs. *ISACA Journal, 6.* Available at www.isaca.org/journal

Hashmi, A. R. (2018). Security and Compliance Management in Cloud Computing. *International Journal of Advanced Studies in Computers, Science and Engineering.*

Huang, S. Y., Lin, C.-C., Chiu, A.-A., & Yen, D. C. (2016). Fraud detection using fraud triangle risk factors. *Information Systems Frontiers, 18,* 1–14.

Hui, L. C. K., Chow, K. P., & Yiu, S. M. (2007.). Tools and Technology for Computer Forensics: Research and Development in Hong Kong. Information Security Practice and Experience Lecture Notes in Computer Science, 11–19. doi:10.1007/978-3-540-72163-5_2

Hunt, R. (2012). New Developments. In *Network Forensics – Tools and Techniques* (pp. 377–381). IEEE.

Hurt, R. L. (2016). *Accounting information systems – Basic concepts and current Issues.* New York: McGraw Hill.

Husain, M. S. (2017). Cloud Computing in E-Governance: Indian Perspective. In Securing Government Information and Data in Developing Countries (pp. 104-114). IGI Global.

I. C. e. a. Fidel Reb_on. (2015). An antifraud system for tourism smes in the context of electronic operations with credit cards. *American Journal of Intelligent Systems*.

Important cyber laws case studies. (n.d.). Retrieved from http://www.cyberralegalservices.com/detail-casestudies.php

Inc SysTools. (2019). *Mailxaminer: Email forensic redefined.* Retrieved from https://www.mailxaminer.com/: https://www.mailxaminer.com/features.html

Independent Investigation Committee (IIC). (2015). *Investigation Report, 20 July 2015.* Available at https://www.toshiba.co.jp/about/ir/en/news/20151208_2.pdf

indiatoday. (2019). *Google removes 28 fake apps from Play Store, Delete Now If You Have Any Of These Apps On Your Phone.* Retrieved from https://www.indiatoday.in/technology/news/story/google-removes-28-fakes-app-from-play-store-delete-now-if-you-have

ISO/IEC 17799:2005. (2005). *Information technology — Security techniques — Code of practice for information security management.* Available at http://www.iso.org/iso/iso_catalogue/catalogue_ics/catalogue_detail_ics.htm?csnumber=39612

Jan, C. (2018). An effective financial statements fraud detection model for the sustainable development of financial markets: Evidence from Taiwan. *Sustainability*, *10*(513), 1–14. PMID:30607262

Janczewski & Colarik. (2007). *Warfare and Cyber Terrorism.* Academic Press.

Jansen, W., & Ayers, R. (2004). *Guidelines on PDA forensics* [NIST 800-72]. Gaithersburg, MD: National Institute of Standards and Technology. doi:10.6028/NIST.SP.800-72

Japan fines Ernst and Young affiliate $17.4 million over Toshiba audit. (2015). *Reuters*. Retrieved from https://www.reuters.com

Jayaram, P., Ranganatha, H. R., & Anupama, H. S. (2011). Information hiding using audio steganography–a survey. *The International Journal of Multimedia & Its Applications*, *3*(3), 86–96. doi:10.5121/ijma.2011.3308

Juliana De Groot. (2019). *A History of Ransomware Attacks: The Biggest and Worst Ransomware Attacks of All Time.* Retrieved from https://digitalguardian.com/blog/history-ransomware-attacks-biggest-and-worst-ransomware-attacks-all-time

Justickis, V. (2010). Criminal Datamining. In Security Handbook of Electronic Security and Digital Forensics. Academic Press.

Kacy Zurkus. (2019). *A Spot of Ransomware Hits AriZona's Tea.* Retrieved from https://www.infosecurity-magazine.com/news/a-spot-of-ransomware-hits-arizonas/

Kanapickienė, R., & Grundienė, Ž. (2015). The model of fraud detection in financial statements by means of financial ratios. *Procedia: Social and Behavioral Sciences*, *213*, 321–327. doi:10.1016/j.sbspro.2015.11.545

Kara Nance, B. H. (2009). Digital Forensics: Defining a Research Agenda. *42nd Hawaii International Conference on System Sciences.*

Karampidis, K., Kavallieratou, E., & Papadourakis, G. (2018). A review of image steganalysis techniques for digital forensics. *Journal of Information Security and Applications, 40*, 217-235.

Kaspersky Lab. (2019). *Kaspersky Lab Survey: One-in-Four Hide Cybersecurity Incidents From Their Employers.* Retrieved from https://usa.kaspersky.com/about/press-releases/2017_kaseprsky-lab-survey-one-in-four-hide-cybersecurity-incidents-from-their-employers

Kassem, R. (2019). Understanding financial reporting fraud in Egypt: Evidence from the audit field. *Third World Quarterly, 40*(11), 1996–2015. doi:10.1080/01436597.2019.1626709

Kataria,, M. (2014). BIG DATA: A Review. *International Journal of Computer Science and Mobile Computing, 3*(7), 106–110.

Kelman, H. C., & Hamilton, V. L. (1989). *Crimes of obedience.* New Haven, CT: Yale University Press.

Kendall, K. (2007). *Practical Malware Analysis.* Mandiant Intelligent Information Security. Available at http://www.blackhat.com/presentations/bh-dc-07/Kendall_McMillan/Paper/bh-dc-07-Kendall_McMillan-WP.pdf

Kenney, M. (2015). Cyber-Terrorism in a Post-Stuxnet World. *Orbis, 59*(1), 111–128. doi:10.1016/j.orbis.2014.11.009

Kent, Chevalier, Grance, & Dang. (2006). *Guide to integrating forensic techniques into incident response.* Academic Press.

Kent, K., & Grance, T. (2006). *Guide to Integrating Forensic Techniques into Incident Response.* Available at: http://csrc.nist.gov/publications/nistpubs/800-86/SP800-86.pdf

Kent, S. C. (2006). *Guide to Integrating Forensic Techniques into Incident Response.* NIST SP800-86 Notes.

Kent, K. (2006). *Guide to Integrating Forensic Techniques into Incident Response. Special Publication 800-86.* National Institute of Standards and Technology.

Ke, Y., Liu, J., Zhang, M. Q., Su, T. T., & Yang, X. Y. (2018). Steganography Security: Principle and Practice. *IEEE Access: Practical Innovations, Open Solutions, 6*, 73009–73022. doi:10.1109/ACCESS.2018.2881680

Khairallah, T. (2018). *Wearables as Digital Evidence Fitbit evidence case study.* Retrieved from https://www.preprints.org/manuscript/201812.0313/v1/download

Khan, M. N. A. (2008). *Digital Forensics using Machine Learning Methods* (Ph.D. thesis). University of Sussex.

Khanuja, H. K., & Adane, D. S. (2011). Database Security Threats and Challenges in Database Forensic: A Survey. In *IPCSIT* (Vol. 20). Singapore: IACSIT Press.

Kolla, A. (2017). *List of 10 Best Steganography Tools to Hide Data*. Retrieved from https://www. geekdashboard.com/best-steganography-tools/

Kotsiantis, S., Koumanakos, E., Tzelepis, D., & Tampakas, V. (2006). Forecasting fraudulent financial statements using data mining. *International Journal of Computational Intelligence*, *3*(2), 104–110.

Kranacher, M., Riley, R., & Wells, J. T. (2010). *Forensic accounting and fraud examination*. Wiley.

Kruse, W. (2015). Your Employee May Be Wearing Their Alibi - Or Your Evidence Vice President for Digital Forensics. Academic Press.

Kruse, W. G. II, & Heiser, J. G. (2010). *Computer Forensics: Incident Response Essentials* (14th ed.). Indianapolis, IN: Pearson Education.

Lachow. (2009). Cyber Terrorism: Menace or Myth? *Cyber Power and National Security*.

Lee, W. (1998). Data Mining Approaches for Intrusion Detection. *Proceedings of the 7th USENIX Security Symposium*.

Lenard, M. J., Petruska, K. A., Alam, P., & Yu, B. (2016). Internal control weaknesses and evidence of real activities manipulation. *Advances in Accounting*, *33*, 47–58. doi:10.1016/j. adiac.2016.04.008

Leroux, O. (2007). Legal Admissibility of Electronic Evidence. *International Review of Law Computers & Technology*, *18*(2), 193–220. doi:10.1080/1360086042000223508

Lewis, J. A. (2002). *Assessing the Risks of Cyber Terrorism, Cyber War and Other Cyber Threats*. In Center for Strategic and International Studies.

Li, H. (2014). Challenges and Trends of Big Data Analytics. In *Ninth International Conference on P2P, Parallel, Grid, Cloud and Internet Computing (3PGCIC)* (pp. 566-567). IEEE.

Lily Hay Newman. (2018). *The Worst Cybersecurity Breaches of 2018 So Far*. Retrieved from https://www.wired.com/story/2018-worst-hacks-so-far/

Liu, Y. L. X. (2010). Analysis and design of heterogeneous bioinformatics database integration system based on middleware. In *International Conference on Information Management and Engineering (ICIME)*. IEEE. 10.1109/ICIME.2010.5477628

Loja, N., Morocho, R., & Novillo, J. (2016). Digital Forensics Tools. *International Journal of Applied Engineering Research.*, *11*, 9754–9762.

Magee, K. (2018). *CISSP – Steganography, An Introduction Using S-Tools*. Retrieved from https:// resources.infosecinstitute.com/cissp-steganography-an-introduction-using-s-tools/

Malviya, S., Saxena, M., & Khare, D. A. (2012). Audio steganography by different methods. *International Journal of Emerging Technology and Advanced Engineering*, *2*(7), 371–375.

Malwarebytes Lab. (2019). *2019 State of Malware*. Retrieved from https://resources.malwarebytes.com/resource/2019-state-malware-malwarebytes-labs-report/

malwarebytes. (2019). *What is a backdoor?* Retrieved from https://www.malwarebytes.com/backdoor/

Manning, P. K. (1992). Information Technologies and the Police. In Modern Policing. Chicago: The University of Chicago. doi:10.1086/449197

Marsico, C. M. (2005). *Rogers iPod forensics*. Available from: https://www.cerias.purdue.edu/tools_and_resources/bibtex_archive/archive/2005-13.pdf

Meyers, M. M. (2004). *Rogers Computer forensics: the need for standardization and certification*. Available from: http://www2.tech.purdue.edu/cpt/courses/CPT499S/meyersrogers_ijde.pdf

Mezghani, E. E. E. (2015). A Semantic Big Data Platform for Integrating Heterogeneous Wearable Data in Health- care. *Journal of Medical Systems*, 1–8. PMID:26490143

Mieke Jans, J. M. (2011). A business process mining application for internal transaction fraud mitigation. *Expert Systems with Applications*, 38(10), 13351–13359. doi:10.1016/j.eswa.2011.04.159

Millan, L. (2011, March 25). Insurers and Social Media: Insurers' use of social networks impinges on privacy rights. *The Lawyers Weekly*. Retrieved from https://www.google.com/search?q=http%3A%2F%2Fwww.lawyersweekly.ca%2Findex.php%3Fsection%3Darticle%26articleid%3D908&ie=&oe=

Milley & Seabolt. (1998). *Data mining and the case for sampling solving business problems using sas R enterprise minertm software*. SAS Institute Inc.

Mishra, N. S. (2015). A compendium over cloud computing cryptographic algorithms and security issues. *BVICA M's International Journal of Information Technology*, 810.

Mitnick, K. (2019). *Exclusive Interview with Kevin Mitnick Ask Me Anything*. Retrieved from https://blog.knowbe4.com/exclusive-interview-with-kevin-mitnick-ask-me-anything-video

N. C. J. U.S. Department of Justice. (2001). Electronic Crime Scene Investigation: A Guide for First Responders. *NIJ Res. Rep., no. NCJ, 187736*, 96.

Nadeem Alherbawi, Z. S. (2013). Systematic Literature Review on Data Carving in Digital Forensic. *Procedia Technology*. Retrieved from https://www.sciencedirect.com/science/article/pii/S2212017313003198

Najafabadi, M. M. (2015). Deep learning applications and challenges in big data analytics. *Journal of Big Data*, 1-21.

Natarajan Meghanathan, S. R. (2009). *Tools and Techniques For Network Forensic. International Journal of Network Security & Its Applications*.

National Forensic Science Technology Center. (2009). *A Simplified Guide to Digital Evidence.* Author.

National Institute of Justice Electronic Crime Scene Investigation: A Guide for First Responders (NCJ 187736). (2001). Washington, DC: Office of Justice Programs.

Nawawi, A., & Salin, A. (2018). Internal control and employees' occupational fraud on expenditure claims. *Journal of Financial Crime, 25*(3), 891–906. doi:10.1108/JFC-07-2017-0067

Neely, P. R. Jr, & Allen, M. T. (2018). Policing Cyber Terrorism. *Journal of Cybersecurity Research, 3*(1), 13–18. doi:10.19030/jcr.v3i1.10227

Neil Rowe, S. L. (2012). Finding Anomalous and Suspicious Files from Directory Metadata on a Large Corpus. *International Conference on Digital Forensics and Cyber Crime.* 10.1007/978-3-642-35515-8_10

Nelson, B. (2008). *Guide to Computer Forensics and Investigations* (3rd ed.). Course Technology.

Nelson, M., Wright, A., Lowry, R. G., & Mutrie, N. (2008). Where is the Theoretical Basis for Understanding and Measuring the Environment for Physical Activity? *Environmental Health Insights, 2,* 111–116. doi:10.4137/EHI.S1048 PMID:21572837

New, Y. C. F. (n.d.). *The Computer Forensics Process.* Retrieved from https://newyorkcomputerforensics.com/computer-forensics-process

News Team. (2017). *What is digital forensics and why is it important?* Retrieved from https://www.firstlegal.com/what-is-digital-forensics-and-why-is-it-important

Nigrini, M. (1999a). Adding value with digital analysis. *The Internal Auditor, 56,* 21–23.

Nigrini, M. (1999b, May). I've got your number. *Journal of Accountancy, 187*(5), 79–83.

Noel, G. E., & Peterson, G. L. (2014). Applicability of Latent Dirichlet Allocation to multi-disk search. *Digital Investigation, 11*(1), 43–56. doi:10.1016/j.diin.2014.02.001

Oberheide, J. E. C. (2008). CloudAV: N-version antivirus in the network cloud. *Proceedings of the Seventeenth USENIX Security Conference,* 91–106.

Olguin, J. (2016). Steganography... what is that? [Web log post]. Retrieved from https://www.trustwave.com/en-us/resources/blogs/spiderlabs-blog/steganography-what-is-that/

Omidi, M., Min, Q., Moradinaftchali, V., & Piri, M. (2019). The Efficacy of Predictive Methods in Financial Statement Fraud. *Discrete Dynamics in Nature and Society, 2019*(4), 1–12. doi:10.1155/2019/4989140

OpenText Corp. (2019). *EnCase Forensic.* Retrieved from http://www.guidancesoftware.com

Othman, R., Ameer, R., & Laswad, F. (2019). *Strategic camouflage: Toshiba's deception tactics 2019.* Asia-Pacific Interdisciplinary Research in Accounting Conference, AUT, Auckland, New Zealand.

Outpost24. (2018). *TOP 10 of the World's Largest Cyberattacks*. Retrieved from https://outpost24. com/blog/top-10-of-the-world-biggest-cyberattacks

Padhraic Smyth, D. H. (2001). *Principles of Data Mining*. MIT Press.

Palmer, G. (2001). A road map for digital forensic research. *First Digital Forensic Research Workshop*, Utica, NY.

Palmer, G. (2001). DTR-T001-01 Technical Report. A Road Map for Digital Forensic Research. *Digital Forensics Workshop (DFRWS)*, Utica, NY.

Passi, H. (2018). *Top 20 Trending Computer Forensics Tools of 2018*. Retrieved from https:// www.greycampus.com/blog/information-security/top-twenty-trending-computer-forensics-tools

Patrascu, A. (2013). Beyond digital forensics. A cloud computing perspective over incident response and reporting. In *8th International Symposium on Applied Computational Intelligence and Informatics (SACI)*. IEEE. 10.1109/SACI.2013.6609018

Pawar, S. S., & Kakde, V. (2014). Review on Steganography for Hiding Data. *International Journal of Computer Science and Mobile Computing, 4*, 225–229.

Peisert, S., Bishop, M., & Marzullo, K. (2008). Computer forensics in forensic. *Operating Systems Review, 42*(3), 112. doi:10.1145/1368506.1368521

Perols, J. (2011). Financial statement fraud detection: An analysis of statistical and machine learning algorithms. *Auditing, 30*(2), 19–50. doi:10.2308/ajpt-50009

Phua, C. L. (2010). *A comprehensive survey of data mining-based fraud detection research*. arXiv preprint arXiv:1009.6119

Pollitt, M. M. (1995). Computer Forensics: An Approach to Evidence in Cyberspace. *Proceeding of the National Information Systems Security Conference, 2*, 487-491.

Pollitt, M. M. (2007). An Ad Hoc Review of Digital Forensic Models. *Proceeding of the Second International Workshop on Systematic Approaches to Digital Forensic Engineering (SADFE'07)*. 10.1109/SADFE.2007.3

prabhu490730. (2015, March). Retrieved from https://prabhurockstar.wordpress.com/

Prichard, J. J., & MacDonald, L. E. (2004). Cyber Terrorism: A Study of the Extent of Coverage in Computer Science Text Books. *JITE-Research, 3*(1).

Ramamoorti, S., Morrison, D., & Koletar, J. W. (2009). *Bringing Freud to fraud: Understanding the state-of-mind of the C-level suite/white collar offender through "A-B-C" analysis* (Working paper). Institute of Fraud Prevention.

Rani, N., & Chaudhary, J. (2013). Text Steganography Techniques: A Review. *International Journal of Engineering Trends and Technology, 4*(7), 2231–5381.

Rathmell. (2008). Cyber-terrorism: The shape of future conflict? *Defense & International Security*, 40-45.

Rathore, S. (2015). Steganography: Basics and Digital Forensics. *International Journal of Science. Engineering and Technology Research*, 4(7), 2589–2593.

RCCF. (n.d.). *EmailTracer*. Retrieved from http://www.cyberforensics.in: http://www.cyberforensics.in/OnlineEmailTracer/index.aspx

Reddy, H. M., & Raja, K. B. (2009). High capacity and security steganography using discrete wavelet transform. *International Journal of Computer Science and Security*, 3(6), 462.

Reith, Carr, & Gunsh. (2002). An Examination of Digital Forensics Models. *International Journal of Digital Evidence, 1*(3).

Resnick, P. (Ed.). (2001). Internet message format. Internet Engineering Task Force (IETF); RFC 2822.

retruster. (2019). *2019 Phishing Statistics and Email Fraud Statistics*. Retrieved from https://retruster.com/blog/2019-phishing-and-email-fraud-statistics.html

Riadi, I., Umar, R., & Firdonsyah, A. (2017). Identification of Digital Evidence On Android's Blackberry Messenger Using NIST Mobile Forensic Method. *International Journal of Computer Science and Information Security*, 15(5), 155–160.

Richards, J. (1999). *Transnational Criminal Organizations, Cybercrime, and Money Laundering: A Handbook for Law Enforcement Officers, Auditors, and Financial Investigators*. Boca Raton, FL: CRC Press.

Richer, P. (2003). Steganalysis: Detecting hidden information with computer forensic analysis. SANS/GIAC Practical Assignment for GSEC Certification, SANS Institute, 6.

Rogers, M. K., Goldman, J., Mislan, R., Wedge, T., & Debrota, S. (2006). Computer Forensics Field Triage Process Model. *Conference on Digital Forensics, Security and Law*, 27-40.

Rosen, D. M. (1982, September). Police and the Computer: The Revolution That Never Happened. *Police Magazine*, 5, 5.

Roussev, V. L. W. (2009). A cloud computing platform for large-scale forensic computing. In Advances in Digital Forensics V (pp. 201-214). Springer.

Roussev, V. (2016). *Digital forensic science: issues, methods, and challenges*. Synthesis Lectures on Information Security, Privacy, & Trust.

Rout, H., & Mishra, B. K. (2014). Pros and Cons of Cryptography, Steganography and Perturbation techniques. *IOSR Journal of Electronics and Communication Engineering*, 76-81.

Rubasundram, G. A. (2015). *Perceived "tone from the top" during a fraud risk assessment*. 7th International Conference on Financial Criminology 2015, Oxford, UK.

Saini, H., Rao, Y.S., & Panda, T.C. (2012). Cyber-Crimes and their Impacts: A Review. *International Journal of Engineering Research and Applications.*

Schilit, H. M., Perler, J., & Engelhart, Y. (2018). Financial shenanigans – How to detect accounting gimmicks and fraud in financial report (4th ed.). New York: McGraw-Hill.

Schoenwaelder & President. (2017). *Role of Wearable Devices for Real World Data Collection: Engagement or Today's.* Academic Press.

Seaskate. (1998). *A Technical Report prepared for The National Committee on Criminal Justice Technology.* National Institute of Justice, By Seaskate, Inc.

securelist. (2018). *DDoS attacks in Q3 2018.* Retrieved from https://securelist.com/ddos-report-in-q3-2018/88617/

serverius. (2019). *Increase of DDoS attacks Q1 2019.* Retrieved from https://serverius.net/increase-of-ddos-attack-q1-2019/

Shankdhar, P. (2019). *Popular Computer Forensics Top 21 Tools.* Retrieved from https://resources.infosecinstitute.com/computer-forensics-tools/

Shiner, D. L. D., & Cross, M. (2002). *Scene of the Cybercrime* (2nd ed.). Burlington: Syncress.

Shi, W., Connelly, B. L., & Hoskisson, R. E. (2017). External corporate governance and financial fraud: Cognitive evaluation theory insights on agency theory prescriptions. *Strategic Management Journal, 38*(6), 1268–1286. doi:10.1002mj.2560

Shrivastava, G. (2016). Network forensics: Methodical literature review. In *3rd International Conference on Computing for Sustainable Global Development (INDIACom)* (pp. 2203-2208). IEEE.

Silke. (2003). *Terrorists, Victims and Society: Psychological Perspectives on Terrorism and its consequences.* Academic Press.

Singh, S. (2015). *Literature Review On Digital Image Steganography and Cryptography Algorithms.* doi:10.13140/RG.2.1.1037.9124

Siper, A., Farley, R., & Lombardo, C. (2005). The Rise of Steganography. In *Computer Science and Information Systems*. Pace University. Retrieved from http://csis.pace.edu/~ctappert/srd2005/d1.pdf

Skoda, M., Slavikova, G., & Lajcin, D. (2016). Fraud accounting in Slovakia after times of financial crisis. *International Journal of Economic Perspectives, 10*(4), 139–146.

Skousen, C., Guan, L., & Wetzel, T. (2004). Anomalies and unusual patterns in reported earnings: Japanese managers round earnings. *Journal of International Financial Management & Accounting, 15*(3), 212–234. doi:10.1111/j.1467-646X.2004.00108.x

Smaili, N., & Arroyo, P. (2019). Categorization of Whistleblowers Using the Whistleblowing Triangle. *Journal of Business Ethics, 157*(1), 95–117. doi:10.100710551-017-3663-7

Smitha, G. L., & Baburaj, E. (2018). Sobel edge detection technique implementation for image steganography analysis. *Biomedical Research.* doi:10.4066/biomedicalresearch.29-17-1212

Solieri, S. A., & Hodowanitz, J. (2016). Electronic Audit Confirmations: Leveraging technology to reduce the risks of fraud. *Journal of Forensic & Investigative Accounting, 8*(1), 68–74.

Sonamjain, T. (2014). A Review of Cloud Forensics Issues & Challenges. *International Journal of Advanced Research in Computer Science & Technology,* 55-57.

Song, S. K. (2008). Computer Forensics: Digital Forensic Analysis Methodology. *Computer Forensics Journal, 56*(1), 1–8.

Spathis, C. (2002). Detecting false financial statements using published data: Some evidence from Greece. *Managerial Auditing Journal, 17*(4), 179–191. doi:10.1108/02686900210424321

Srinivasan, C. R. (2019). *Cyber-security trends to look out for in 2019.* Retrieved from https://telecom.economictimes.indiatimes.com/news/cyber-security-trends-to-look- out-for-in-2019/67471232

Srinivasan, C. R. (2019). *Cyber-security trends to look out for in 2019.* Retrieved from https://telecom.economictimes.indiatimes.com/news/cyber-security-trends-to-look-out-for-in-2019/67471232

Srivastava, S., Haroon, M., & Bajaj, A. (2013). Web document information extraction using class attribute approach. *4th International Conference on Computer and Communication Technology (ICCCT),* 17-22. 10.1109/ICCCT.2013.6749596

Steganos. (2001). *Steganos responds to the current demands for a ban on cryptography and steganography* [Press release]. Retrieved from https://www.steganos.com/uploads/media/Steganos_Press_Release_2001-09-20_Steganography.pdf

Stohl. (2006). Cyber terrorism: a clear and present danger, the sum of all fears, breaking point or patriot games? Crime, Law, and Social Change, 46(4–5), 223–238.

Stuart, T., & Wang, Y. (2016). Who cooks the books in China, and does it pay? Evidence from private, high-technology firms. *Strategic Management Journal, 37*(13), 2658–2676. doi:10.1002mj.2466

Sundresan. (2009). Digital Forensic Model based on Malaysian Investigation Process. *International Journal of Computer Science and Network Security, 9*(8).

Sutherland, E. H. (1983). *White collar crime: The uncut version.* New Haven, CT: Yale University Press.

Suzuki, S. N. M. (2005). Domain Name System—Past, Present, and Future. *IEICE Transactions on Communications, E88-B*(3), 857–864. doi:10.1093/ietcom/e88-b.3.857

Swanson, M. (2001). *NIST Security Self-Assessment Guide for Information Technology Systems.* Available at http://www.itl.nist.gov/lab/bulletns/bltnsep01.htm

Taylor, M., Haggerty, J., Gresty, D., & Lamb, D. (2011, March). Forensic investigation of cloud computing systems. *Network Security, 2011*(3), 4–9. doi:10.1016/S1353-4858(11)70024-1

thebestvpn. (2019). *14 Most Alarming Cyber Security Statistics in 2019*. Retrieved from https://thebestvpn.com/cyber-security-statistics-2019/

thesslstore. (2019). *80 Eye-Opening Cyber Security Statistics for 2019*. Retrieved from https://www.thesslstore.com/blog/80-eye-opening-cyber-security-statistics-for-2019/

Tilstone, W. J. (2006). *Forensic science: An encyclopaedia of history, methods, and techniques.* Academic Press.

Tzerefos, S. S. (1997). A comparative study of Simple Mail Transfer Protocol (SMTP), Post Office Protocol (POP) and X.400 Electronic Mail Protocols. *22nd Annual IEEE Conference on Local Computer Networks*, 545–554. 10.1109/LCN.1997.631025

US-CERT. a. g. (2008). Retrieved from https://www.us-cert.gov/sites/default/files/publications/forensics.pdf

Uzel, V. N., Saraç Eşsiz, E., & Ayşe Özel, S. (2018). Using Fuzzy Sets for Detecting Cyber Terrorism and Extremism in the Text. *2018 Innovations in Intelligent Systems and Applications Conference (ASYU),* 1-4. 10.1109/ASYU.2018.8554017

Vacca, R. (2005). Computer Forensics Computer Crime Scene Investigation (2nd ed.). Academic Press.

Verma, A. A. (2018). Analysis of DDOS attack Detection and Prevention in Cloud Environment: A Review. *International Journal of Advanced Research in Computer Science*.

Vinez, K. E. (2017). The Admissibility of Data Collected from Wearable Devices. *Stetson J. Advocacy Law, 1*, 1–23.

Visualware Inc. (2014). *eMailTrackerPro*. Retrieved from http://www.emailtrackerpro.com/: http://www.emailtrackerpro.com/

Wagner, E. J. (2006). *The Science of Sherlock Holmes*. Chichester, UK: Wiley.

Walters, A. (2007). *Integrating volatile memory forensics into the digital investigation process*. Black Hat, DC.

Wei, D., Shaoyi, L., & Zhongju, Z. (2018). Leveraging Financial Social Media Data for Corporate Fraud Detection. *Journal of Management Information Systems, 35*(2), 461–487. doi:10.1080/07421222.2018.1451954

Weimann. (2005). Cyber Terrorism: The Sum of all Fears? Studies in Conflict and Terrorism, 28(2).

Willer, L. (2006). *Computer forensics*. Available from: http://www.giac.org/certified_professionals/practicals/gsec/0854.php

Wolfe, D. T., & Hermanson, D. R. (2004). The fraud diamond: Considering the four elements of fraud. *The CPA Journal, 74*(12), 38–42.

X-Ways Software Technology. (n.d.). *X-Ways Forensics: Integrated Computer Forensics Software.* Retrieved from www.x-ways.net/forensics

Yassir, A., & Nayak, S. (2012). Cybercrime: A threat to Network Security. *International Journal of Computer Science and Network Security.*

Ziese, K. J. (1996). Computer based forensics-a case study-U.S. support to the U.N. *Proceedings of CMAD IV: Computer Misuse and Anomaly Detection.*

Zourrig, H., & Park, J. (2019). The effects of cultural tightness and perceived unfairness on Japanese consumers' attitude towards insurance fraud: The mediating effect of rationalization. *Journal of Financial Services Marketing, 24*(1-2), 21–30. doi:10.105741264-019-00061-w

About the Contributors

Mohammad Shahid Husain is a Research professional and Faculty member with more than twelve years of teaching and research experience. He is currently working as Assistant Professor in College of Applied Sciences, Ministry of Higher Education, Oman. He has done his M.Tech. in Information Technology (spl: Intelligent System) from the Indian Institute of Information Technology, Allahabad (www.iiita.ac.in), India, which is one among the premier research Institute of India. He has done his PhD in Computer Science & Engineering from Integral University, Lucknow (www.iul.ac.in), India. His area of interest are Artificial Intelligence, Information Retrieval, Natural Language Processing, Data Mining, Web mining, Sentiment Analysis and Computer Networks & Security. Dr. Mohd. Shahid Husain has published 2 books, 4 book chapters & more than 30 research papers. He is contributing his knowledge and experience as member of Editorial Board/Advisory committee and TPC in various international Journals/Conferences of repute. Dr. Mohd Shahid Husain is active member of different professional bodies including ACM, IEEE young professionals, IEEE-TCII, ISTE, CSTA, IACSIT. Dr. Mohd Shahid Husain qualified UGC-NET (National Eligibility Test) in June 2014 and GATE (Graduate Aptitude Test in Engineering) in 2008.

Mohammad Khan is working as an assistant professor in the department of computer science and engineering at Integral University, Lucknow, and having more than 10 years of teaching research experience. He had completed his Ph.D. in Computer Science & Engineering, published around 20 research articles in different reputed/refereed journals and conferences. He has also served various National & International Conferences and Journals as an Editorial Board member.

* * *

Alka Agrawal has earned her Doctoral Degree from Babasaheb Bhimrao Ambedkar University, (A Central University), Vidya Vihar, Raibareli Road, Lucknow and she is currently working as an Assistant Professor in the same Department. Dr. Alka is a passionate researcher and has also published a number of research papers in national and international journals both. She has research/teaching experience of more than 8 years. Her areas of research include Software Security, Software Vulnerability. She is currently working in the fields of Big Data Security, Genetic Algorithms and Security Durability.

Faiyaz Ahmad is a Cyber Law and Cyber Security Expert. He is working as Assistant Professor in Integral University, Lucknow. He has teaching and research experience of 10 years.

Mohd Akbar is an academician in the field of Cyber Security and Computer Networking. He is an Assistant Professor at Integral University. His thrust areas are "Cloud Network Security, Mobile Ad-hock Network, VANET, Mobile Computing, Cryptography & Network Security etc. He is having around 10 years of teaching experience in the Department of Computer Science and Engineering at Integral University, Lucknow.

Priyadharshini G. is a student in the Department of Information Technology, Thiagarajar College of Engineering.

Mohammad Haroon is working as an associate professor at Integral University, Lucknow.

Divya K. is doing her Undergraduate Program B.Tech Information Technology in Thiagarajar College of Engineering, Madurai, Tamil Nadu, India. Her area of interest includes Computer Forensics, Information Security.

Gayatri Kapil is pursuing a Ph.D. in Information Technology from Babasaheb Bhimrao Ambedkar University (A Central University), Lucknow. Their research domains are MANET, Big Data and its security and Cloud Computing. Before joining this, they got their M.Tech in Digital Communication from Uttarakhand Technical University, Dehradun, Uttarakhand and B.Tech in Electronics and Communication Engineering from Uttar Pradesh Technical University, Lucknow.

Mahmoodul Hasan Khan is a professor in computer science and has more than 25 years of rich teaching and research experience.

Mohammad Khan is working as an assistant professor in the department of computer science and engineering at Integral University, Lucknow, and having more than 10 years of teaching research experience. He had completed his Ph.D. in Computer Science and Engineering, published around 20 research articles in different reputed/refereed journals and conferences. He has also served various National & International Conferences and Journals as an Editorial Board member.

Mohd Waris Khan is currently engaged in teaching in the department of Information Technology, in Babasaheb Bhimrao Ambedkar University (A Central University), Lucknow, U.P., India. Dr Khan has completed his PhD (Information Technology) in 2019 from same University and M.Phil. (Computer Science) in 2013 from Dr. C.V. Raman University, Chhattisgarh. He is also an alumnus of Lucknow University (Bachelor's Degree), Lucknow Christian Inter College. During PhD work, he has also worked on a major Research Project entitled "Analysis of the impact of Ergonomic Deficiencies in Computer Workstations at Government Offices of Uttar Pradesh State". The project was sponsored by Uttar Pradesh Council of Science and Technology, under Young Scientist Scheme, Lucknow, India. His research interests are in the areas of Requirement Engineering, Security Engineering. He published numerous research articles in the journals and conferences of repute.

Raees Ahmad Khan is currently working as a Professor, Head of the Department in the Department of Information Technology and Dean of School for Information Science and Technology, Babasaheb Bhimrao Ambedkar University, (A Central University), Vidya Vihar, Raibareli Road, Lucknow, India. Prof. R. A. Khan has more than 16 years of teaching & research experience. His area of interest is Software Security, Software Quality and Software Testing. He has published a number of National and International Books (including Chinese Language), Technical Article, Research Papers, Reviews and Chapters on Software Security, Software Quality and Software Testing.

Rajeev Kumar is pursuing a Ph.D. in Information Technology from Babasaheb Bhimrao Ambedkar University (A Central University), Vidya Vihar, Raibareli Road, Lucknow and he has completed his Master's Degree in Information Technology from same University in 2014. He has also published & presented papers in refereed journals and conferences. His research interests are in the areas of Software Security, Software Durability, Security Risk and Cyber Security.

Radiah Othman is currently a Senior Lecturer with Massey University, New Zealand. Her Masters in Accountancy (with distinction) is from Curtin University of Technology (Australia), and PhD from Aston University (UK). She is an active researcher and has published papers in the area of fraud and forensic accounting, sustainability, public sector auditing and accountability in book chapters and reputable journals such as Journal of Business Ethics, International Journal of Public Sector Management, Accountancy, Business and Public Interest. Her current research interest is fraud examination and forensic accounting topics. She has received research grants to profile fraudsters and to examine the usefulness of forensic detecting tools.

Abhishek Kumar Pandey received his Bachelor degree in Computer Applications (BCA, Gold Medalist) from Siddhartha University, Kapilvastu in 2018 and pursuing his Master's degree in Cyber Security from Babasaheb Bhimrao Ambedkar University, A central university, Lucknow. His area of interest is Digital Forensic and Cyber Security Methods.

Gayathri R. is doing her Undergraduate Program B.Tech Information Technology in Thiagarajar College of Engineering, Madurai, Tamil Nadu, India. Her area of interest includes Computer Forensics, Information Security.

Parkavi R. is working as Assistant Professor, Department of Information Technology, Thiagarajar College of Engineering, Madurai, Tamil Nadu, India. She completed her B.Tech (Information Technology), at Sree Sowdambika College of Engineering, and M.E (Computer Science and Engineering) at Thiagarajar College of Engineering under Anna University, Chennai. She is pursuing her Ph.D in the domain of Learning Analytics at Anna University Chennai. Her research interests include Biometrics, E-Learning, M-Learning and Educational Technology. She has been awarded as Best Outgoing Student for her excellence in the degree of undergraduate, in the discipline of Information Technology by Sree Sowdambika College of Engineering. She has published research articles in various reputed Journals, National and International Conferences. She has authored various books under IGI Global Publishers, USA. Currently, she is working towards the impact and use of various ICT tools in Educational Technology.

Anitha S. is doing her Undergraduate Program B.Tech Information Technology in Thiagarajar College of Engineering, Madurai, Tamil Nadu, India. Her area of interest includes Computer Forensics, Information Security.

Mohd Shoaib is currently working in the Department of Computer Engineering, Zakir Husain College of Engineering and Technology, Aligarh Muslim University. He has over six years of experience in academics. His area of research are Cyber Security, Web Mining and Parallel Computing.

287

Saurabh Shukla received the B.S. degree in Information Technology from Abdul Kalam Technical University, Lucknow, India, in 2008 and the M.S. degree in Information Technology from Indian Institute of Information Technology, Allahabad, India in 2010. He is currently pursuing the Ph.D. degree in Information Technology at Universiti Teknologi of PETRONAS, Malaysia. From 2011 to 2012, he was an assistant system engineer at Tata Consultancy Services in India. From 2012 to 2017 he was working as a Lecturer in Rajiv Gandhi Institute of Petroleum Technology, Rae-Bareli, India. His research interest includes machine learning, Agent-based system, Fog computing, and Internet-of-Things.

Virendra Singh is a PhD student in Software Engineering. He holds an MSc in Information Technology. His research interest is in Security Requirement Elicitation.

Ashutosh Kumar Tripathi received his Bachelor degree in Information technology (MSc IT) from Lovely Professional University, Panjab in 2017 and pursuing his Master's degree in Cyber Security from Babasaheb Bhimrao Ambedkar University, A central university, Lucknow. His area of interest is digital forensic, cyber security methods, malware, source code, and data mining.

Manish Tripathi is working as an Associate Professor at Integral University, Lucknow. He has18 years of teaching and research experience. He has published more than 50 papers in peer reviewed journals.

Sherry Ruth V. is doing her Undergraduate Program B.Tech Information Technology in Thiagarajar College of Engineering, Madurai, Tamil Nadu, India. Her area of interest includes Computer Forensics, Information Security.

Sonali Yadav is a Research professional and Faculty member with seven years of teaching and research experience. She is currently working as Assistant Professor in Integral University, Lucknow. She has done her M.Tech. in Computer Science (spl: Cloud Computing) from Banasthali Vidyapeeth (Rajasthan), India, which is one among the premier research Institute of India. Her areas of interest are Cloud Computing, Cyber Forensics, Data Sciences. Sonali Yadav has published many research papers. She is also contributing his knowledge and experience as member of Editorial Board and TPC in various international Journals/Conferences of repute. Sonali Yadav qualified GATE (Graduate Aptitude Test in Engineering) in 2010.

Index

A

Accreditation Process 115
Advanced Forensic Format 88, 91
AES 162-163, 173
Android 10-11, 34-35, 46, 209, 213
Anomaly Detection 114, 131, 244, 246-247
Anonymity 87, 117
Anti-Forensic Techniques 40-41, 46
Attack 36, 42-43, 48-52, 54-55, 58, 61-63, 65-67, 70-71, 73, 75, 78-79, 82, 84-85, 87, 137, 167-168, 182-183, 206, 226

B

Bait Tactics 180, 186
Big Data Acquisition and Analytics 98
BPO 254-257, 264

C

Cardinal Rules in Cyber Forensics 28, 30
Case studies 140, 142, 249, 251, 253, 262
Certification 29, 95, 110, 113, 115, 118, 172, 175
Certification Related to Cyber Forensics 115
Cloud Computing 45-46, 101-102, 214-218, 220, 222-226
Cloud Forensics 31, 33-34, 36, 44-46, 104, 215-221, 223-226

Computer 1-4, 7, 9-11, 14-15, 17-19, 25-30, 40-41, 45-46, 55, 64-69, 72-73, 75, 77, 79-80, 82, 86-87, 89-90, 93, 96, 101-103, 114-124, 126, 128-129, 133, 135, 138-139, 141-144, 147, 156, 172-173, 176, 180-181, 183, 185-189, 194-195, 213-214, 216, 221, 226-229, 234, 238-239, 242-243, 246-249, 251-256, 258-264
Computer Forensics Timeline 18, 30
Conceal 180, 190-191, 204-205, 214
Control 4, 12, 51, 69, 73-74, 80, 93, 156, 166, 180, 191-193, 197, 205, 211-212, 214, 218, 221, 254
Corporate Fraud 214, 252, 264
Cryptanalysis 146, 173
Cyber Forensics 1-4, 6-7, 13, 15-17, 26-30, 42, 88, 93, 96-98, 103-104, 107, 115, 175, 182, 215, 219, 225, 228, 238, 240, 242-243, 245-246, 248
Cyberattack 87
Cybercrime 1, 3, 15, 32, 37-40, 44, 51, 70, 94, 103, 116-117, 140, 142-143, 175, 216, 225, 242, 246, 257, 263
Cybersecurity 31, 37, 39, 44, 59, 76, 82, 86-87
Cyberspace 29, 53, 66-68, 70, 72, 75, 82, 87, 241

Ensure Quality Research is Introduced to the Academic Community

Become an IGI Global Reviewer for Authored Book Projects

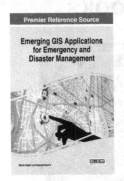

Premier Reference Source

Emerging GIS Applications for Emergency and Disaster Management

Premier Reference Source

Managerial Strategies and Green Solutions for Project Sustainability

Premier Reference Source

Comparative Approaches to Using R and Python for Statistical Data Analysis

Premier Reference Source

Solutions for High-Touch Communications in a High-Tech World

The overall success of an authored book project is dependent on quality and timely reviews.

In this competitive age of scholarly publishing, constructive and timely feedback significantly expedites the turnaround time of manuscripts from submission to acceptance, allowing the publication and discovery of forward-thinking research at a much more expeditious rate. Several IGI Global authored book projects are currently seeking highly-qualified experts in the field to fill vacancies on their respective editorial review boards:

Applications and Inquiries may be sent to:
development@igi-global.com

Applicants must have a doctorate (or an equivalent degree) as well as publishing and reviewing experience. Reviewers are asked to complete the open-ended evaluation questions with as much detail as possible in a timely, collegial, and constructive manner. All reviewers' tenures run for one-year terms on the editorial review boards and are expected to complete at least three reviews per term. Upon successful completion of this term, reviewers can be considered for an additional term.

If you have a colleague that may be interested in this opportunity, we encourage you to share this information with them.

IGI Global Proudly Partners With eContent Pro International

Receive a 25% Discount on all Editorial Services

Editorial Services

IGI Global expects all final manuscripts submitted for publication to be in their final form. This means they must be reviewed, revised, and professionally copy edited prior to their final submission. Not only does this support with accelerating the publication process, but it also ensures that the highest quality scholarly work can be disseminated.

English Language Copy Editing

Let eContent Pro International's expert copy editors perform edits on your manuscript to resolve spelling, punctuaion, grammar, syntax, flow, formatting issues and more.

Scientific and Scholarly Editing

Allow colleagues in your research area to examine the content of your manuscript and provide you with valuable feedback and suggestions before submission.

Figure, Table, Chart & Equation Conversions

Do you have poor quality figures? Do you need visual elements in your manuscript created or converted? A design expert can help!

Translation

Need your documjent translated into English? eContent Pro International's expert translators are fluent in English and more than 40 different languages.

Email: **customerservice@econtentpro.com**   **www.igi-global.com/editorial-service-partners**